LEARNING ACTIVISM

LEARNING ACTIVISM

THE INTELLECTUAL LIFE OF
CONTEMPORARY SOCIAL MOVEMENTS

AZIZ CHOUDRY

UNIVERSITY OF TORONTO PRESS

Copyright © University of Toronto Press 2015
Higher Education Division

www.utppublishing.com

Library and Archives Canada Cataloguing in Publication

    Choudry, Aziz, author
Learning activism : the intellectual life of contemporary social movements / Aziz Choudry.

Includes bibliographical references and index.
Issued in print and electronic formats.
ISBN 978-1-4426-0791-0 (bound).—ISBN 978-1-4426-0790-3 (pbk.).—
ISBN 978-1-4426-0792-7 (pdf).—ISBN 978-1-4426-0793-4 (html).

    1. Social movements. 2. Political activists—Intellectual life. 3. Social reformers—Intellectual
life. I. Title.

HM881.C46 2015   303.48′4   C2015-901439-5
                                                    C2015-901440-9

We welcome comments and suggestions regarding any aspect of our publications—please feel free to
contact us at news@utphighereducation.com or visit our Internet site at www.utppublishing.com.

North America	*UK, Ireland, and continental Europe*
5201 Dufferin Street	NBN International
North York, Ontario, Canada, M3H 5T8	Estover Road, Plymouth, PL6 7PY, UK
	ORDERS PHONE: 44 (0) 1752 202301
2250 Military Road	ORDERS FAX: 44 (0) 1752 202333
Tonawanda, New York, USA, 14150	ORDERS E-MAIL: enquiries@nbninternational.com

ORDERS PHONE: 1–800–565–9523
ORDERS FAX: 1–800–221–9985
ORDERS E-MAIL: utpbooks@utpress.utoronto.ca

Every effort has been made to contact copyright holders; in the event of an error or omission, please
notify the publisher.

This book is printed on paper containing 100% post-consumer fibre.

The University of Toronto Press acknowledges the financial support for its publishing activities of
the Government of Canada through the Canada Book Fund.

Printed in the United States of America.

CONTENTS

FIGURES

ACKNOWLEDGEMENTS

As this book argues, knowledge and learning in social movements and activism are often produced collectively and in interaction with others. *Learning Activism* emerged from, and is very much influenced by and produced through collective efforts in which many people were engaged, both in the past and in the present. This includes too many conversations, shared experiences, and back stories to do justice to here. I started a list of people to thank, but it would be an impossible task to do justice to everyone who should be acknowledged. You know who you are. . . . Despite that, the primary responsibility for the book's contents, including any shortcomings, is mine. I am profoundly grateful for the Indigenous Peoples of Aotearoa and Turtle Island for providing me with places to think and write over many years. I am particularly indebted to Dave Bleakney, Leigh Cookson, Radha D'Souza, Michelle Hartman, Tony Kelly, Orin Langelle, Désirée Rochat, and Salim Vally, who read and commented on earlier drafts of some or all parts of this book. The section on migrant and immigrant workers and knowledge production in Chapter 2 is adapted from part of an article that I co-authored with Mostafa Henaway.[1] Désirée and Nakita Sunar's support with the interview materials on which much of Chapter 4 is based was invaluable, and I also thank all those interviewed for their generosity and reflections. A special debt of gratitude is due to Orin Langelle for his powerful photography that illustrates this book. More of his photos can be seen at photolangelle.org. I acknowledge funding support for my work on activist research from a Social Sciences and Humanities Research Council Standard Research Grant (No. 410-2011-1688). I also thank the anonymous reviewers

....

1 Choudry, A., & Henaway, M. (2014). Temporary agency worker organizing in an era of contingent employment. *Global Labour Journal, 5*(1), 1–22.

of earlier drafts of this book. Finally, I am grateful to Anne Brackenbury at University of Toronto Press for her invitation to write this book and for her support in seeing it through with discussion and editorial input, and to Leanne Rancourt for her careful copyediting and Ashley Rayner, Anna Del Col and Beate Schwirtlich for their efficient assistance.

Note: Some of the material in Chapter 4 is adapted from the following articles:

Choudry, A. (2013). Activist research and organizing: Blurring the boundaries, challenging the binaries. *International Journal of Lifelong Education.* doi:10.1080/02601370.2013.867907

Choudry, A. (2013). Activist research practice: Exploring research and knowledge production for social action. *Socialist Studies, 9*(1), 128–151.

Choudry, A. (2014). Activist research for education and social movement mobilization. *Post-Colonial Directions in Education, 3*(1), 88–121.

All royalties from this book will go to the Immigrant Workers Centre in Montreal.

PREFACE

I am a bit of a hoarder. When I interviewed for a tenure-track academic position in McGill University's Faculty of Education in 2007, I arrived as a doctoral student without any university degrees except for a one-year graduate diploma but with some two decades worth of baggage of activism, popular education, and organizing work. This was not just metaphorical baggage. I actually turned up to the interview room with a suitcase full of publications, DVDs, and other documentation that I had written, edited, contributed to, researched, or had otherwise been directly involved with in the course of my activist work. This material was published in numerous countries across the Asia-Pacific, North America, and Europe by movements, nongovernmental organizations (NGOs), trade unions, and independent progressive media, often with little or no involvement of academic researchers. I spread it out on a table before the interview began. I did this not just to illustrate my productivity but to make a point to the hiring committee—my soon-to-be colleagues—that this material was important. I wanted to show that popular/activist knowledge produced outside of the academy and academic scholarship can each have their own integrity, strengths, and weaknesses.

I played a film clip of a workshop on resistance against bilateral free trade and investment agreements that I facilitated at the November 2004 People's Convention on Food Sovereignty in Dhaka, Bangladesh. Among the publications on the table was a book I had edited on strategies for confronting transnational corporations in the Asia-Pacific, reports I had written on topics including childcare and workers' rights, and a controversial overseas aid-funded forestry development project in the Philippines. There were fact sheets on subjects like free trade and the Pacific Islands, intellectual property rights, corporate control over agriculture, and threats to the future of rice. There were pieces that I had written for Australian migrant and refugee justice networks on racism, colonialism, and immigration detention policies, and a critical analysis of a major US environmental NGO that was published in Spanish in a Latin American magazine on biodiversity. And there were interview articles with a range of activists and organizers adapted from transcripts of broadcasts of a radio show that I co-produced and hosted in Christchurch (Aotearoa/New Zealand) in the 1990s. All of these resources were shared as examples of the education, thinking, theorizing, and other forms of knowledge produced in movements and activist circles. This intellectual work is too rarely acknowledged in faculties of education or universities as a whole. This public show-and-tell activity with some of my personal activist archives was intended to emphasize its importance and to challenge the fact that these kinds of knowledge, research, and ideas are not often seen to be on equal terms with academic knowledge.

The ideas in this book took shape out of reflections on the approximately 30 years of my own political engagements. By drawing on my experiences and research, I highlight the intellectual contributions of the knowledge produced, informal and non-formal learning, and research within activism. I also connect all of these to the fields of education and learning. Through this, I propose that social, political, and environmental activist movements can best be understood if we engage with the learning, knowledge, debates, and theorizing that go on within them. I draw on my own experiences and learning in my activist involvements to share what I have learned and to inform and inspire further reflection and critical inquiry in others. These experiences and the ideas behind them are drawn from many places, times, and struggles. They range from organizing experiences in Aotearoa/New Zealand to progressive social movements and people's organizations in the Philippines, and from support for Indigenous Peoples' struggles for self-determination to migrant and immigrant workers' struggles in Canada to the 2012 student strike in Quebec.

My own experiences inevitably shape what is written here—but this is not a memoir. I do not claim to have any special powers of divination or recipes for movement success. I do, however, strongly believe in the collective nature of most knowledge production. I don't claim to write on anyone else's behalf. But most of what I have written here rests on the shoulders of many people's work and generations of struggles for a better world.

This book also comes out of a life of personal and political struggles against racism and a grounding in anti-colonial politics, which are not always central to either scholarship or many of today's movements. I wish there was less need to address concerns about social and economic injustice, colonialism, and gendered and racial oppression today. But unfortunately there are few indications—in struggles for social change; in schools, colleges, and universities; or in society at large—that these have become less urgent or relevant. In Chapter 1, I outline this framework for understanding and action to ground the discussion throughout the rest of the book in these ideas. I have been greatly influenced by the crucial work of many anti-racist, anti-colonial, socialist, and feminist struggles and thinkers while insisting upon the continued importance of class politics and struggles. My thinking is also deeply informed by the tenacity and sharp insights of Indigenous Peoples who have refused to be silenced, brushed aside in an era of "free" market "democracy," or alternatively tucked into a watered down, liberal left set of visions, demands, and declarations of the kind frequently put forward in so many "civil society" initiatives.

Some of these struggles, people, and perspectives have been dismissed as marginal and radical; others are simply overlooked and ignored. Yet I believe that it is important for us to take into account how ideas about what and who is considered radical and what is thought to constitute the margins and the centre can shift over time and place. It is also vital to grasp the significance of the insights from people who are viewed to be at the margins and seriously engage with their ideas. Perhaps this orientation may feel a bit "outside of the box" for some scholars and students interested in social movements in North America (and beyond). Or perhaps not. But these perspectives are foundational to my own academic and movement collaborations and commitments—including this book.

At my PhD defence which took place a few months after I had started my job as a professor, two members of my examining committee quizzed me about whether I was "now" an academic or an activist—as if a two-hour examination, being hired as a professor, or academic study for several years necessarily changes one's identity or vision. This book was partly born from needing to bridge academia and activist ideas and to explore what it is to work with both. In part, it is a product of questions and reservations about dominant academic trends, particularly in studies of activism, social movements, and social movement learning. This book is organized to encourage a deeper engagement with knowledge produced in activist contexts and learning processes within social movements. It does not offer a romanticized version of social and political activism. Indeed, my analysis has been influenced by encountering, examining, and often challenging power relations within movements, and conflicts and contradictions within networks espousing social justice. It is informed by experiences arising from the co-optation or orchestration of dissent in the interests of elites. It is shaped by an exasperation with nostalgias—including some versions of history circulating in supposedly progressive circles—that both erase and exclude the experiences of many people in an attempt to conjure up imagined, better pasts. It challenges white saviours, professionalized "civil society" experts and lobbyists, NGO and trade union bureaucracies and other elites, as well as the subtle and not-so-subtle disciplining of dissent within activist groups and movement and NGO networks. Yet equally it draws inspiration and hope from the visions, ideas, and collective efforts of ordinary people engaged in struggles for liberation, self-determination, and justice.

This book addresses theoretical and analytical questions in ways that are relevant to both organizers/activists and scholars. It wasn't written to be a conventional textbook or a typical research-based text (although research has shaped and influenced its ideas). It also wasn't designed to make a "novel" theoretical contribution. Instead, it consciously falls somewhere in between, bringing a relatively light touch and a synthetic tone to a number of developments in the field. In order to do this, it is punctuated at points with personal reflections derived from my activist, organizing, and scholarly experiences. In more ways than one, this book was conceived as going "against the grain" of most academic texts.

To offer a better sense of how it works against the grain, I can provide an idea of what the book is and what it is not. It is neither a social movement studies reader nor a traditional text on social movement learning. Rather, it engages critically with some of the literature in the field of social movement studies as part of a broader project. It tries to break the serious analysis of social movement learning out of the particular sites where it usually takes place (like adult education programs and literature) to make it more widely accessible. Since it is not an exhaustive text on the study of social movements, I point readers to further sources that include many theoretical works as well as more popular or activist literature. By no means do I set out to provide an overview of the state of the world's contemporary protest and social movements.

Whether inside formal classrooms or outside of them, I have noticed that people interested in understanding social, political, and ecological struggles are hungry to read about other organizers' experiences. They want to read about how others think through possibilities and articulate dilemmas and ideas. They want to know how others have thought, acted, educated, and learned to make a better world. They might want to challenge or test their ideas and experiences.

This book fills this need by integrating examples drawn from experience in social struggles and the lessons learned there with critical scholarship. It is intended for teaching purposes as well as bridging the everyday worlds of activists and students and scholars. It is a critical intervention into debates on social movements, learning, and knowledge politics. It can be used as a complementary text in courses on social movements, critical adult education, and community education. It offers a grounded approach to thinking through questions of social movements combined with discussions about knowledge and learning. The chapters can be interwoven with more formal texts through-out a course, or they can be used as a base—as jumping-off points for deeper theoretical discussions—in a way that connects people's practical activities to scholarship. There are multiple points of entry here through the more "theoret-ical" sections or via the vignettes and examples given throughout the chapters; or indeed by going behind the powerful images of veteran activist/photojour-nalist Orin Langelle that are included throughout this book.

The structure of this book reflects its intended audience; it is meant to be approachable by students, teachers, and people involved in struggles for social change. I do not believe that activism can be neatly packaged into boxes labelled "organizing," "education/learning," "research," and "action." Academic scholarship commonly demands and generates such categories, but attempting to carve up and analyze people's activities in the world is not always analyt-ically helpful or an accurate reflection of how things actually happen. Thus this book's division into chapters and sections reflects convenience rather than rigid categorization or narrow compartmentalization. The book can be read in the order in which it is presented, or its chapters can be read to comple-ment themes of courses in any order.

For teaching purposes, I am often drawn to books that incorporate, in differ-ent ways, narrations of the author's everyday observations and experiences—to make their points as well as review and reference selective areas of scholar-ship. As you read this book, you will see that I am upfront about my biases and where I am coming from. All knowledge is necessarily partial. I don't aspire to be an educator who can somehow adopt a "neutral" or "distanced" stance. This is not a tradition of scholarship and teaching in which I situate my work. One of the tensions in writing this book has been how to balance insights derived from activism and activist education practice with scholarship about activist learning, knowledge production, and research in sufficient depth to be helpful to both student and broader audiences. Such a relatively small book inevitably demands being selective rather than offering a comprehensive or exhaustive treatment of wide fields of scholarship about social movements and activism.

Yet through following the references and examples provided, readers can track and trace ideas, concepts, and arguments, including some of the differ-ent ways in which these have been studied. You can explore how and why particular perspectives have been erased or silenced. In my own university teaching, and in the non-formal education work I do in community orga-nizations, activist/movement networks, and unions, I draw from a range of ideas, texts, films, and multimedia that span conventional academic work and the reflections of organizers as presented in activist media and other materials, including cultural and artistic forms. I hope this book will also be useful to teachers and students who want to explore relations between the broader social, economic, ecological, and political moment in which our classes take place. I hope it can usefully help to tease out the interconnections between what is being read and discussed in the classroom and the struggles of people down the street or around the world. I also hope that it helps focus attention on some questions that are relevant to organizers/activists.

I am often left with more questions than answers. Perhaps open questions can sometimes be more useful than what we think are the "right answers." Books can sometimes provide fuel for further reflection; they can hook us into thinking critically about historical lessons, concepts and understandings, new discussions, learning, education, and organizing processes. Through unsettling us and taking us out of our comfort zones from time to time, books can encourage us to ask ourselves questions and challenge the assumptions we have about the world. Books can affirm that alternatives to the status quo have been, can be, must be, and are being built. Alternatives that are rooted in people's own activities and collective capacities allow us to critically think about and act upon the world we live in. At the heart of this book lies a belief that we can engage with ways of seeing the world and building counterpower to bring about social change—and all its tensions—without succumbing to cynicism, the limited horizons of possibility and imagination seemingly on offer, or a disconnect born of too much abstraction. I hope that it spurs you—as a reader, student, teacher, organizer, or activist, as a person engaged in changing the world—to think about and take seriously the knowledge produced and the imagination developed, as well as the learning and research that happen in the course of struggles for a better future.

CHAPTER I

KNOWLEDGE PRODUCTION, LEARNING, AND EDUCATION IN SOCIAL MOVEMENT ACTIVISM

This book looks at the intellectual and educational work of social movements and activism. It engages with the kinds of knowledge produced and the informal and non-formal learning that takes place in the course of activism. It suggests that such work can greatly enrich, broaden, and challenge dominant understandings of how and where education, learning, and knowledge production occur and what these look like. It argues that these are resources that can provide critical conceptual tools with which to understand, inform, imagine, and bring about social change. It contends that the success of organizing to fight injustice and create a better, fairer world depends on taking such knowledge and learning seriously. But this also requires being able to reflect critically, build spaces where people can come together to act and learn collectively, and appreciate the unfinished nature of popular struggles for social and political change.

The forms of activist knowledge, learning, and research discussed here are often concerned with exposing the contradictions, cracks, and fault lines in the structures and systems that produce and reproduce inequality, injustice, and environmental devastation. To do so requires practices and strategies that are grounded in critical (including self-critical) historical perspectives as well as emerging ideas born of current struggles. Ideas, insights, and visions produced in the course of people collectively trying to change things and reflecting on their experiences, the knowledge about systems of power and exploitation developed as people find themselves in confrontation with states and capital, the rich but often underexplored archives of social movement and activist publications, memories and other resources from earlier generations, and challenges from below to notions of expertise are just some examples of activist knowledge and learning discussed in this book. Communities, movements, and people around the world can learn from and build upon the powerful insights that emerge out of past and present movements for change. We are in dire need of thinking, acting, theorizing, and imagining "outside of the box" to make fundamental changes and dramatic differences in the communities, societies, and world we live in. Whether the struggles of today and tomorrow will be sufficient to address our current unprecedented social and ecological crises remains to be seen.

But the future is not entirely determined for us. What people choose to do as individuals and collectively—by learning from history and from each other—can influence the kind of future we can look forward to and, indeed, shape. People can sometimes be rather quick to dismiss and label ideas and actions they do not understand or disagree with as "radical." But I think it is precisely the kind of radical imagination glimpsed in moments of learning and action in organizing spaces and activism, including tensions and contradictions, mistakes, setbacks and losses, and the opportunities to reflect on them, that keeps dreams and possibilities for a better and different world afloat. It certainly should not be a radical idea to acknowledge that ordinary people can think and theorize as they act collectively.

Beginnings: A Point of Departure

A point of departure for this book is my own engagement in political, social, and environmental justice organizing and activism. Today, as I write this book, I am a university professor. However, to write it I am drawing not only on scholarship on these issues but on knowledge that comes from a wide range of my activist, community, labour, popular education, and organizing experience, as well as independent media work, writing, and research in and for various movements and NGOs.

My experiences of racism growing up in England in the 1970s and early 1980s profoundly shaped my social and political perspectives, especially the ways I understand power relations. Some of my earliest concerns included struggles against racism in the UK, opposition to apartheid in South Africa and the British occupation of Northern Ireland, and nuclear disarmament. From a relatively young age I identified with emancipatory movements for justice in the Third World[2] as well as various freedom struggles in the First World. My interest and involvement in anti-nuclear, environmental, anti-racist, anti-colonial, anti-imperialist, and labour politics, as well as activist/community

2 "Third World" and "South," and "First World" and "North" are used interchangeably in this book.

media, further developed after I relocated to Aotearoa/New Zealand[3] in the late 1980s. There I spent many years working in activist groups and small NGOs supporting Third World people's struggles for liberation from oppression and domination, independent trade unions and workers' organizations, Indigenous sovereignty struggles, and economic and environmental justice at home and abroad. Many of the groups that I was part of were in some way committed to fighting injustice locally while highlighting ways in which the "local" is connected to the "global." Thus this book draws from lessons I have learned from organizing and activism in Aotearoa/New Zealand, Canada, as well as globally/transnationally. As Gary Kinsman (2006, p. 145) notes, protests against a World Trade Organization (WTO) meeting in a particular city "are not simply global events but also occur in particular local settings, just as global relations are always accomplished in local settings and have impacts in people's local worlds." This idea is certainly true in relation to much of the "global justice" and anti-corporate organizing in Aotearoa/New Zealand in which I was involved. This work targeted both local manifestations of capitalist globalization and also international processes and structures.

For example, during the 1990s and into the start of the following decade, I was an organizer, educator, and researcher for two small Aotearoa/New Zealand–based activist groups: GATT[4] Watchdog and the Aotearoa/New Zealand APEC Monitoring Group. These groups operated autonomously, although they were formed from and comprised coalitions and networks of small NGOs, activist groups, and members of trade unions. Years before, and on the other side of the Pacific, from the "battle of Seattle" protests around the 1999 WTO Ministerial Conference, these groups educated and built opposition to free trade and investment agreements at domestic and regional (Asia-Pacific) levels. These organizations, like most others in which I have worked, existed on shoestring budgets largely independently of state or other institutional funding. In my roles as organizer and educator with these groups, sometimes I was paid, sometimes not. We did research, education, and action work in close collaboration with Maori sovereignty activists and representatives of other struggles for self-determination across the Pacific, several community organizations, NGOs, and activist groups, and the more oppositional arm of the national trade union movement at that time, the New Zealand Trade Union Federation. From time to time, some of us were arrested, and through defending ourselves

....

3 Aotearoa is the Maori word for New Zealand. I use the term "Aotearoa/New Zealand" when referring to the country and "New Zealand" when referring to the government or other institutions.
4 "GATT" stands for the General Agreement on Tariffs and Trade. It is a multilateral agreement regulating international trade that was replaced by the World Trade Organization (WTO) in 1995.

in court, tried to use the proceedings for political purposes. We learnt about the law, police tactics and strategy, and ourselves. We linked local struggles against poverty and free market policies with resistance to global economic processes and institutions. One focus of this activism was the Asia–Pacific Economic Cooperation (APEC) process that includes 21 "member economies" in the region, with a goal to advance trade and investment liberalization. APEC's highest-profile annual event, the leaders' summit, rotated among the member countries and was targeted by mobilizations against neoliberal globalization and others advocating for a range of environmental, social, and democratic rights concerns. Much of the anti-APEC activism in which I was involved sought to delegitimize the APEC forum and expose APEC governments' claims of "civil society" involvement in the process as a sham. I was, and continue to be, involved in organizing, education, and research initiatives against bilateral free trade and investment agreements (FTAs) that have proliferated in recent years.

Exchanging Margaret Thatcher's Britain for life in Aotearoa/New Zealand had placed me in a small country that was a veritable petri dish for testing free market capitalism. From 1984 onwards, starting with the fourth Labour government which is also remembered for its "nuclear-free" ban on nuclear-powered or nuclear-armed ships, successive New Zealand governments imposed neoliberal policies to an extent hitherto unseen in any OECD (Organisation for Economic Co-operation and Development) member country. These reforms mirrored key elements of structural adjustment programs in the Third World. Between 1988 and 1993, Aotearoa/New Zealand led the world in state-owned asset sales, often at bargain prices. In the mid-1980s, the country went into recession with the highest unemployment since the Great Depression of the 1930s, with huge job losses in the manufacturing sector. The number of New Zealanders estimated to be below the poverty line rose by at least 35 per cent between 1989 and 1992. By 1996 about one in five New Zealanders—and one-third of all children—were considered to be living in poverty. That same year, UNICEF reported New Zealand's youth suicide rate to be the third highest in the world. Maori and Pacific Island families were more likely to be poor than Pakeha (European) New Zealanders. Underfunding, user-pay charges in health and education, and the introduction of market rentals for state house tenants (low-cost public housing) severely impacted the poor.

By the mid-1990s, most of Aotearoa/New Zealand's productive, financial, energy, retail, transport, media, and communications sectors were controlled by transnational corporations that drained huge profits out of the country. The pursuit of FTAs made explicit the state's legal responsibility to serve corporate interests. Meanwhile, many "civil society" players, including NGOs and trade unions, were uncritical of being co-opted into supposedly consultative meetings on trade and economic policy with officials that were largely exercises in manufacturing consent and constraining dissent. Those experiences of living through, organizing against, and resisting the extreme market fundamentalism of that place and time have led to countless conversations and connections with others about the parallels between policies in different places and opportunities for resisting them. This includes, for example, people challenging privatized models of fisheries management and its impact on small fisherfolk and Indigenous communities in Canada, South Africa, and Mexico. It also includes trade unionists for Thailand's state railways where the New Zealand government's privatization of the national rail network was held up as a model, and those mobilizing against a raft of free market policies including radical health and education "reforms" in many other countries. Indeed, despite its small size as a country, the "New Zealand Experiment" has been aggressively marketed across the world as a model for economic reform—including in Canada (see Kelsey, 1999).

When reflecting on the contours of my own informal, incidental learning in these many contexts, my mind travels back to standing over an old photocopier in Christchurch, Aotearoa/New Zealand. I remember days of stuffing envelopes with fundraising and campaign mailouts for various organizations and activist groups; the hours of photocopying, printing, and folding fact sheets, flyers for demonstrations, posters, and newsletters; sitting on uncomfortable chairs at wobbly tables where people and conversations came and went, numerous cups of tea were made and drunk, and food shared. There were often people from at least three generations: some who had been jailed as conscientious objectors during World War II, remarkable older women who were unassuming anchors of local anti-nuclear/peace and environment groups, and younger folks and their children. Those hours, spent in an old inner-city building that was like a freezer in winter and an oven in summer, could pass by remarkably quickly. Many different groups used the space. Conversations ranged from social inequalities in Aotearoa/New Zealand and the imposition of free market policies, to the politics of the peace movement, to the independence struggles in East Timor and other non–self-governing Pacific territories, to people's individual frustrations with restructured health and social welfare systems, to Maori struggles for self-determination, to many other topics. Apart from film screenings, workshops, or public talks we organized, most of these activities were not defined as "learning" or seen as being explicitly related to the production of knowledge. Yet they occurred in spaces that were very much about people coming together, sharing ideas, learning from and challenging each other, and reflecting and strategizing.

I also recall the many often furtive or discreet conversations held with hushed voices in corridors outside of countless meetings, assemblies, workshops, or conferences of community organizations, NGOs, and activist coalitions, along with the terse whispering, note-passing, and body language inside of them. For all of the positive experiences and celebratory accounts of such activities, many of us have felt excluded from organizing spaces, "alternative" conferences, teach-ins, meetings, and workshops that were proclaimed to be open and democratic. Whether or not they claimed to be horizontally structured, they made us feel marginalized and alienated. This is not to foster a sense of victimhood, but rather to highlight the kinds of learning that can take place when, for example, we face racism or sexism within movements supposedly committed to social justice. Or when we come up against ritualized ways of talking and doing things which are not seemingly open to challenge. How do we draw on such experiences to inform and sharpen our strategy to address these problems? Another crucial example is to think about what we learn from coming up against state power during protest actions and in campaign work—repression, harassment, surveillance, and the criminalization of dissent. This is equally true of more subtle forms of policing dissent internally within movements. And while overhearing yet another person dismissing demonstrations as useless and ineffective or becoming angry because of the inconvenience they caused, I think about those collective spaces on the streets where people come together and talk, share, and learn—what really happens there, and not just the decontextualized, disembodied two-second TV news clips that tell us very little about the reasons to protest.

LEARNING IN THE QUEBEC STUDENT STRIKE

The 2012 Quebec student strike saw some of the largest and most sustained mobilizations of dissent in recent years in North America. Alongside the groundswell of support and sympathy for the cause, there was no shortage of commentary about how the many thousands of striking students did not really care about their education, did not want to learn, and were wasting their lives by not attending classes. The strike was directed against university tuition increases and the further commodification of education, but an underlying assumption behind such comments was that the status quo was working fine for everybody. Another assumption was that education and learning happen only through formal education in institutional settings like schools, colleges, and universities. But this is at odds with what many of us experience in our lives, in the "how," "where," "when," "why," and "what" we learn. In this particular case it was also deeply disconnected from what was actually happening across Quebec for many participants in this movement. As an academic who was active in support for the student movement, inside and outside of campus, at the time I wrote:

> Long-term efforts at coordination and education by student organizers
> and their allies have built and sustained this major mobilization. . . .

These organization and education efforts are happening in the general assemblies in which students have been organizing the strike, debating ideas, making decisions, voting, building strategies and solidarity. They're happening in teach-ins and other forums organized by striking students and in coalition work with other communities and movements to build connections and common fronts of struggle. They're happening in anti-racist organizing within the student movement, challenging racism and the ongoing marginalization of many racialized students in Quebec. This mobilization and education has spread to the neighbourhood marches, casseroles, and popular assemblies springing up across Quebec.

There's a lot happening in the streets, every day/every night—incrementally, incidentally, informally, through talking, exchanging, marching together, claiming and creating space, confronting power, building solidarities and trust—learning that could not take place in a classroom. (Choudry, 2012)

For many days and nights demonstrations throughout Montreal were, in a very real sense, "universities of the streets" that were full of rich discussions, conversations, and exchanges. My participation in striking student–initiated teach-ins and hearing from students about their experiences in their assemblies and other deliberative and decision-making spaces made it obvious to me that there was a wealth of informal and non-formal learning taking place. Activist research had played an important role in providing organizers with tools to argue against the tuition hike and commodification of education. A well-conceived, accessible brochure by IRIS (Institut de recherche et d'informations socio-économiques), an independent progressive nonprofit research organization, debunked eight arguments commonly used to promote tuition fee increases and was distributed widely in French and English in both hard copy and virtual forms (Martin & Tremblay-Pepin, 2011). Yet as the complaints and negative comments about the student strike continually revealed, many people tend to see activism as action/practice that is somehow separate from learning, education, theory, and theorizing. Knowledge production and research were seen as things that happen elsewhere—in schools, colleges, and universities.

Earlier movements have attracted the interest of academic study and broader publics. Recent student movements in Quebec and Chile, Occupy protests and occupations (primarily, although not exclusively, in Europe, North America, and Australasia), Palestine solidarity and anti-war, anti-globalization/global justice mobilizations, and climate justice movements throughout the world have certainly contributed to renewed academic and public interest in social movements and political, social, and environmental activism. So too have uprisings in the Middle East and North Africa and the continuing resistance of Indigenous Peoples and other struggles.

This book centres on the project of analyzing activist knowledge and explaining the power of the worldviews generated through projects of change. It does this in part through a discussion of the relationship between activist and academic knowledge. Throughout this book I highlight the intellectual contributions of informal and non-formal learning, knowledge production, activist research, and organizing to the academic field of education and learning and educators in general. I also address some theoretical and analytical questions in ways that should be relevant to organizers and activists. In doing so, the book integrates a wide range of issues within a single frame, including the ways activists learn through doing; the current state of social movements; feminist, anti-racist, and anti-colonial perspectives on knowledge; and the academic theorization of social movements. In some respects, this frame pushes toward an integrative perspective that clarifies the relations between these issues and viewpoints. This book draws from relevant scholarly literature, my own activist experience, and interviews with activist researchers. This first chapter introduces the book's main ideas and framework. It explains the many interconnections between activist knowledge production, informal and non-formal learning, activist research and theorizing, consciousness, and activist practice/social action. It ties different parts of the book together and locates them within a bigger picture.

Although there is a considerable body of scholarly literature on adult education and learning, relatively few attempts have been made to understand how people produce knowledge and learn (especially through informal learning) through involvement in social action. This learning and knowledge is not only relevant to participants in movements and mobilizations or those who study them. As John Holford (1995) suggests, studying social movements' organizational knowledge is to study a key site of interaction between learning, knowledge, and society. Hall and Turay (2006) suggest that social movements can also play a major educative role for broader publics who are not engaged in them. Dominant strands of adult education literature tend to dismiss or overlook the importance and nature of learning in social movements. I agree with John Holst (2002, pp. 80–81), who says that this reluctance "stems from (a) viewing social movement practice as political and not educative; (b) the tendency in adult education to dismiss informal education in everyday life; and (c) the increasing professionalization of the field, which has moved the field away from its historical roots within social movements themselves." This book challenges these trends in adult education and the assumptions underlying them. In what follows, I show how activists and organizers through their practices do indeed generate various forms of sophisticated knowledge and engage in significant learning and research.

Some individuals achieve extraordinary things, but I believe that social change is driven mainly by ordinary people organizing, learning, and creating knowledge together—by people consciously and collectively taking steps to bring about change. Not to rule out spontaneity, but most struggles emerge from the hard work of organizing, incremental learning, lineages of earlier movements, and efforts to organize together. Although it is often overlooked, this work is both informed by and contributes to the intellectual work that takes place within social movements, as in social, political, and ecological activism. Everyday acts of resistance are not always visible, nor is much of the long-haul work of organizing that takes place in communities, workplaces, fields, homes, and other spaces down the street and around the world, 365 days a year. This work is often slow, painful, and painstaking. It involves a lot of patient work in small groups and organizations. Across the centuries, movements of people have come together to organize in the face of discrimination, injustice, exploitation, and oppression—from numerous anti-colonial and Third World liberation movements; to struggles against slavery, apartheid, patriarchy, and occupation; to migrant workers mobilizing for fair wages and conditions; to outrage at the continued colonial violence of the Israeli state against Palestine; to campaigns for justice for the hundreds of missing and murdered Indigenous women and their families across Canada. They tap into a sense of collective social anger at injustice.

Incremental, below-the-radar learning and knowledge production in the course of organizing and action is so important, but it is often hard to recognize, document, or theorize. Often, "learning by doing" leaves the deepest footprints. Staughton Lynd (2010, p. 74) puts it so clearly, claiming "Everything we know about learning instructs that people do not learn by reading Left-wing newspapers, nor by attending lectures . . . at which some learned person offers correct theory. **People learn by experience . . .** People must touch and taste an alternative way of doing things, they must however briefly live inside that hope, in order to come to believe that an alternative might really come true" (emphasis in original). Yet as Alan Sears (2014, p. 117) reminds us, although people learn through experience, "the development of deep vision also requires access to things others have learned, in the past, or elsewhere, or from a different positioning in society."

I believe in the importance of the learning and the radical imagination found in movements as vital conceptual resources to change the world. I still live inside a hope for a better world and other ways of doing things. I believe in the power of social movements, in people coming together to build counterpower to bring about social change and to contest governments and capital. Historian Robin Kelley's (2002, p. ix) words are particularly helpful for thinking about the significance of social movements:

> Unfortunately, too often our standards for evaluating social movements
> pivot around whether or not they "succeeded" in realizing their visions
> rather than on the merits or power of the visions themselves. By such a
> measure, virtually every radical movement failed because the basic power
> relations they sought to change remained pretty much intact. And yet it is
> precisely these alternative visions and dreams that inspire new generations
> to continue to struggle for change.

What Kelley points to that is so important to think about is that in practice there are both possibilities and tensions when working between a sense of connectedness to ideas from past struggles that are in danger of being erased, and the way of understanding how the world we now live in has changed.

Learning from Tensions and Contradictions in Struggles

Tensions exist between the past, present, and future. Indeed, processes of learning and producing knowledge in movements and activism can also be fraught with many different tensions and contradictions. I will examine some of these in detail while connecting movement knowledge production, learning, education, action, research, and organizing. I start from the premise that to discuss the emancipatory potential and prospects of activist learning and knowledge production we must at the outset address questions of power—particularly processes of disciplining dissent within movements. We change our thinking about the world in the course of working to change it. Reflecting on community organizing in North America, DeFilippis, Fisher, and Shragge (2010, p. 180) write that learning and education within community organizations are often ignored, or education is limited to teaching specific skills. They say that political education is the basis for unmasking the central issues of power and inequality in the system and building a longer-term vision and political culture. For them, the first of many levels of learning is the kind that people gain through engaging in action, which is "often experiential, growing from their everyday lives. Critical reflection contributes to greater awareness of the interconnection between the specific issues in which an organization is engaged and the wider political economy." Fostering such critical reflection in learning is one way to build the kind of reflections that challenge power and can productively work within tensions and contradictions.

All movements for change themselves, and the learning and knowledge that they produce, are contested terrain. One reason for this is expressed well by historian and educator David Austin, who asserts that a primary measure of a social movement's validity "is the degree to which society's most marginalized and dispossessed are part of and genuinely reflected in the social vision proposed by the movement" (Austin, 2013, p. 12). The connections and relations between the people working in movements and their relation to structures of power are crucial. How we work within movements as well as study or evaluate them itself demands reflection and critical engagement.

My perspective on movements, reflected throughout this book, is engaged and critically sympathetic but unromantic. I am sensitive to the sometimes complex contradictions, tensions, and dynamics in the relationship between learning and action, but I am firm in my belief that organizing and building movements are key to creating counterpower to resist and transform capitalist exploitation and oppression, colonial relations, racism, and patriarchy. Yet the term *social movement* equally includes explicitly xenophobic, homophobic, racist, sexist, and fascist movements, which exist in many parts of the world. While it might be of great interest, and indeed useful, to study those movements, that is not my focus here. However, it is crucial for us to recognize that ostensibly "progressive" movements and activist spaces are not immune to these tendencies. There are frequent power struggles over the direction of campaigns and movements, strategies and tactics, priority issues, and the words, phrases, images, symbols, and targets. The power struggles about who speaks and who "we" are and who "we" claim to stand for, be accountable to, and speak on behalf of exist everywhere. As does the question of who is excluded—subtly or not so subtly. Claims made about commitment to "safe space," anti-oppressive practice, and prefigurative politics in activist contexts should not be immune from critique (Hanhardt, 2013; A. Smith, 2013). What I am highlighting here is that struggles to confront hostility toward working-class people, along with the existence of racism, sexism, and homophobia within activist movements and alternative social formations, cannot be disconnected from bigger goals and broader tensions and injustices in societies. People often talk of activist bubbles or cocoons, but these are not hermetically sealed spaces and often reproduce patterns and relations that they seek to oppose or challenge. I have experienced many conflicts within organizations, coalitions, and other spaces that are ostensibly committed to working for peace and justice because their programs or campaigns dismissed colonialism, class politics, racism, and sexism as being unrelated to the "real issue"—as defined by dominant cliques and perspectives within these groups. Ego and personality politics as well as other forms of power relations can be as embedded in these networks as they are in the world we supposedly want to transform. We live, learn, and organize in a web of contradictions.

At the same time, while working within these contradictions I have often been buoyed by others' solidarity, struggle, and strength in campaigns and mobilizations. I have experienced many moments that seemed personally and politically transformative. These sources of inspiration support us in moving through the difficult challenges that we must pose to ourselves and others. Through cumulative experiences of movements, community organizations, NGOs, and activist groups, for example, I also developed the skills and confidence to critically examine claims about working for a better world. It can be difficult to challenge ideas, assumptions, practices, and power dynamics within such spaces, but building this kind of critique within contradictions is partly what we all must do and what this book is arguing for.

To be clear, I am not arguing that all learning, evaluation, and analysis embedded in various forms of organizing are rigorous or adequate. Indeed, a critical analysis of learning in "progressive" movements necessitates looking critically at their claims in relation to actual practices and, for example, the ways these are experienced by racialized people, Indigenous Peoples, and women. Michael Newman (2000, pp. 275–276) states that

> everyday experience and learning can as easily reproduce ways of thinking and acting which support the often oppressive status quo as it can produce recognitions that enable people to critique and challenge the existing order. And even when learning is emancipatory it is not so in some linear, development sense: it is complex and contradictory, shaped as it is by intrapersonal, interpersonal and broader social forces.

Learning within social movements, therefore, is embedded within all of its contradictions and must be understood as something that actual people within the movements do.

Movements are made up of ordinary people. Activists and organizers are ordinary people. But ordinary people make change. Myths and narratives that attribute change to a few great men (or, occasionally, women), thus reproducing a view of social change as dependent on individual achievements, characteristics, or charisma, often do a great disservice to understanding social movements and the learning that takes place within and about them. Such accounts of history and of movements can obscure or divert attention away from the real nature of the dynamics of broader struggles for social change, rendering invisible the role of a wider array of social forces for transformation. In doing so, they can misinform people about how to organize to bring about change. Highlighting the role of *collective action* in addressing injustices, rather than fetishizing individuals and individual leadership, is both a matter of intellectual honesty as well as empowerment. Kinsman (2010) reminds us of the need to overcome social and historical amnesia about histories of resistance to oppression that have hindered "our remembrance of past social struggles that won the social gains, programs, spaces, and human rights that we so often take for granted." Through what he terms the "social organization of forgetting," the more radical roots of movements and community resistance can be erased and replaced with liberal, respectable constructions of history. He suggests that we have been "forced to forget where we have come from, our histories are rarely being recorded, and we are denied the embodied social and historical literacy that allow us to pass down knowledge, relive our pasts and, therefore, to grasp our present."

As people, we need to feel that we have some agency and can take action, that we have a responsibility to do so that cannot be outsourced to "leaders," and that we appreciate that different people may well have different roles and different skills to offer. In an era of individualism and the atomization of society, such treatments of history and social movements serve to undermine people's sense of agency—that they can play a part in bringing about change. It also therefore undermines the importance of organizing, militant resistance, and collective action. Here the role of critical historians—scholarly and movement varieties—is important in excavating and bringing into question the nature of social and political realities of struggles involving mass movements or long-haul organizing. This is crucial to bring forth and learn about the social relations embedded in collective action and learning in struggle.

Without daily struggles, larger systemic change cannot come about. It is in these daily, local struggles that people learn, reflect, strategize, and act. They build analysis, skills, strategies, and a base needed for longer-term, broader change. Some idealists all too easily dismiss these activities as reformist—this is a mistake. Adult educator Paula Allman (2010, p. 128) insists that

> critical revolutionary praxis develops through and within the struggles
> for reform, whether these pertain to issues emanating from the shop

floor, the community, the environment or any other site where the ramifications of capitalism are experienced. . . . These struggles are some of the most important sites in which critical education can and must take place. Moreover, if this critical education takes place within changed relations, people will be transforming not only their consciousness but their subjectivity and sensibility as well.

Putting it another way, perhaps freedom then becomes, as Angela Davis (2007) suggests, "not a state for which one yearns, but rather an incessant struggle to remake our lives, our relations, our communities, and our futures."

Activism and Social Movements in the Era of Global Capitalism, Ecological Crisis, and War

For several years after the September 11, 2001, attacks on the Pentagon and the World Trade Center, there seemed to be a growing disconnect between activism in the North and South. People's struggles against global free market capitalism, particularly peasant farmer movements, Indigenous Peoples, and militant trade unionists in Latin America and Asia, continued to vigorously challenge the power of states and transnational capital, notwithstanding increasing militarization and the use of draconian anti-terror legislation against activists and communities of resistance. For example, there continued to be major popular movement mobilizations in several countries throughout Asia, Africa, and Latin America against bilateral free trade and investment agreements. These deals threatened to accelerate even more radical trade and investment liberalization regimes than multilateral agreements like the WTO. With few exceptions, very little activism confronted these agreements in the North. In many Northern activist networks, the frames for understanding and mobilizing around the connections between war and links to political economy and global free market capitalism were often limited to articulating how US oil interests in the Middle East related to the invasion of Iraq. However, for many on the frontlines of movements against FTAs—in Colombia, South Korea, or the Philippines, for example, and in the daily struggles for justice and dignity by Indigenous Peoples and immigrant communities in the North—these links were often identified and articulated in ways informed by longer histories of popular struggle against imperialism and colonialism.

Yet in the wake of the 2008 world financial crisis, there were once again mass movements of ordinary people taking to the streets and occupying spaces—and in the North, too—organizing and learning as they worked to oppose government austerity policies, cuts to social spending, and spiralling unemployment. There are examples in many countries in Europe, for example, like Spain's *Los Indignados* ("the outraged"). Indeed, outrage and anger against injustice are important resources to channel into organizing for change, when not harnessed by fascist and racist movements as they sometimes are. In many countries there are new waves, or a resurgence, of struggles of immigrant and migrant workers. Often self-organized, sometimes these are in mass movements, though at other times their resistance takes less visible forms. These workers not only have stood up against labour and immigration injustice, demanding dignity and respect, but also have raised important challenges about the future composition and dynamics of working-class movements, typically occupied by trade unions. They have organized locally, but with global reverberations.

Another important example can be found in Toronto, which saw major protests against the G20 Summit in 2010. These protests were accompanied by mass arrests and police brutality in yet another militarized state security operation at a summit of the world's economic and political elites which was a showpiece for Stephen Harper's Conservative government. Similar challenges to the impact of free market capitalist policies in education sparked the Quebec student movement that built and sustained the 2012 strike, leading to the fall of the Liberal government that had proposed the provincial tuition hikes. As the box earlier in this chapter suggests, there were rich sites of critical learning both within the movement and outside it, reaffirming the power and hard work of methodical long-haul organizing. Further, the level of engagement, sacrifice, creativity, and collective struggle that many thousands of Quebec students displayed so consistently is forcing some to re-examine their cynical view of today's youth as inherently individualistic and self-absorbed. While it may be too soon to predict the course and outcomes of this movement, the process of developing critical consciousness and the politicization of a generation of students—and their courage in taking action—offer hope for the future for many people who do not see "business as usual" as a viable response to today's profound economic, political, and ecological crises. Within these contexts and from these collective experiences are many ordinary people with rich insights into the way society works, arising from their reflections on the world as they are engaged in their lives and struggles rather than from classes in formal education settings like schools, colleges, and universities. As I write in the spring of 2015, thousands of students and others are back on the streets throughout Quebec to protest the provincial government's austerity budget and the petro-economy.

Today, prospects for change can sometimes seem quite grim. On a bad day, it is not always clear to me how much has changed. Take one outcome of the student strike. After months of sustained student-led protests, Quebec's besieged Liberals were replaced by a Parti Québécois government that cynically fuelled a brand of xenophobic white nationalism through its so-called Charter of Quebec Values, which constructed real or perceived religious and cultural practices—particularly those of Muslims living in the province—as a threat. And, as I argue throughout this book, colonialism never disappeared—it just wears different clothes in the twenty-first century. It operates through other names, practices, policies, and institutions—but it is still there. There is an unrelenting assault on Indigenous Peoples and occupation of their territories throughout the world. The doomsday scenario of corporate rule, transnational plunder, and environmental and social disaster that many critics of the global free market economy warn of has long been everyday reality for many Indigenous Peoples.

On the other hand, however, there is continued resistance throughout the Americas, such as the Elsipogtog First Nation's direct action against hydraulic fracking in Mi'kmaq territory (New Brunswick) or the struggle at the other end of the continent against the same process by Mapuche communities in Neuquen, Argentina. These struggles—many of which never make the news—keep alive concepts and practices of relating to the earth and each other in a way that acknowledges we live on a finite planet and we need to think more carefully about whose land we live on and how we are complicit in using and abusing it for corporate profit.

A recurring theme that runs through parts of this book is that we often seem to collude with what we critique. The above example of the ongoing assaults upon Indigenous Peoples and their territories is one to begin with. There is much talk about decolonization in some academic and activist circles. But how much of it is bound up within and limited by the parameters and worldview of the very liberal democratic notions and nations that have taken root on occupied Indigenous territories and dispossessed millions? Similarly, community organizations and global justice movements exist in tension with the very neoliberal capitalism that established and nourished the local and international political and social spaces for NGOs—that nebulous thing called "civil society" and the community sector. Indeed, some of these organizations had picked up increased roles and responsibilities for social provision and economic development as states restructured. Many local community organizations and international development and advocacy NGOs share certain characteristics that impact struggles for justice in both the North and South. These include professionalization, collaboration with, and recognition and support from, the state or international institutions, and a detachment from more critical forms of resistance. There are often disjunctures between what is declared and what is done in the name of social justice; there are tensions between funded projects and campaigns and politically independent forms of social struggle. Such tensions are often mirrored in academic activities and the relationship between universities and communities, movements, and social and political struggles.

Theory and Theorizing

When we think about the learning that takes place in movements, sometimes it is construed as merely factual or contextual. But this is far from true. Theory and theorizing are in fact crucial to the ways in which learning happens in movements. Austin (2009, p. 115) explains that theory is far from being abstract; it "is congealed experience, which, in a concentrated form, can bring years of accumulated knowledge to bear on a particular issue or cause and help to prevent strategic mishaps." But the voices, ideas, and indeed theories produced by those engaged in social struggles are often ignored, rendered invisible, or overwritten with accounts by professionalized "experts" or university-based intellectuals. Deeper theoretical work is crucial to movements and activism, but formally educated specialized theorists do not have a monopoly over it, as Alan Sears (2005a) has argued so well. Kinsman (2006) similarly contends that research and theorizing is a broader everyday/every night part of the life of social movements, whether explicitly recognized or not. I will return to take a deeper look at activist/movement research in Chapter 4.

So what is the relationship of theory to knowledge arising from experience? How do we effectively mediate between experiential knowledge and theoretical concepts? How can we apply concepts to concrete experiences in struggles to help reorganize understandings in ways that support effective strategy and action? Some answers are given by Lynd (in Lynd and Grubacic 2009, p. 40), who says "there are examples of homegrown, close-to-the-earth kind of theory that evolved directly from folks' experience in organizing . . . [but] I think there is another kind of theory that is needed, too." For example, "in the absence of a theory to explain what is going on economically the best-intentioned, most grassroots and democratic sort of movement is likely to flounder." Theoretical and analytical frameworks can provide powerful tools for analysis, strategy, and action, whether produced in institutional spaces like universities or outside of them.

One factor contributing to the failure to acknowledge the intellectual contributions of activism—including the lineages of ideas and theories forged in struggles and learning largely outside of universities that often occur incrementally, collectively, informally, and sometimes incidentally—is the high value accorded to "original" single authorship in the realm of academic knowledge. But Lynd (2010, p. 144) reminds us that the most significant contributions to

Marxist thought came from people who were not academics, "who passed through the university but did not remain there." This is only one example, of course, and it is not only Marxist theory that has been deeply influenced by non-academics.

In affirming the concept of activist knowledge production, theorizing, research, and other forms of intellectual work in struggle, Italian Marxist activist and thinker Antonio Gramsci's (1971, p. 62) articulation of different groups of intellectuals is also helpful here. Gramsci theorized two groups of intellectuals. First, there are "traditional" intellectuals, scholars and scientists who, although seemingly detached from class positions, are produced by specific historical class formations. Gramsci argued that they are produced within the ruling systems and that they play a part in and are connected to them in particular ways that constrain them from being able to think and profoundly change systems of power. They function according to their positions. Second, there are the "organic" intellectuals, the thinking and organizing persons in any class. According to Gramsci, such people articulate a "philosophy of praxis" that develops in the course of political struggle, the "concrete historicisation of philosophy and its identification with history." Often organizers and "permanent persuaders" emerging from the grassroots/working class are not seen as intellectuals capable of creating knowledge. Yet in Gramsci's understanding of intellectuals, these people have a greater potential to effect change because they are not tied to the system in the same way. Moreover, they develop theories and ideas in relation to where they come from in powerful ways that push and challenge their thought further.

It is not particularly important to me to categorize intellectuals or thinkers into groups, but rather to take from Gramsci's articulations a way to recognize and validate theorization and theories that are deeply informed by practice and struggle. Some examples may help to make this clearer and more concrete. One example of scholarly work that has explored the impact of anti-colonial struggles on an influential academic theoretical tradition is the attention that Tavares (1992) and Buck-Morss (2009) have brought to how the Haitian revolution influenced Hegel's theorizing—in particular its influence upon the master–slave dialectic. Another good example is that Karl Marx (1984) rewrote his influential theory of the state under the impact of the Paris Commune on his thinking. Raya Dunayevskaya (1958) points out that the spur to Marx finishing the first volume of *Capital* came from the revival of the British working-class movement in the context of the US Civil War.

Another example to think about in this context is the suggestion by both Brady Heiner (2007) and David Austin (2013) that Michel Foucault's extremely influential *Discipline and Punish* might never have been written without ideas and insights of Black Panther Party members with whom the French sociologist met on a United States visit. The Panthers' influence on Foucault is recorded in the documentation of meetings of his Prison Information Group (GIP) with George Jackson and Angela Davis while they were jailed. These encounters happened before Foucault started writing on prisons, power–knowledge, genealogy, discipline, biopolitics, and biopower. Heiner and Austin suggest that Foucault rendered invisible the theoretical contributions of Jackson and Davis, appropriating the experience of incarcerated Black individuals in the US prison–industrial complex while failing to acknowledge them. Austin suggests that notwithstanding Foucault's contributions to theory, this means erasing the memory of Black struggles and the theories that arose from this experience.

These examples are far from isolated. Numerous examples of feminist, anti-racist, and Indigenous scholarship have also arisen and benefited from popular forms of resistance challenging patriarchal, racist, colonial, and capitalist relations. Indeed, upsurges in social movement studies research itself can be attributed to periods of widespread social protest and mobilization. These

FIGURE 1.1: Cecilia Rodriguez, US spokesperson for the EZLN (Zapatista Army of National Liberation), speaks at a rally in Washington, DC, protesting the World Bank's 50th anniversary and Mexican President Ernesto Zedillo's visit to the United States in 1995. (Photograph by Orin Langelle)

include the multiple worldwide movements in the late 1960s and the emergence of global justice, climate justice, and anti-austerity movements more
recently. Such dynamics should call into further question dominant tendencies, even among those on the left, within the academy and outside it, to make
assumptions about the relative value and significance of the location of intellectual work. We must think about how much we valorize and legitimate
work done in universities compared to everyday social action settings, what
processes of knowledge production we recognize, and what counts as knowledge, theory, research, or expertise.

Power in a Globalized World

> Power concedes nothing without a demand. It never did and it
> never will. Find out just what any people will quietly admit to
> and you have found out the exact measure of injustice and wrong
> which will be imposed upon them, and these will continue till
> they are resisted with either words or blows, or with both. The
> limits of tyrants are prescribed by the endurance of those whom
> they oppress.
>
> Frederick Douglass (1857/1985, p. 204)

We hear a lot about *globalization*. Dominant media and official accounts tend
to claim that this is a relatively new phenomenon and that all of the world's
peoples will benefit through opportunities to compete in a global market as
trade, investment, and economies become more open. This is supposed to bring
people closer together and lead to peace, prosperity, and greater understanding
between people. To begin with, there are real dangers in treating globalization
as something new. Many, including Petras and Veltmeyer (2001), note that the
question of whether globalization does actually represent a qualitatively new
phenomenon or yet another phase in a longer historical period of imperi-
alist expansion is highly disputed. This points to one of the dangers we face:
the failure to learn from historical antecedents, particularly older phases of
capitalism, imperialism, and colonialism and the struggles against them. Ellen
Wood (1998, p. 14) argues that the term *globalization* itself can obscure and
mystify collusion between states and capital and infer a kind of inevitability
about the process. She warns that

> [w]e have to guard against treating the trends that go under that name
> [globalization] as if they were natural, inevitable processes, instead

of historically specific *capitalist* processes, the capitalist exploitation
of human beings and natural resources, aided and abetted by a direct
collaboration between the state and capital.

Global free market capitalism is not like evolution or the moon's pull on
the tide. It is not a natural, inevitable, or organic process, nor is it a mystical, deterministic force that is somehow driven by technological advances
detached from human activities, as some would have us believe. The World
Bank, the International Monetary Fund (IMF), and the WTO—three of the
most powerful institutional vehicles for extending, maintaining, and enforc-
ing global free market capitalism—are not somehow outside of or above
social relations; nor are the transnational corporations that have emerged over
recent decades as major actors in both global and national economies. Their
political and economic power is often viewed as more significant than that
exercised by governments. By 1995, the United Nations Conference on Trade
and Development (1995) noted that several of the world's biggest corporations had total revenues larger than the gross domestic product of countries
in which they operated; two-thirds of global trade in goods and services
were occurring between subsidiaries of transnational corporations. Another
report (Anderson & Cavanaugh, 1996) illustrated that by the same year, 51 of
the world's largest 100 economies were corporations, not countries.[5] While
most large corporations have been headquartered in the North, a significant
number of corporations from the South are now major global and regional
players. This ongoing concentration, consolidation, and expansion of corporate interests and power—which has advanced through a swathe of mergers
and acquisitions, diversification, takeovers, alliances, changes in production,
transportation, information technology, and the financialization of the global
economy—has only further concentrated economic power in fewer hands in
recent years. Finance capital, including banks, pension schemes, hedge funds,
private equity funds, and other public and private financial institutions, along
with governments and corporations, are engaged in massive land and water
grabs in the global South, undermining food sovereignty and the livelihoods
of millions of people. Yet across the planet such corporations and financial
institutions also meet with resistance from communities and movements that
organize, learn, educate, research, resist—and sometimes win!

In this book you will see the word *dialectic* a lot, drawing from the thoughts
of Karl Marx and others. To think dialectically means to understand things that

....

5 Calculated by comparing corporate sales with countries' gross domestic product (GDP).

appear to be "givens" as actually being made through relations. Talking about a dialectic means that there is a unity of two opposites—they could not have developed in the way they did or even exist as they do outside of the way in which they are internally related to each other. The famous example of this is labour and capital; others include the global North/First World and global South/Third World, and human societies and nature. We can think about the "big picture" of the global economy and our own communities, the "local." More abstractly, there is the past, present, and future. The relationships between these things are constantly moving and changing as they make up our social world. As people struggle with problems and injustice in their everyday lives, through the unity of theory and action—also called *praxis*—they can learn, think, and act to bring about broader social, economic, political, and ecological change, rejecting "common sense" assumptions and explanations and building a deeper understanding of power structures and relations. One of this book's tasks is to look past artificial divides between theory and practice, particularly in relation to learning, pedagogy, research, theorizing, and social movements. I suggest that we need to break down distinctions between various forms of human activity. Rather than considering movements, learning and education, organizing, knowledge production, and activist research as separate categories and activities, I highlight how these are dialectically linked. Citing the ideas of political scientist Bertell Ollman, Carroll (2006, pp. 235–236) explains that to understand a social issue—poverty, for example—we need to uncover "the ways in which it is hooked into other social issues and relations. . . . Marx's method rejects metaphysical conceptions that view the present as 'walled off' from either the past or the future. Such conceptions, all too common in social science and policy discourses, can become 'a prison for thinking,' as the present form of something—'the family,' 'the economy,' 'retirement'—is mistaken for 'what it is in full, and what it could only be'" (Ollman, 1998, p. 345).

So capitalism is not a reified system or structure external to human beings, but a human structure, as Allman (2010, p. 39) reminds us, which means

> the structured relations of human beings into which they enter routinely in order to produce their material existence. Forms of organization and physical structures, as well as the legal system that gives legitimacy to the structure, are created in order to "cement" this structuring of human relations, but the real or material substance of the structure is the daily, sensuous activity of human beings.

Thus she argues that capitalism is created and sustained by human beings who are actively engaged in capitalist social relations and can be challenged and resisted in the course of a struggle to transform capitalist structures and relations.

As Holst (2002, p. 10) observes, Marx "views society dialectically, but the dialectic is not some mystical, deterministic force pushing history forward but the way in which things and people come into relations; it is the human agency (class struggle) characteristic of these relations that moves history." Contrary to caricatures of Marxism or ossified, mechanistic versions (Biel, 2015), therefore, the very idea of the dialectic is not about determinism. People—and how they engage each other—are what matter. People's everyday activities create, sustain, reshape, and remake social relations. This is why mapping power is a crucial element of activist knowledge production: to uncover, explain, explore, and analyze the ways in which capitalist relations—through global and local institutions, corporations, financial instruments, processes, and policies—shape our lives and those of others with whom we share this planet. In turn, such knowledge can try to identify weaknesses, contradictions, conjunctures, or pressure points that organizers and movements can exploit.

There remain many challenges to building counterpower from below to challenge the power of states and capital and bring about social and environmental justice. My own activism began during the Cold War, when the threat of mutually assured destruction through nuclear annihilation often seemed perilously close. Today, the so-called War on Terror continues apace, social and economic inequalities are deepening and growing within and among societies, and the planet faces a climate/ecological crisis the magnitude of which seems like the sum of all environmental fears. Since the death of Margaret Thatcher—who reigned over my own politicization and that of many others of my generation—I have had countless conversations about the long-term impacts of the imposition of free market capitalist policies in several contexts. These include not only Thatcher's Britain, but also the United States since Ronald Reagan, Canada since Brian Mulroney, and Aotearoa/New Zealand's radical free market transformation. These processes wreaked havoc on communities and social movements. This era can be characterized by the atomization of society; the exalting of the capitalist free market and its mechanisms as the favoured means of distributing income and wealth; the demonization and pulverizing of community, trade unions, and left-wing social movements; and the intensification of the idea that individuals are defined primarily and narrowly by their market value, including what and how they consume: the perfect neoliberal subjects.

With the Cold War's end and the Soviet Union's collapse, we entered a unipolar world of supposed capitalist triumph over socialism, neoliberal transformations, and a crisis of the left in many places. The ascendancy of neoliberalism has transformed society in multiple ways. I agree with David McNally (2011, p. 149), who emphasizes that neoliberalism was more than just a set of policies imposed from above. As he writes, the neoliberal turn "also involved molecular transformations at the most basic levels of everyday life. Senses of self, ways of relating to others, and the organization of communities were all restructured. Essential here were the social and cultural processes that eroded older forms of working-class organization, spaces of resistance, and solidarities." Since the 2007–08 global financial meltdown, many governments have implemented austerity measures to launch an assault on wages, working conditions, and social services while bailing out corporations and banks. Like the term "globalization," perhaps "austerity" serves to obscure both the structural crisis and nature of capitalism. These transformations pose serious challenges for collective action, not least for youth—"generation NGO"—for whom models of NGO or community entrepreneurialism are the most visible kind of social engagement on display. This model of "civic engagement" arguably supports and reifies free market capitalism and neoliberal subjectivities. Such activity often claims to be nonpartisan, apolitical, or anti-political and encourages individuals to adopt these positions.

Despite these challenges—or perhaps in part because of them—the first decade and a half of the twenty-first century has seen major resistance movements and vigorous organizing for social change in many places. Some of this can be explained through the fact that effective collective action is nurtured by what Sears (2005b, 2014) calls the "infrastructure of dissent," that is to say, a range of formal and informal organizations through which people develop their capacities to analyze and map the system, communicate using official and alternative media, and take strategic action in solidarity with others. In different ways Gramsci (1971), Holst (2002), Boughton (2013), and Sears (2014) have all highlighted the significance and overlooked nature of the informal and non-formal forms of learning and knowledge production that take place in revolutionary political parties. Having never been a member of a party, I have not had that experience. Yet I have experienced this in other movement/organizing spaces and indeed, as John Hilary (2013, p. 5) reminds us, alternatives exist "not only in the everyday resistance of social movements to the threat of capitalist expansion, but in the existing operations of those movements and cooperative ventures that are already constructing their own paths out of capitalism. The fact that such alternatives are so often hidden from public view is a result of the power exercised by transnational capital over the economic development discourse, often with the active connivance of 'respectable' NGOs." Such alternatives arise from struggle, active engagement, reflection, and action. The traditions, trajectories, hopes, visions, and challenges of today's struggles—and yesterday's—invite us to think, to resist, and to organize. However, while today's economic and unprecedented ecological crises arguably add both a real sense of urgency for systemic change and new opportunities for resistance, this is not a given. Some lessons in how to go forward may be found by engaging histories from the past, but also avoiding false nostalgia about past struggles.

Engaging History

> . . . and still our history gets written in a liar's scrawl.
> Buffy Sainte-Marie (1992; Cree singer-songwriter).

> [P]eople who imagine that history flatters them (as it does, indeed, since they wrote it) are impaled like a butterfly on a pin, and become incapable of seeing or changing themselves or their world.
> James Baldwin (1985, p. 410).

To analyze activism in the present, it is important not only to learn from history in activist contexts but also to problematize the production of histories. The theme of looking back to move forward runs throughout this book. This means not only understanding dominant versions of history, but also critically engaging with histories about and by movement actors. The politics of knowledge production and learning in contemporary social movements are located in (and sometimes in tension with) older histories of struggle and contestation. This is central in the organizing and thinking that many organizers and activists do. Crucial to the notion of history in this book is the suggestion made by Robin Kelley (in Holtzman, 2010, p. 320) that we place a lot of emphasis on studying the history of social movements, successes, and failures, but that we should spend more time looking "at the reproduction of power and how things work. What are the weaknesses in a system? How are decisions made?" History is not merely what came before but a process of working through and evaluating these things in our own contexts, with our own insights. So history is as much about the present and the future as it is about the past.

In thinking through education and action strategies in contemporary struggles, it is crucial to appreciate historical continuities and change as well as a critical eye for interrogating the sense of newness one often experiences about new campaigns and actions. History serves the present and the future in many critical ways, as DeFilippis, Fisher, and Shragge (2010, p. 181) suggest, "including providing a collective memory of prior struggles, strategies, victories, and defeats. It offers an instant comparative perspective with the present, filled with lessons for those with interest and time. One of the critical lessons from the past . . . is the powerful role played by the broader political-economic context. These structural factors heavily influence the opportunities and limits, the potential success and constrained barriers that shape contemporary community practices." This attention to broader contexts reminds us that merely trying to reproduce past mobilizations, framings, and modes of organizing without attending to their relevance and horizons of possibility can be problematic. Moreover, in referring to history, questions must always be asked about the politics behind which accounts of earlier struggles are documented and preserved. No history is neutral; we must always learn from the past through a critical lens.

Just as no history is neutral, history is also not just what is written in books. Recently I was sitting with a friend in Johannesburg, sifting through trade union and other publications that he had edited or written that were banned by the apartheid regime in South Africa. This was a familiar experience and reminded me of flyers, handbills, newsletters, publications, and posters from my own organizing and activism. In the preface to this book I talk about bringing these materials to an academic job interview; and I also referred to myself as a hoarder. If this is a tongue-in-cheek way of putting it, there is nonetheless very real work to be done in collecting, documenting, and archiving these materials. They contain rich movement histories, debates, and knowledge, and it is important they not be lost or erased. One of the challenges is that these visions, and the learning and experience-based knowledge produced within them, do not often end up neatly packaged for our consumption on websites, in academic studies of social movements, in glossy NGO publications, or in more popularly written books or articles. In his obituary for Black British historian and educationalist Len Garrison (founder of the Black Cultural Archives and the Afro-Caribbean Education Resource Centre in Britain), Mike Phillips's (2003, p. 297) words ring so true for many other contexts: "[t]he handbills, flyers, posters, programmes for a wide range of events, including political meetings, art exhibitions, concerts, plays, community meetings about education, welfare and politics . . . may be not only the only surviving record of transient organizations, but the only way of understanding whole movements and trends." Sometimes these are kept intentionally. More often than not this kind of material languishes in boxes, plastic bags, basements, and garages before ending up getting thrown away, perhaps not without some guilt, because we don't have space and can't afford the costs of storage and we wonder if anyone is interested in them. Maybe someone will digitize them someday, to preserve and make them available for future generations? What are the possibilities for community and movement control over the way such hidden histories can be recovered? Histories are transmitted in many struggles through such informal collections. They are also transmitted through stories, songs, and poems, particularly in contexts where oral transmission of knowledge, values, and visions is more significant than written versions.

Poets, musicians, and other artists also play vital roles as historians, educators, and transmitters of ideas. Cree singer-songwriter, educator, and activist Buffy Sainte-Marie's song "Bury My Heart at Wounded Knee," for example, directly confronts dominant versions of history in North America. The song passionately documents and condemns corporate greed and US exploitation and oppression against Indigenous Peoples and their territories. It narrates events surrounding the 1973 FBI siege of Wounded Knee on the Pine Ridge Oglala Lakota reservation and the subsequent jailing of Lakota/Anishinabe activist Leonard Peltier and murder of Mi'kmaq activist Annie Mae Aquash. South Africa's Miriam Makeba sang searing songs like "Soweto Blues," reminding the world about the June 1976 Soweto uprising when thousands of Black students rose up against an apartheid government decree that made Afrikaans the medium of school instruction and where many were brutally massacred by police. Black British dub poet Linton Kwesi Johnson insightfully chronicled struggles against racism and capitalism in Britain, the conundrums of left politics, immigration justice, police brutality, and the legacies of fallen activists and thinkers like assassinated Guyanese historian Walter Rodney ("Reggae fi Radni"). These three performers tell histories in profound and challenging ways. But more than this, as Montreal-based anarchist artist, musician, writer, and activist Norman Nawrocki (2012, p. 106) writes, music "can help tell community stories uncensored, from a fresh perspective. It encourages people to explore and reinvent the oral tradition and introduce it into their daily routine. It helps broaden discussion and reclaim silenced voices. Moreover, it combats the ever-passive consumerism of our own culture, allowing people to take music back." Many artists record and transmit (hi)stories of resistance around the world, sometimes at times or about events, periods, or perspectives on which "official histories" are conveniently or deliberately silent. Many movements have had poets and musicians in their ranks who have creatively told the stories of struggle, affirmed their experiences, and inspired people to stay strong. I will return to the role of music and the arts in relation to consciousness, popular education, learning, and organizing in Chapter 3. But these art forms are as much history and knowledge as are more official sources, and they can help us in documenting, theorizing, and nourishing social action.

In Search of the Big Picture

To give a further example of the relevance of a historical perspective that bridges both theoretical literature and concrete experience, I will discuss Frantz Fanon, an especially insightful anti-colonial thinker of the twentieth century. His classic book *The Wretched of the Earth* (Fanon, 1968) remains one of the most important books I have ever read. When one reads Fanon against the times that we live in, the materiality and intensity of his writing from the 1950s and 1960s still leap from every page. Of course, we cannot and should not overlook the geo-historical aspects of the moment(s) in which he wrote. The time and place, the political and social contexts were shaped by his experiences in Martinique, France, Tunisia, and the independence struggle in Algeria, and informed by his political commitments and engagements in the 1940s, 50s, and early 60s. His legacy and analysis remain relevant—as evidenced by the many commemorations of his life, work, and struggles in so many places in 2011–12 to mark the 50th anniversary of his death in December 1961. For example, talking with friends and comrades in South Africa affirmed to me how Fanon's ideas still resonate with many of those who struggled against apartheid only to find the old regime replaced by governments led by new elites who have prioritized the interests of capital over those of the majority of the population in the name of liberation. It is also encouraging to see new generations of organizers—and students—encountering Fanon for the first time and finding his insights useful to their own processes of thinking.

The divide between what are viewed as "old" and "new" social movements has introduced a disjuncture between the historical experiences in social transformation and the present. This in turn has thwarted the development of theoretical and conceptual resources that are needed to act in transformative ways. Rejecting or forgetting the history of capitalism and colonialism and the struggles against them has produced what critical scholars describe as "capitalist triumphalism." *Triumphalism* is the ideology of transnational finance corporations; it sees all struggles everywhere as failures and therefore proclaims that there is no alternative to capitalism. It is necessary to bring ideas of emancipation, decolonization, and freedom back into social movements and the work of organizing. This is a move that makes it imperative to restore the unity of the past and the future in the present and will be revisited in Chapter 2.

Understanding Capitalist Globalization as (Re)Colonization

To critically analyze capitalist triumphalism from a historical and engaged perspective, Fanon's writing on colonialism and anti-colonial struggles—particularly *The Wretched of the Earth*—remains a profound source of inspiration and insight. Fanon's visionary analysis of imperialism in post-independence Third World nations predicts a scenario where decolonized societies contend with attendant capital flight, and direct colonial rule is replaced by the intensification of foreign investment imperialism that locks newly independent peoples into new forms of exploitation. In doing so, Fanon accurately predicts the past three decades of experience with neoliberal capitalism.

A fuller debate on the nature of contemporary capitalist relations and global-ization falls outside the scope of this book. But undoubtedly the positions that social movement actors have taken on this question influence their actions. Despite the very real and rapid economic and political changes sweeping the world—such as the transnationalization of production, resource exploitation, and the internationalization of finance—the structure of capitalism has not fundamentally changed, though its intensity and scope have. This is especially true of Third World countries. As Eqbal Ahmad (2000) argues, globalization has changed neither the political nor the economic reality of many parts of the world since the days of direct colonial rule. Rather, they are living through another phase of colonialism and imperialism. This resonates with ideas voiced by many Indigenous Peoples in settler–colonial states like Canada, Australia, and Aotearoa/New Zealand. For example, Maori lawyer Moana Jackson (1999, p. 105) argues that for Indigenous Peoples, globalization is not a new phenom-enon. Instead, they are "faced with a two-fold challenge, to struggle as best we can to deal with the immediate consequences of globalization. Secondly, and more difficult, to contextualize those problems within the 500-year-and-more history of the culture of colonization."

Thinking back to one moment when this analysis was clearly laid out, I vividly remember an evening in November 1991, when Maori trade union-ist and Indigenous sovereignty activist Syd Jackson addressed a packed public meeting in Christchurch on free trade and GATT (the General Agreement on Tariffs and Trade). Jackson spoke about how free market economics and free trade were nothing new for Maori. He reminded the audience that the sense of loss of sovereignty that many non-Maori New Zealanders were expressing at that time—as radical privatization and deregulation delivered the economy into the hands of transnational corporations—was something that Maori had experienced far more deeply for generations. Jackson clearly wove together the threads of colonialism, dispossession, neoliberalism, Aotearoa/New Zealand's history, and Indigenous Peoples' resistance in a way that was at once firmly located in a local context but cognizant of global capitalist relations.

In those days it was difficult to avoid thinking about these issues. I was living on a low income at the height of New Zealand's application of almost pure free market economic doctrine, complete with privatizations, job layoffs, increased poverty, and other negative social effects. I knew about the effects of World Bank/IMF structural adjustment in the Third World and could see parallels with Aotearoa/New Zealand's transformation into a lean, mean, free market state. Indeed, exchanges with Third World activists helped us frame and think through what Jane Kelsey (1995) calls "the New Zealand experiment." Such exchanges were crucial in building an analysis and understanding of similarities and differences and historical continuities, and informing our action. An anti-colonial analysis has remained at the core of my political activism, and later my academic research. This critical historical understanding meant that I could see that this was not the first time there had been such sweeping changes in Aotearoa/New Zealand. A colonial continuum connected contemporary "reforms" with the radical changes wrought by British colonization since the nineteenth century. Land and resource theft, invasion and occupation lie at the heart of colonialism. For me, anti-colonial politics necessarily embrace strong and active opposition to capitalism and all forms of imperialism—and it places the issue of self-determination front and centre.

Key elements of modern-day global free market capitalism are not new—the commodification of peoples, of nature, and of social relations; the exalting of individual over collective rights; and indeed the forebears of some of its major drivers and beneficiaries, transnational corporations (charter colonizing companies like the East India Company in South Asia or the Hudson's Bay Company in North America). Such insights are fundamental to my understandings of social movements, activism, learning, knowledge, and the world. They also inevitably draw me to look for conceptual resources from older struggles, compel me to pay attention to local contexts, and highlight the importance of thinking critically about historical processes. Raghavan (1990) used the term *recolonization* to refer to the GATT negotiations. This frame is quite common in Third World scholarly literature and activist networks—although some, such as Eqbal Ahmad, ask whether it is accurate to talk of recolonization, questioning if genuine decolonization ever really occurred. Indeed.

Indigenous and other colonized peoples are often at the forefront of both the analysis of and resistance to capitalist globalization. Some have taken the lead in critiquing and resisting free market capitalism by emphasizing how it commodifies everything and is founded on the exploitation of people and nature—from land to water, to climate change, to the corporate enclosure of nature through biotechnology and bioprospecting.[6] At a macroeconomic level, a debt-driven model of colonialism has been imposed on the South through IMF/World Bank structural adjustment programs that is connected to the "repauperization of the North" (Faraclas, 2001, p. 70). Kelsey (1999, p. 167) observes that contemporary conflicts between transnational corporations and Indigenous Peoples are rooted in colonization, with the former being new actors in an older, ongoing struggle for self-determination. "Yet," she argues, "power is also

....

6 It would be a gross misrepresentation, however, to homogenize all Indigenous Peoples' positions as inherently anti-capitalist and anti-colonial. There are many internal debates and conflicts among Indigenous Peoples regarding values and models of "development" (see, for example, Kelsey, 1999; Bargh, 2007).

being transferred from the colonial state, which can be challenged at the very least on moral grounds . . . to more remote international corporations whose sole responsibility is to their shareholders." The 1994 Zapatista uprising in Mexico's southern state of Chiapas and its subsequent articulation—transmitted worldwide through solidarity networks, the Internet, and alternative media—as an Indigenous Peoples' struggle rooted in resistance to five centuries of colonial injustice also drew attention to the relationship between contemporary and older forms of imperialism. One reason for this was that it explicitly confronted the North American Free Trade Agreement (NAFTA), which was signed between Canada, Mexico, and the United States and took effect on 1 January 1994, as well as other forms of global free market capitalism.

Indigenous Peoples' struggles for self-determination are useful contributions to theorizing a convincing alternative to neoliberalism, according to Burgmann and Ure (2004, p. 57). These authors assert that "the practical critique of neoliberalism embodied in Indigenous People's resistance to their incorporation into the global market is one informed by an often acute recognition of not only the global dimensions of such resistance but also an acknowledgement of anti-imperialist struggles stretching back over many hundreds of years." This has "enabled non-indigenous groups and movements to root their critique in an anti-capitalist perspective that emanates from non-Western sources." They further argue that the desire for self-determination in the face of neoliberalism is often expressed most intensely in the struggles of Indigenous Peoples, and thus their role has been crucially significant to its spread to other sectors of global society.

I believe that to overlook or underestimate the value of Indigenous Peoples' critical analyses and strategies of resistance in relation to capitalist globalization is to seriously constrain analysis and action that could meaningfully transform the dominant economic, political, and social order—both locally and internationally. This body of knowledge and the conceptualization of the various institutions and processes that drive capitalist globalization as new forms of colonial actors are important to inform and frame our analysis. This perspective problematizes the legitimacy, role, and mandate of nation-states to commit to economic and social policies that further marginalize and dispossess Indigenous Peoples within the territories that they govern, and challenges many dominant "civil society" narratives, accounts of history, and claims to representation. It forces us to rethink relations between people, land, and nature. Moreover, it invites us to bring back and re-centre conceptual space, relocating the terrain of struggle around ideas about decolonization and self-determination.

This historical understanding of the relations between colonialism and capitalist globalization is very present in the Third World. As Biel (2015) remarks,

capitalism is a world system premised on colonialism. Imperialism's fundamental features, as described in the early twentieth century, are unchanged
but intensified, as Argentinian sociologist Atilio Boron (2005, pp. 3–4) notes:

> The acceleration of globalization that took place in the final quarter
> of the last century, instead of weakening or dissolving the imperialist
> structures of the world economy, magnified the structural asymmetries
> that define the insertion of the different countries in it. While a handful
> of developed capitalist nations increased their capacity to control, at least
> partially, the productive processes at a global level, the financialization
> of the international economy and the growing circulation of goods and
> services, the great majority of countries witnessed the growth of their
> external dependency and the widening of the gap that separated them
> from the centre. Globalization, in short, consolidated the imperialist
> domination and deepened the submission of peripheral capitalisms,
> which became more and more incapable of controlling their domestic
> economic processes even minimally.

As this passage by Boron indicates, perhaps echoing Fanon, global restructuring led to new forms of colonial relationships as nominally independent Third
World countries were made dependent on exports, desperately trying to earn
foreign exchange while their local economies were undermined. Non-market
forms of social relations—subsistence economies and traditional or customary
land tenure systems that sustain millions of people—were targeted for elimina-
tion and incorporation into a global market. Rising interest rates on loans and
falling world prices for exports cemented this exploitative colonial relationship.
Many critics charged that corporations and Northern governments worked
together to recolonize the Third World, aided by local elites. Workers, Indigenous
Peoples, and small farmers were under renewed and intensified attack worldwide.
Meanwhile, women were often expected to pick up the pieces as social services
were dismantled, and were further marginalized as low-paid, highly exploited
agricultural or factory workers in global supply chains. Millions became migrant
workers. Indigenous Peoples, small farmers, and Third World workers were also on
the frontlines of struggles against global capitalism and "domestic" neoliberalism.

On a recent visit to Buenos Aires, I talked with Argentinian activists who
were pondering the meaning of two centuries of "independence." They stated
that massive corporate-owned soya plantations had taken the place of the Spanish
colonizers. These plantations, cropping up throughout the country, generate profits for transnational agribusiness but take over land from Indigenous
Peoples and *campesinos* to grow crops for export or agrofuels. Fanon's words

once again resonate (1968, pp. 79–80): "Colonialism and imperialism have not paid their score when they withdraw their flags and their police forces from our territories. For centuries the capitalists have behaved in the under-developed world like nothing more than war criminals." In other words, even if countries, peoples, or territories may be nominally independent or self-governing, the process of colonization continues through globalized free market capitalism. It is resistance to pervasive forms of colonialism and imperialism from which I draw experience, research, analysis, and theoretical/conceptual materials for this book—as well as inspiration.

Consciousness, Knowledge Production, Learning, and Education

Having made explicit some of the thinking that underpins my activism and perspectives on social change, struggles, and knowledge politics, I would now like to introduce some ideas about the significance of knowledge production, informal and non-formal learning, and research in activism. In reflecting on my own political education, I concur with Budd Hall (1978, pp. 13–14), who writes that "knowledge is produced and renewed by continuous testing, by acting upon one's theories, by reflecting upon one's actions, and by beginning the cycle again. It is the combination of social transformation and education that has created the kind of knowledge which forges the personal and communal commitment for sustained engagement." This rings true to me because it captures the continual cycle of learning in action that occurs in the course of long-term campaigns, short-term mobilizations, and daily struggles.

Beginning to work with the question of how consciousness is formed, I am drawn to Marxist dialectical understandings of how this works through and by our relationship with a material, social world. Allman (2010, p. 152) suggests that "our action in and on the material world is the mediation or link between our consciousness and objective reality. Our consciousness develops from our active engagement with other people, nature, and the objects or processes we produce. In other words, it develops from the sensuous experiencing of reality from within the social relations in which we exist." A major focus throughout this book is to think about how real, material experiences form our learning and consciousness in ways not normally addressed through formal education—school, university, and so on—but in other kinds of ways. For example, a migrant worker whose race, gender, and class analysis is grounded in and shaped by her experiences—exploited in a low-wage job with lousy conditions by a racist employer who refuses to treat her with dignity and respect, and an immigration regime which facilitates this exploitation, can offer important perspectives that are not necessarily central to dominant trade union understandings of such a case.

Strategic learning through struggle and contestation encompasses a dialectic that includes incidental, formal, informal, and non-formal education. This implies an engagement in strategic analysis, which leads to strategic action, then to intended and unintended consequences of action, and finally to further reflection/analysis and action (Novelli, 2010). Griff Foley (1999) highlights the importance of embracing a broad conception of education and learning, the relationship between struggle and learning, and an analytical framework that connects learning to its context. A Marxist theory of praxis that insists upon the unity of thought and action necessitates a "[d]ialectical theory of consciousness in which thought, action, and social relations are inseparable" (Carpenter & Mojab, 2012, p. 13). Human activity and thought are mutually constitutive; they are shaped by each other.

At the same time that we focus on how different kinds of learning are done in different educational milieus, there remains much work to be done in thinking through what kinds of social relations, contexts, and circumstances help people move from consciousness to action. How do people move from learning only to adapt, to learning that supports resistance? Learning that can generate theoretical insights and more complex understandings about the world? Foley (1999, p. 3) once again is helpful here, because he discusses learning in movements and activist contexts in a way that analyzes and validates the importance of the incidental, informal learning in social struggles. He writes that while "systematic education does occur in some social movement sites and actions, learning in such situations is largely informal and often incidental—it is tacit, embedded in action and is often not recognised as learning." Foley highlights the complicated and contradictory nature of learning in movements. One of the most important questions then becomes how to build time and space for collective reflection—bringing people together to build understandings and analyses that start with their lives, experiences, and actions. Foley emphasizes the importance of theorizing experience, standing back from it, and reordering it using categories like power, conflict, structure, values, and choice. He emphasizes that critical learning is gained informally through experience by acting and reflecting on action, rather than in formal courses. Informal learning can be profound and significant. But is it enough? I will return to this question in Chapter 3.

Building a social analysis that informs and is informed by grounded practice often draws on informal and non-formal learning that occurs in the process of doing things. This involves dynamic relations between more structured forms and processes of popular education in social movements and informal and incidental learning and knowledge production that takes place within them as well. People learn a lot in the process of doing things. Kelley puts it so well (in Holtzman, 2010, p. 323):

> They learn about what the weaknesses are in the system, but they're not learning about whether or not they want another system, or what's wrong with that system. They may just see it as their personal problem. That's why all these forms of activities have to be followed up with political education. How does the system work? . . . Why are so many people in prison? How come wages aren't going up, but CEO bonuses keep going up? Why is that? Where are the answers to those questions? Those answers don't come out of everyday forms of resistance. They come out of political engagement and conversation and information.

Chapter 3 focuses on these relations between different forms of education and learning in more depth.

FIGURE 1.2: On 3 December 2011, thousands of people from around the world hit the streets of Durban, South Africa, to protest the UN Climate Conference. (Photograph by Orin Langelle)

Activist Research and Producing Knowledge That Counts

Murdered South African activist Steve Biko (1978, p. 68) wrote that "the most potent weapon in the hands of the oppressor is the mind of the oppressed." To talk and think critically about knowledge is inevitably to engage with social and political power. Whose knowledge counts and by what criteria do we assess its value? To paraphrase Allman (2010, p. 167), is knowledge an object that can be possessed, or rather (as she asserts) a process of continuous unfolding and deepening? I have already introduced some ways in which social movements and activists have contributed to theory. Research is a fundamental component of social struggles, including the Quebec student strike example highlighted earlier in this chapter. This discussion will be broadened considerably in Chapter 4, which delves more deeply into activist research and not only shows how knowledge is constructed and mobilized as a tool for effective social action by and for movements, but also discusses the relations of the production of the research itself to collective struggles. In that chapter I draw from interviews with activist researchers—many of whom are also educators and organizers—to explore how they research and develop theory within movements.

Movement research is generated and organized in diverse ways. But there has been little focus on the actual micropolitics of processes of research activism in the context of generating alternatives to hegemonic development paradigms. I attempt to fill in some of these gaps by exploring how a range of activist researchers understand, practise, and validate research and processes of knowledge production, and also how such research contributes to movement struggles. I show how activist research and organizing are often mutually constitutive; knowledge production in many movements is dialectically related to the material conditions experienced in struggles for social and economic justice.

To help us think about how we evaluate intellectual work, knowledge, and learning, it can once again be useful to turn to Fanon's insights. An enduring aspect of Fanon's thought is his recognition of the importance of the intellectual work—the dialectic of learning—in the struggle, with all of its tensions and contradictions. He steers clear of dualistic notions about "the brain" and "the brawn" of movements, viewing that both reason and force have great importance in popular mobilization and are, indeed, dialectically related. Fanon was insistent on change depending on the muscles and brains at the bottom, not a top-down revolution imposed by the elite. Writing from within the Algerian struggle for liberation, when many other colonized peoples were also rising up to demand independence throughout Africa and Asia, Fanon noted how ordinary people have the potential to take control over their lives and pointed out that their consciousness emerges through struggle, and he articulated a faith in the intelligence and consciousness of ordinary people.

Like many others who have struggled against racism and colonialism in different contexts, I find that Fanon and Biko helped to produce a vocabulary that allows us to reimagine ourselves and believe in our own sense of agency. Another anti-colonial thinker and revolutionary, Amilcar Cabral (1973, p. 54), also remarks on how leaders of the liberation movement (in the independence struggle of Guinea and Cape Verde from Portuguese colonial rule) came to "realize, not without a certain astonishment, the richness of spirit, the capacity for reasoned discussion and clear exposition of ideas, the facility for understanding and assimilating concepts on the part of populations, groups who yesterday were forgotten, if not despised, and who were considered incompetent by the colonizer and even by some nationals." Fanon's and Cabral's observations still resonate today in different movements and organizing contexts. This appreciation for their ideas is deeply connected to my emphasis on the social character of all knowledge production, and the ways in which everyday struggles not only are the means to build movements, alliances, and counterpower, but also are generative of and in turn informed by the learning/knowledge aspects of this activity.

One pertinent example of how ordinary people know more than they are often given credit for immediately comes to mind. In 1997, I travelled with a trade union colleague to several worksites in small towns on the South Island of Aotearoa/New Zealand, en route to address a public meeting on the Multilateral Agreement on Investment (MAI), the stalled international treaty among OECD governments that many critics described as a charter of rights and privileges for transnational corporations. At one food-processing plant, I was invited to talk with workers about globalization. In our short time together, it was clear that many of the workers were critically reading their world and had a strong sense of the impacts of privatization and deregulation in their community, fostered by concrete examples from what they observed happening in their town. This came through just in asking a couple of questions and a go-round. The workers produced knowledge and an analysis about their own situations from their own experiences that was different from what I could provide as an activist educator and campaigner coming in from the outside.

This division between mental and manual labour is famously described by Karl Marx as a hallmark of capitalist society. The false disconnect, which I have encountered at university between forms of academic theorizing about movements and both activist practice and theorizing grounded in practice, is certainly mirrored by divisions within movement networks that reproduce—rather than challenge—capitalist relations. For example, there is often a tension between professionalized actors who speak at conferences and "teach-ins" and write NGO policy analysis documents and those everyday organizers and movement activists who participate in the daily grind of organizing and mobilizing. I discuss this further in Chapters 2 and 3. The elevation and promotion of elite forms of knowledge as "expert" and "authoritative" creates a disjuncture within organizations and movements that claim to espouse democracy and to equally value different knowledge traditions and experiences. Those who can convincingly talk and write in a language and style that mesh with academically (and officially) sanctioned forms of expression are readily reified and recognized as experts. Even within many networks and organizations that claim to be alternative and radical, the value of learning by doing is undervalued and ignored in actual practice. This illustrates Newman's point that movements and community organizing can also reproduce the status quo, dominant positions, and power. NGOs and activist groups often define issues—and themselves—in a narrow, compartmentalized way and therefore set narrow and compartmentalized parameters for campaigns, political action, and vision.

Coalition politics have positive and negative sides. In the US context, for example, Armstrong and Prashad (2005, pp. 184–185) see this as a result of fragmentation and the "NGOization" of the left: "[E]ach of our groups carves out areas of expertise or special interest, gets intensely informed about the area, and then uses this market specialization to attract members and funds. Organizations that 'do too much' bewilder the landscape." While they argue that specialization can result in valuable analytical and strategic resources for a broader movement, these authors suggest that fragmentation is problematic because it leaves us without a sense of common strategy, tactics, or movement, or even political agreement about how the systems operate and reproduce themselves. They continue: "As we extend coalitional politics from our local and national contexts to webs of networking fostered by international conferences, we need to ask again about how we know what we fight, and what alternate futures we see emerging from our often delinked, but not disparate struggles." How does this tendency to compartmentalize, to carve the world up, relate to the common call to connect the dots? How have we come to see "issues" such as climate change, colonialism, human rights violations, capitalism, violence against women, or labour justice as "dots" that are separate from each other? Where does this compartmentalizing lens take us, both analytically and strategically?

These are some of the questions that will recur in Chapters 2 and 3, which critically discuss some of the theories used to analyze social movements as well as others that theorize learning in social action. As I discuss there in more detail, it is helpful to think through whether and to what extent social movement theory largely emanating from, and developed in, specific geographical and historical conditions in Europe and North America can be unproblematically applied to Southern movements and networks. Such theorizing sometimes overlooks or misconstrues historical, economic, social, political, and cultural questions in contexts with which theorists have little familiarity. Another disconnect can exist between such academic research and activist networks. Within the university, there remains relatively little awareness of many important debates and thinking occurring within those networks of activists, social movements, trade unions, community organizations, and NGOs that take critical stances in relation to state power and capital. We need to question the borders and institutional boundaries of knowledge production. I particularly like Kelley's (2002, p. 8) suggestion about where new knowledge is being produced: "[T]he most powerful, visionary dreams of a new society don't come from little think tanks of smart people or out of the atomized, individualistic world of consumer capitalism, where raging against the status quo is simply the hip thing to do. Revolutionary dreams erupt out of political engagement; collective social movements are incubators of new knowledge."

All of this brings me back to the importance of recognizing the politics of knowledge production. For me, a pivotal moment in thinking about these questions arose when I saw some of my own "non-academic" activist writings being taught or cited by academics in institutions that wouldn't accept me as a graduate student because I didn't have an undergraduate degree. This kind of tension reinforced to me how the institutional context, and presumptions about standards of rigour through which knowledge is created, is clearly a factor in how and what knowledge is valued. While an anti-intellectual and anti-theory stance permeates some activist spaces, a real hunger for debate, discussion, and ideas exists in many organizing milieus. Many activists and organizers are voracious readers of histories of earlier social struggles and movements with an interest in gleaning practical, conceptual resources for their own engagement and challenges. This book also aims to intervene directly into these politics of knowledge production by arguing that theoretical and experiential forms of knowledge can enrich each other and that the academy does not have a monopoly on research and knowledge production on social movements and social change.

Concluding Thoughts

Earlier I claimed to have an unromantic view of social movements and activism. But it is not a cynical one. We can learn as much from mistakes, pitfalls, and challenges from earlier struggles as from what goes right—perhaps even more. As Vancouver-based organizer and writer Harsha Walia (2013, p. 174) writes, building movements requires reflexivity and a willingness to analyze, critique, and unsettle activist practices that we may be invested and implicated in: "Rather than shying away from debate and dialogue, transformative and effective movement organizing requires us to kindle a consciousness within the Left that fosters deliberate thought aimed at effectively challenging exploitation and oppression beyond ritualized 'petition to workshop to rally' activism."

In closing, I would like to invoke South African scholar and activist Neville Alexander's thoughts (cited in Magnien, 2012, n.p.) on the process of education on Robben Island, where he was jailed for a decade under apartheid:

> We taught one another what we knew, discovering each other's resourcefulness. We also learned how people with little or no formal education could not only themselves participate in education programmes but actually teach others a range of different insights and skills. The "University of Robben Island" was one of the best universities in the country. It also showed me that you don't need professors.

People struggle, learn, educate, and theorize wherever they find themselves. The forms this takes may change, but the importance of spaces and places for collective action, learning, reflection, and intergenerational sharing is crucial to building, sustaining, and broadening resistance. A critical eye to history is vital, together with an openness to valuing processes of informal and non-formal learning and knowledge created from the ground up—produced from within people's everyday struggles and experiences. Indeed, this lens is necessary for those who want to link critical knowledge to action and for action to be informed by deeper historical understandings of how and why we are in the state we are in.

CHAPTER 2

CRITIQUING THE STUDY OF SOCIAL MOVEMENTS: THEORIES, KNOWLEDGE, HISTORY, ACTION

This chapter critically discusses some of the theories used to understand activism, knowledge production, and social movements in tandem with the following chapter, which discusses learning in activism. It is not intended to be a comprehensive overview of social movement theory. Rather, I present here a rationale for the need to bridge these areas of inquiry. A broad, critical sense of theory—both from a scholarly perspective and with respect to the body of ideas and visions emerging from social struggles—can help us understand movements and activism. While this chapter does not seek to satisfy those seeking new contributions to social movement studies, it will illuminate some of the concerns and approaches of these strands of theory. At the outset, it is crucial to emphasize that there is a wide range of literature and writing related to social movements, not just the dominant strands of social movement theory as sketched out here. To do this, I will touch on several important examples of works that make up an emerging body of literature that engages with both scholarly and activist communities and also the knowledge produced within them.

There are many places to start, but here I will first mention Chris Dixon's (2014) *Another Politics: Talking across Today's Transformational Movements*, Harsha Walia's (2013) *Undoing Border Imperialism*, Anandi Ramamurthy's (2013) activist archive and oral-history–based *Black Star: Britain's Asian Youth Movements*, INCITE! Women of Color Against Violence's (2007) *The Revolution Will Not Be Funded: Beyond the Non-profit Industrial Complex*, Scott Neigh's (2012) *Resisting the State: Canadian History through the Stories of Activists*, Alan Sears's (2014) historically informed *The Next New Left: A History of the Future*, and Eric Shragge's (2013) *Activism and Social Change: Lessons for Community Organizing*, second edition, among others. I highlight these works in particular to indicate the new moves in the field and the possibility that the field might itself be changing and may even be construed differently. They also fit in well with

the other issue that this chapter discusses: the importance of critical historical perspectives for understanding movements and movement knowledge
production and the implications of the politics of writing movement histories.

I appreciate some of the insights of the scholarship on social movements,
those works often categorized as "social movement studies." I am, however,
troubled at the ways in which many movements, networks, organizations,
and struggles are constructed as objects of study as if they are things that
can best be known from the outside by disinterested observers. There are
tensions between understandings of movements that objectify them and the
dynamic nature of practice, knowledge production, learning on the ground,
and self-knowledge generated by movements. In much of this literature, these
approaches are coupled with a relative lack of attention to, awareness of, and
sometimes even condescension toward the processes and practices of learning
or producing knowledge in movements. Relatively little social movement
studies literature focuses on learning and knowledge production, but the
emerging trends in this literature are promising as well. They include possibilities for further contributions to knowledge about—and for—movements
arising from creative tensions between academic and activist thinking.

Pointing out the tensions between social movement scholarship and activism is not new. The disconnect between scholars and activists comes at a price
for both activism and theory, according to Croteau, Haynes, and Ryan (2005,
p. xiii), for example. They contend that activism

> uninformed by broader theories of power and social change is more
> likely to fall prey to common pitfalls and less likely to maximize the
> potential for change. Social movements without access to routine
> reflection on practice are prisoners of their present conditions. Theory
> uninformed by and isolated from social movement struggles is more
> likely to be sterile and less likely to capture the vibrant heart and subtle
> nuances of movement efforts. Theorists without significant connections
> to social movements can end up constructing elegant abstractions with
> little real insight or utility.

As I emphasize throughout this book, I do not consider academic scholarship to have a monopoly on theorizing and intellectual work. I firmly believe
that theories and theoretical thinking circulate much more widely than within
academic institutions alone. Moreover, as Dixon, Neigh, Ramamurthy, Sears,
Shragge, Walia, and others illustrate, there are other approaches we can take
to analyzing and understanding movements and activism for social change.
These books centre and build upon the experiences of organizers, and draw

readers into conversations about hard-earned lessons, tensions, and challenges in collective efforts to transform social relations and remake the world. It is important to acknowledge the legacy for academic theorizing of collective knowledge production in movements.

To establish my discussion of the field, the first part of this chapter draws from exchanges among sociologists and social movement studies scholars who are critical of the dominant trends and tendencies of scholarship in social movement theory. Another set of ideas then comes from critiques levelled by movement activists themselves about the limitations of academic studies to engage with and understand the nature of processes and practices of organizing, learning, and knowledge production. Finally, I discuss the implications of reading and writing the histories of past movements for understanding contemporary struggles. Given the recent triumph of far-right Hindu nationalist prime minister Narendra Modi and the highly charged politics around history in India, I reflect upon the tensions over different approaches to historical understandings of India's social movements. I use this as an example to extrapolate wider lessons that we can draw from this.

A Brief Critique of Social Movement Studies

As I mentioned at the outset, this chapter is not a comprehensive interdisciplinary introduction to social movement studies scholarship, but rather a critical intervention into the field. If we begin where most histories of the study of social movements do, we might start off with collective behaviour theory, which tends to treat social movements as social problems. This approach focuses heavily on participants' psychological states, often emphasizing the allegedly irrational or even deviant behaviour of those taking part in mass movements, protests, and other forms of collective action. While many more recent scholars have distanced themselves from French social psychologist Gustave Le Bon's (1960) interest in "the crowd," his work has arguably left marked conceptual footprints on the way in which individual and collective participation in movements is at times still viewed today. Le Bon was writing in late-nineteenth-century France, the era of the Paris Commune and major labour unrest with the emergence of trade unions, and his conservative views of such popular mass mobilizations were negative and condemnatory. Le Bon (p. 16) wrote to inform the social forces seeking to maintain class power, privilege—and control: "Today the claims of the masses are becoming more and more sharply defined, and amount to nothing less than a determination to utterly destroy society as it now exists, with a view to making it hark back to that primitive communism."

Le Bon's writings resound with alarm and opposition to working-class social movements, which he saw as irrational and pathological. For example, he wrote that

> by the mere fact that he forms part of an organised crowd, a man [*sic*] descends several rungs in the ladder of civilisation. Isolated, he may be a cultivated individual; in a crowd, he is a barbarian—that is, a creature acting by instinct. He possesses the spontaneity, the violence, the ferocity, and also the enthusiasm and heroism of primitive beings, whom he further tends to resemble by the facility with which he allows himself to be impressed by words and images—which would be entirely without action on each of the isolated individuals composing the crowd—and to be induced to commit acts contrary to his most obvious interests and his best-known habits. (p. 36)

I find it interesting and useful to read Le Bon's writing alongside accounts of rebellion/resistance in colonial administrative documents which portray this as irrational criminal activity, and indeed some similar constructions of contemporary movements and activists by contemporary state security agencies, some media outlets, and politicians. One such project is the current US Department of Defense–sponsored, university-based Minerva Initiative social sciences research program that funds academics to study social movements and current and projected conflicts in the interests of US national security. Other examples range from recent characterizations of Quebec student activists as rioting spoiled children; to the preoccupation with dominant constructions of "radicalization" of Muslim (and other) racialized youth that largely ignores social, political, and economic contexts and factors; from viewing resistance to the oil and gas industries as threats to Canada's "national security"; to the security intelligence reports on anti-globalization activists (discussed in Chapter 3). One specific example taken from the latter is former New Zealand politician and WTO Director-General Mike Moore's (1997) description of GATT Watchdog and other opponents of free trade as "grumpy geriatric communists . . . a mutant strain of the left . . . primitives who if they had their way would plunge our nation and the region into chaos and depression."

In the 1920s, Robert Park, Ernest Burgess, and later Herbert Blumer developed the Chicago School perspective on collective behaviour that began to consider how various forms of groups or associations might, as critical rational actors, help form and change society. Yet collective behaviour approaches tend to view mass mobilizations and movements as abnormal, deviating from and existing outside of the political process. Central to Neil Smelser's theory of collective behaviour is the notion of structural strain existing in a (normally stable) society for a movement to occur. One critique of these approaches, mounted by Holst (2002), contends that they were unconcerned with the socioeconomic conditions that led to these actions, an analysis of which might render the inequalities of the ruling-class order visible and provide a justification for working-class movements. Moreover, Holst notes the "ultimately psychologistic stigmatization of social movement leaders and participants as lacking critical ability" (p. 31). This framing of activists and their capacity for knowledge and consciousness contributes to some scholarly and official treatments that largely overlook or fail to engage with the capacity and significance of intellectual work in movements. In portraying such movements as destructive, deviant, and spontaneous, such theories ignore the behind-the-scenes work of organizing, deliberation, education, and learning.

Resource Mobilization and Political Process Theories

Since the 1960s, two theoretical approaches have dominated social movement theory, which has largely been a European–North American academic project. Resource mobilization theory (RMT) emerged primarily in North America, while the new social movements paradigms arose mainly in Western Europe. Cross-national collaborations between North Americans and Europeans have helped to extend and integrate these two approaches (Staggenborg, 2011). Resource mobilization theorists—including Tilly (1988), Tarrow (1998), and McAdam, McCarthy, and Zald (1996)—depart from collective behaviour theory in proposing that people who are engaged in social movements act as rational actors (whether as individuals or collectively) pursuing common interests, primarily through building formal organizations. Resource mobilization theorists understand people in movements to be making rational choices between costs and benefits of involvement in social movement activity. They argue that people pool or seek to gain control of resources to follow a common end, and this gaining or sharing of resources gives a group the capacity to engage in collective actions and to mobilize. RMT emphasizes supposedly objective variables—organization, interests, resources, opportunities, and strategies—to account for large-scale mobilizations (Cohen & Arato, 1994). It views social organization—and organizations involving shared consciousness and collective identity—as both a prerequisite for and the end result of mobilizations. This, theorists argue, tends to lead to the establishment of organizations to institutionalize the control of resources and to mobilize support. Such resources might include funding, labour, time, commitment, land, technical expertise, or facilities.

There have been two main strands within RMT. Zald and McCarthy's (1987) entrepreneurial mobilization model emphasizes the role of "movement entrepreneurs" believed necessary to sustain social movement organizations and the technical and practical aspects of movements. This model, they argue, leads toward a professionalization of movement leadership with paid middle-class staff displacing grassroots leaders. In this analysis, organizations and organizers tap into middle-class supporters by appealing to their consciences, even if they are not directly affected by a movement's issues and concerns. Zald and McCarthy also explore cultural framing—the ways in which a movement's grievances, demands, or message are framed to both those in power and the public, and how they are used to mobilize support among its members to take collective action (McAdam, McCarthy, & Zald, 1996).

The other main strand is Charles Tilly's (1988) political process theory (PPT). This approach focuses on the political opportunities for movements to act in terms of the balance of social forces and the relationship between the state, a given movement, and other forces in "civil society." It also sets the parameters for the timing, types, and levels of action that a movement may take, as well as its outcomes. PPT emphasizes the role of grassroots movement leadership, contending that there are frequently struggles between this base and middle-class supporters who see the movement as an opportunity to use or control it for their own interests. Tilly and Tarrow (2007) have written more recently about social movements as a form of "contentious politics," meaning that movements "involve collective making of claims that, if realized, would conflict with someone else's interest, political in the sense that governments of one sort or another figure somehow in the claim making, whether as claimants, objects of claims, allies of the objects, or monitors of the contention" (Tilly, 2004, p. 3).

New Social Movement Theory

Across the Atlantic, another approach came to dominate scholarship: new social movement (NSM) theory. NSM theorists, such as Touraine (1981) and Melucci (1980; 1989), seek to understand the processes whereby people consciously construct group or collective identities, values, and lifestyles rather than, or in addition to, developed ideologies. They tend to ask why "new" social actors emerge, whereas RMT approaches emphasize how people mobilize. Broadly, NSM proponents felt that Marxist analyses, which explained social movements in terms of class conflict, structural contradictions, and crises of capitalism, were reductionist and inadequate to understand emergent social movements in Europe during the 1960s and 1970s. NSM theorists held that many of these movements seemed to emerge from middle-class rather than working-class constituencies. They saw the peace, environmental, queer, and women's movements of that era as struggles against old and new kinds of domination in a supposedly postindustrial society with shifting boundaries between public, private, and social life.

Instead of concerns about material resources and redistribution, they characterized these struggles as being about quality-of-life issues, democracy, and the articulation of identities. NSM theory focuses on new forms of collective identity rather than common interests, viewing these movements as laboratories in which people's self-understandings are transformed and where they create cultural codes to contest the legitimacy of received points of view. This approach pays considerable attention to language, viewed as constitutive of social life in a vaguely defined "complex society" (Melucci, 1980). Most NSM theory deals with symbolic challenges and discourse, temporary spaces and identities, in a clean break from Marxism. These movements open up spaces and expose power, but they do not directly challenge ruling groups to take that power. For NSM theorists, movement actors' focus is very much on self-realization rather than contesting state/political power.

Critiques of Dominant Social Movement Theories

Categorization, Compartmentalization, and Confusion

This is, of course, a very brief overview of a complex field. I give just a sketch here in part so I can emphasize that there are many other ways to look at activism and social movements that fall outside of these strands of scholarship. There are scholars who are invested in the project of social movement theory and extending its explanatory reach, who insist that it is always evolving. This does not mean, however, that it must remain the dominant set of ideas for interpreting social movements. Critiques of this field of scholarship are important, too. For example, Frampton, Kinsman, Thompson, and Tilleczek (2006, p. 11) charge that "[b]y researching social movements rather than the social world that movements aim to unsettle, social movement theory often reifies activists and movements and establishes regulatory practices within academia by classifying activists and their work." They note, for example, that NSM theorists tend to categorize some movements as "new" and others as "old," and that some movements become classified as "cultural" and others as "economic" or "resource allocation." They suggest that such distinctions are arbitrary and "often result in an inability to describe and account for how social movements actually work and tend to increase the divide between 'activist' and 'researcher.' . . . Social movement theory regulates activism by slotting it into categories, rather than explicating the importance of what a movement produces in the social world and what its confrontations with ruling relations bring into view."

This strand of critique suggests that seeing social movements through only one of these theoretical lenses leads to a fragmented view of complex, perhaps even contradictory, and multifaceted movements. Notwithstanding the sense in which many of these movements appear fragmented, focused on a single issue, and identity centred, there is a danger in theorizing them in ways which construct or interpret them to fit narrow theoretical frameworks. While RMT and NSM theories usefully draw attention to some aspects of some movements, their levels of abstraction and generalization—as well as the overextension of key concepts—make them problematic and limited. By focusing on a small set of variables, theorists in both dominant schools tend to ignore the dynamic and shifting nature of movements. In other respects, these theories are rather vague. PPT theorists tend to view anything as a political opportunity if it appears to help movement mobilization. This concept, while potentially useful in drawing attention to the importance of situating the movement in a specific political moment and context, has become overextended. RMT focuses too much on single-issue reform movements and their organizations, while NSM emphasizes micropolitics and identity. Neither of these two dominant approaches deals satisfactorily with the relationship between capitalism and the causes and concerns of movements and organizations, and in their own way often fall back on analysis that is rather reductive.

What is the relation, then, between social movements and politics? Both schools of thought are vague about what constitutes a social movement. For example, Touraine (1981) argued that a movement must be more than just oppositional and that it must propose alternatives. Following this, should we then recognize only those movements that articulate alternatives in some programmatic form? Or do we understand the importance of using oppositional mobilization (whether or not this involves formal organizational structures and institutions) to create spaces of resistance and processes such as direct democracy and nonhierarchical organizing as the creation of alternatives? Here it is worth mentioning Holloway's (2002) work on power, revolution, and autonomy, which draws on the Zapatista movement in Chiapas, Mexico, and which has been both influential and hotly debated in some academic and activist circles. Critical of the fetishization of state and power relations, his approach emphasizes struggles and a politics that seek to build forms of social relations, social organizations, autonomous communities, and counterpower from below to "change the world without seizing [state] power." In a similar vein, Zibechi (2003) and Sitrin (2012) discuss the creation of what they see as new social relationships based on horizontalism and autonomy in specific locations in Argentina that are sites of protest, creation, and mutual aid, from worker-run factories to land that is taken over to grow food and build homes and schools.

Issues of resource mobilization and cultural/personal factors are both important to examine in understanding movements. But political and cultural aspects are interdependent. RMT theorists construct a rigid notion of movements and movement organizations, implying that institutionalization is the key to success. This idea has been disputed by many. One example is where Piven and Cloward (1977) state that the drive toward formally structured organizations by organizers and activists in poor people's movements in the United States during the 1930s and 1960s led to the abandonment of oppositional politics and co-optation by elites, and diverted energy away from mobilization and escalating protest movements toward the sustenance and growth of organizations that become preoccupied with financial survival. They emphasize the importance of gaining as much as possible from periods of militancy rather than phases of building organizations and amassing resources.

Another transnational example is Petras and Veltmeyer (2001, 2003, 2005) and Veltmeyer's (2007) argument that the rise of international development NGOs and increased funding for development from governments funnelled through NGOs has led to the co-optation of grassroots movements and organizations in the Third World by elite interests and actors. This, they argue, has increased pressures on grassroots organizations and local NGOs to become professionalized subcontractors to governments or international financial institutions and to distance themselves from confrontational or other oppositional forms of action. Indeed, institutionalized international and local NGOs active in global justice, human rights, or development networks, for example, may be deemed by RMT theorists as "successful" in gaining financial, professional, and other resources. But they may also serve to depoliticize and dampen more radical social movement activity while purporting to represent the voices of the poor and oppressed. These organizations may lack any accountability or mandate for their work and yet still fit a definition of successful movement organizations for RMT theorists.

This is very much supported by my own experiences. The movements, NGOs, and other groups in which I have worked are diverse and often defy neat categorization. They frequently draw from and enact local social, political, and cultural forms of resistance. But they also struggle over resources and frequently over relationships with the state. Some are hybrid organizations, and some are broad-based movements and networks with little apparent formal or institutional structure. Some work at building movements and community mobilization but are constituted in such a way that they can be recognized in an organizational form. This sometimes allows them to seek support from philanthropic foundations, get state funding, or achieve charitable status. But other organizations cannot, or do not, seek such support. Brazil's MST (Movimento dos Trabalhadores Rurais Sem Terra—the landless rural workers' movement) has strategic relationships with NGOs, many of which, as Burrowes, Cousins, Rojas, and Ude (2007, p. 231) note, "were started at the request of the movements, usually to provide specific skills or resources" but "ultimately . . . are not essential. If those NGOs collapsed tomorrow, the movements would remain intact." Such organizations and movements sometimes exist in the North, but also defy neat categorization by frameworks employing a limited set of variables that objectify them rather than seeking to understand the processes and practices within them.

We need not discard social movement theory altogether. But I believe that there is scope for important analysis and understandings from the tensions between this body of literature and the critical writing on social movements and activism that exists outside of these approaches. For example, much of the scholarship on both national and transnational/international movements tends to overlook connections between such movements and local/community organizing. DeFilippis, Fisher, and Shragge (2010, pp. 55–56) remark that history shows that

> local organizing gives birth to, galvanizes, and sustains social movements. The core issue is not organization versus movement building, but rather the content and structure of social movement organization and its relationship to local practices. Clearly there are tensions. Community organizing is premised on the assumption that building a relatively permanent structure with clear processes of delegation of power and roles facilitates longevity and democracy. Social movements tend to be by definition much looser. Groups mobilize for specific campaigns or actions and then disband. It is impossible to impose a single structure on a movement. Social movements are short lived and cannot be reproduced or channeled into traditional organizations. And yet, at all levels of social movement building, organizing, even local organizing, provides the activists, relationships, resources and organization without which it is difficult for movements to emerge, be sustained, and develop. Just as community efforts need movements, movements do not develop out of or exist in a vacuum. The populist, labor, or civil rights movement, or the feminist movements of the past century, all developed out of local organizing and became, as social movements, far greater than the sum of their local organizational parts.

These kinds of connections are crucial. Dixon (2014) and Walia (2013) address the same issues in similar ways in their recent interventions. Individuals and organizations become involved in social action for many reasons, bring

diverse perspectives about the world with them, and consequently have different interests invested in the direction, success, or failure of a movement or
campaign. As Long (1997, p. 168) notes, "[u]nderstanding why coalitions and
larger social movements exist, fail, or succeed depends on understanding them
in historical context and examining the interaction of their particular social
characteristics." But NSM theorists often overlook crucial issues of class and
the continuation of capitalist relations. Indeed, they tend toward a "postclass"
analysis, ignore the importance of political engagements with the state, and
adopt a micropolitical focus on resistance that adopts a decentred concept of
power being everywhere. This approach underestimates or even ignores the
continuing power of states and capital. Wood (1998, p. 12) reminds us of
the importance of the state as the main agent of globalization, noting that in
the global market, capital needs the state "to maintain the conditions of accu-
mulation to preserve labor discipline, to enhance the mobility of capital while
suppressing the mobility of labor . . . if anything, the nation-state is the main
agent of globalization." Moreover, even when NSM theorists limit their focus
to Western Europe, such theorizing overlooks working-class struggles, such as
major strike activities during the 1970s and 1980s, and the dialectical relations
between class, gender, and race in milieus described as "new" movements and
the societies they struggle in.

FIGURE 2.1: A guerilla theatre during the 1972 Republican National
Convention in Miami Beach, Florida. Thousands gathered outside of the
convention to protest the Vietnam War. (Photograph by Orin Langelle)

Troubling the Histories and Geographies of Theory

It is questionable just how new these concerns are, given longer histories of struggles around women's rights, peace, and the environment throughout the world. Perhaps these claims of ruptures with the past or of "newness" in particular contemporary movements have overlooked aspects of earlier struggles about these issues because of their focus on other things. This draws attention to the importance of recovering and constructing movement histories from below, rather than creating theories that deny this historicity. Challenges to the dominant fields of social movement theory have come from within social movement theory itself, and also from scholars located in or addressing aspects of social action in the Third World. Some Indigenous and Third World scholars frame their critiques around the tendency to elevate and universalize "Western" theories about knowledge, power, and history. This, they charge, can misunderstand, misrepresent, or overlook the specificities of social relations and the lived experience of peoples' struggles in the South.

Should the fact that the major strands of social movement theory emerge from particular geo-historical contexts in North America and Europe lead to caution in applying them unreflexively to the rest of the world? The reductionism of the debates within dominant Northern social movement and "civil society" theories tends to exclude or belittle the importance of modes of struggle at street level or on the land in many countries, which may be far more extensive and effective for the actors involved than conventional, institutionalized forms of struggle (Bayat, 1997). The existence of these modes of struggle is often difficult enough for people engaged in social activism to acknowledge, let alone for academics to see.

Older histories of some strands of movements, especially in the South, inform and influence modern struggles. The histories of anti-colonial and anti-imperialist struggles, for example, have different kinds of relevance for contemporary movement strategies. Not unrelated to Kinsman's discussion of the social organization of forgetting in the previous chapter, Radha D'Souza (2002, pp. 25–26) argues that many contemporary "global civil society" actors such as NGOs de-link the present from the past, seriously limiting their vision:

> The struggle against imperialism and colonisation in the early 20th century against project "progress" was inextricably linked to the idea of self-determination. De-linking "corporate globalisation" from history, the state from capital/corporation nexus and the UN organisations from their context and role in the contemporary world . . . promotes amnesia of history that is dis-empowering. . . . As the idea of self-determination fades from historical memory, the political space concedes, by proxy,

to those seeking to make poverty and exploitation of people and nature more sustainable.

Another valuable contribution for thinking through the ideas, concepts, and trajectories of radical thought and action in social movements across borders and the colonial divide is David Austin's (2009, 2013) scholarship on the Caribbean left, anti-colonial thinking and their interconnectedness with radical politics in North America. Sohail Daulatzai (2012) has also done important work on the ideological and political influences of the politics of decolonization and racism in the ideas that circulated between Black radical thought and freedom struggles in the United States and the Muslim Third World after World War II. These recoveries of radical transnational histories are useful not only for understanding the past but thinking through our challenges in the present.

Some charge that in the South and in those parts of the North that were colonized, dominant strands of political theory ignore, devalue, and render invisible ideas and theory produced from there. Two scholars who problematize the universalizability of theory developed in the West in crossing the colonial difference into Indigenous worlds or to the Third World are Maori scholar Linda Smith (1999) and Walter Mignolo (2000). They problematize the positional superiority of canonical forms of knowledge and theory that came from Europe and North America and have dominated and displaced other worldviews. Both discuss the importance of understanding that theories and theorists emerge from concrete geo-historical, social, and cultural contexts. Smith (1999, p. 28) writes that

> imperialism and colonialism brought complete disorder to colonized peoples, disconnecting them from their histories, their landscapes, their social relations and their own ways of thinking, feeling and interacting with the world. It was a process of systematic fragmentation which can still be seen in the disciplinary carve-up of the indigenous world: bones, mummies and skulls to the museums, art work to private collectors, languages to linguistics, "customs" to anthropologists, beliefs and behaviours to psychologists.

This imperially wrought disorder and disciplinary carve-up has implications for understanding movements and struggles in many parts of the world through theoretical lenses that claim a position of intellectual superiority and universality. There are limitations to uncritically applying theories fashioned primarily in the "West" to contexts where local forms of organizing have shaped or influenced contemporary movements and popular resistance. This process of systematic fragmentation that

Smith describes has influenced the way in which many scholars have sought to understand peoples' struggles. But among and within movement networks it also influences which ideas are heard and valued and which movements and organizations we see as significant, representative, and accountable to a broader base.

This kind of theorizing frequently overlooks or misconstrues historical, economic, political, and cultural questions in contexts about which the theorists, based in and largely focused on Europe and North America, have little understanding. The processes of producing knowledge, whether one is an academic or an activist—or both, are profoundly influenced by our experiences of social relations. Third World Marxists and anti-colonial thinkers have extended and sometimes contested dominant strands of European and North American Marxist thought, particularly in regard to questions of "development," race, and colonialism. D'Souza (2006, p. 17), for example, notes.

> Several centuries of colonialism and imperialism have given to the societies of the "Third World" general attributes that are constituted by distinctive geo-historical developments. Class, gender, race, ethnicity, environment, ecology as well as political economy are constituted by distinctive historical and geographical processes that qualify the categories of analysis developed within the context of capitalism in the "West."

D'Souza's comments remind us that we should also pay attention to such processes to more fully understand social movements, activism, and the rise of NGOs. The devaluation of Indigenous knowledge(s) is intrinsic to colonization, and thus thinkers like Fanon (1968) and Smith (1999) emphasize the importance of history for struggle against old and new forms of colonization.

However, in thinking through these ideas, we also must be wary of not falling into what Himani Bannerji (2011, p. 3) has described as "the trap of fixed spatialization." Bannerji develops this idea as follows: "Rooted as the historical and social realities are in constantly constitutive relations that have marked the world in the last few hundred years through colonialism, nationalisms and imperialism, we do not need to forge two separate sets of theoretical/critical apparatuses for 'the West' and 'the rest.' . . . [H]istorical and social realities of the world are neither macro-spaces of free-floating imaginaries and abstractions nor bounded within micro-formations and spaces of geographically discrete cultural identities." What we can take from this is that questioning the ways that theory "travels"—and the possible limitations interpretative frameworks may have when applied with little regard for geo-historical specificities of the context being analyzed—does not mean we must simply and

crudely reject knowledge or theory on the grounds that it has been generated in the "West." Instead, we should recognize the need to build knowledge
about social movements and the world they exist in through dialogue with
other people, other perspectives.

Abstracted Empiricism and Theoretical Paradigms/Activist Lives and Practices

Noting the recent explosion of research and theorizing about social movements, Richard Flacks (2005, p. 4) argues that much of the social movement
studies scholarship defining the field resembles a "mix of inflated theorizing
and abstracted empiricism" rather than illuminating movements. This scholarship, as Charlotte Ryan (2004, p. 111) contends, imposes theories on activists,
ignoring the fact that ordinary people can theorize. As she warns, "[s]ubjected
to practice, only the most robust theoretical constructs survive. Most theoretical
models are under-developed offering a vague sense of relationships between
ideas, sometimes little more than a direction for future inquiry. In practice, one
quickly knows which concepts are under-specified." Similar caution is advised
by Catherine Eschle (2001, p. 74), who tells us that constructing categories
of analysis and political projects that "universalize the particular and located
experience of the theorist" leads to many social movement scholars failing
to account for "multiple differences in power, form, strategy and ideology"
between and within movements. She sees Eurocentrism and a tendency to
presuppose that diverse movements share a unified perspective as fatal flaws of
the "universalist aspirations of global civil society theory." Eschle suggests that
this approach lends itself to redefining movements to fit predetermined theoretical constructs, and in doing so, making conscious decisions about which
movements are documented and cited in academic accounts, and which are not.

Flacks (2005, pp. 7–8) puts forward a similar critique to Eschle, saying that
academic writings aimed at establishing, critiquing, or refining paradigms have
proliferated: "More and more, the work of younger scholars seems driven by
their felt need to 'relate' to one or another of such 'paradigms'—or to try
to synthesize them in some way. Journal articles increasingly analyze social
movement experience as grist for the testing of hypotheses as the illustration of concepts." It can be tempting and seemingly easy to conflate different
movements that occur in different moments, locations, and contexts to make
a point. This is particularly true when one's focus is applying a paradigm or
theoretical concept. This means that theoretical approaches become ways of
knowing in which ideas and concepts are prioritized over the material practices by which these ideas are produced. Frampton, Kinsman, Thompson, and
Tilleczek (2006, p. 7) suggest that this is how "real lives are transposed into

concepts and representations." An overattachment to paradigms, typologies, and criteria for describing movements and their perceived success or failure can displace potentially fruitful engagement through dialogue with knowledge generated by activists.

Within these typologies and paradigms, specialization and specialized terminology can also be problematic. The fact that academic social movement theorizing generates specialized terminology and venues, "scholarly presses, conferences, and peer-reviewed publications—is neither surprising nor necessarily problematic. Specialization becomes problematic only if it produces isolation, i.e., if social movement theorists lose exchanges with collective actors regarding ideas, experiences, and needs. The problem is not that framing theorists debate concepts; the problem is terminological proliferation as a symptom of withering dialogue with activists. More troubling still, theorists do not seem to recognize that the dialogues they are missing are valuable" (Ryan, 2005, p. 118). To put this into a larger context, a return to a dialectical Marxist framework is useful. Flacks (2005, p. 15) points out how contemporary social movement scholars overlook Marx's "effort to embed power relations in an analysis of the political economy as a whole. Opportunity was not fixed. The more that capitalism organized a global economy and society, the more potential the world's proletariat would have for transformative change. Much of Marx's intellectual career involved the effort to analyze capitalism as a developing and contradictory system, and the ways in which such development would necessitate and make possible collective action from below." To think about how useful and relevant social movement theory can be to movements themselves, it is crucial to locate analytical insights within a contextualization of movements and organizing and a broader understanding of contemporary power relations.

So while it can be helpful to read social movement studies literature, it is equally fruitful to engage with other critical works that look at organizing and activism outside of the dominant paradigms, as sketched above. An emerging area of social movement scholarship urges that theory on movements must be relevant to social activism, building upon ideas, literature, and discussions within movements. My own experiences in activism, as someone who then navigated disjunctures between these and academic engagements, lead me to propose linking these issues to further questions. How, where, and when does theorization take place? Who does it? Whose knowledge is valued and by what criteria? What are the political, economic, and social conditions in which knowledge is produced, given that the academic mode of knowledge production is only one among many? How do we value the importance of insurgent skills and knowledge, what some call "struggle knowledge"? How do we reconceptualize knowledge–power relations? What are the tensions and possibilities associated with processes of trying to systematize experiential forms of knowledge and learning that occur in the context of activism? How concerned should we be regarding valuing knowledge for its difference rather than its similarity to academic expertise? To what extent should we try to justify or prove the worth of knowledge produced or gained through active engagement with the world outside of the social and institutional context of the university? I return to discuss these ideas in further detail in Chapters 3 and 4.

Making Theory That Is Relevant (and Useful) for Social Change

> Many of those who studied social movements in the 1960s and 1970s were themselves politically active. My impression then was that most of them believed the study of social movements ought to provide movement activists with intellectual resources they might not readily obtain otherwise. . . . Work in that vein indeed proved to be directly useful to activists; some of the research and theorizing of academic sociologists helped shape movement training programs and handbooks. It was possible to imagine, if you were engaged in social movement studies, that your teaching, consulting, and direct participation as well as your research efforts themselves, might have some relevance to the practices and understandings of political activists. (Flacks, 2004, p. 136)

Within academia, I have encountered relatively little awareness of the many important debates within the networks of activists, movements, and NGOs that take critical stances in relation to state power and capital. Moreover, with a few exceptions—including Dixon (2014) and Walia (2013), who are mentioned above—it is relatively rare to find serious, sustained attention paid to internal dynamics in movements. This is especially true in relation to dynamics involving race and class, which are often pushed to one side or ignored in much of what has been written on the global justice movement or on anti-authoritarian and horizontal forms of organizing, for example. Since these are hardly new concerns or critiques, it is interesting to consider why this is the case. For example, when I was writing my doctoral thesis, I found that much of the literature on the "global justice movement" tended toward either abstracted, universalized, or generalized views, or case studies written from the point of view of people not associated closely enough with the practice to be aware of the dynamics of these movements. Some studies rely too heavily on the Internet for their information and conclusions about movements and activism. This raises questions about sound methodologies for researching and theorizing this field. Movements or activists that are less visible on the Internet or other digital media—either because of time, security concerns, resources, or strategic priorities—may be less likely to be noticed by scholars, even when they are significant actors. Indeed the heightened focus on technology and social media brings with it risks of overestimating its significance in social movements and organizing spaces, and an over-reliance on what and who is being represented in these forums. The contributions of movements that are either composed of largely non-literate people or in which written documentation is never or rarely produced may also be similarly excluded. Another tension is the issue of violence/nonviolence debates, given that this is a line that is firmly drawn by most social movement scholarship. What are the implications of effectively excising armed movements (e.g., within past anti-colonial and liberation struggles and contemporary revolutionary organizations) from the definition of "social movements" and understandings about politics, history, and social change? Moreover, the scholarly literature is dominated by a focus on movements and mobilizations in North America and Europe and often misconstrues movements in other parts of the world. Even where academics have been located as activists/participant observers in these networks, it is instructive to see who is written about, interviewed, and framed as significant or authoritative among NGO and movement actors, and who is overlooked, missing, or invisible.

This resonates with my own experiences as an activist. Before completing a doctorate and working as a professor, I had encountered academic researchers seeking to study groups and movements that I was part of. Many clearly believed that they had "the theory," a virtual monopoly on rigorous analysis and theorizing, and showed little appreciation for the intellectual work within—and fundamental to—everyday activism. Activists and organizers were to supply the data, the empirical material from their struggles and movements for others to interpret. Yet much of the foundational work in classic social theory about organization had its roots in the experience of activist intellectuals and is still an important resource for contemporary activists, as Flacks (2005) reminds us. Ryan's (2004, pp. 111–112) observation is particularly pertinent here and speaks to my experiences. As she observes, collective actors "who do not speak the secret language of social movement theory are seen as atheoretical, or as sources of raw material in the colonial tradition. This hurts relation building. Activists rarely see social movement theories honor their ideas much less recognize that activists theorize constantly. Perceiving theorists as being more interested in each other than in front line experience, activists withdraw as well."

Activists and organizers strive to anticipate the future, assess opportunities, and work out ways to understand them. But as Flacks (2005, pp. 9–10) argues, research using the political opportunity perspective rarely looks at how activists, "in the movements being studied, understood and determined their own opportunities. Indeed, how organizers figure out their opportunities and how movements expand on them are largely unstudied and untheorized by [political opportunity] practitioners." He argues that activists and organizers with any strategic attitude already know that they should try to understand "potential points of access and possibilities for alliance in the political environment. Their fundamental practice includes efforts to assess the vulnerabilities of elites and themselves. They are likely to start with the assumption that the established opportunity structure is in fact not hospitable to their efforts and so they have to try to figure out how to make opportunities when those seem largely absent. In a crucial sense, organizers embedded in strategic debate and planning are likely to be more knowledgeable about the nature of political opportunity than are academics who are separated from movement scenes."

What purpose does such theorizing serve if it is detached from and of no use to social movements? This crucial question is central to the themes of this book. It is raised by several scholars, including Bevington and Dixon (2005) and Flacks (2004). They note that few movement activists read academic social movement theory. They further charge that these theoretical endeavours seem to be driven by attempts to define and refine concepts that are likely to be irrelevant or obvious to organizers. Bevington and Dixon call for recognition of existing movement-generated theory and also dynamic reciprocal engagement by theorists and movement activists in formulating, producing, refining, and applying research. This is where I would situate this book and my previous work with Dip Kapoor (Choudry & Kapoor, 2010, 2013), alongside other works mentioned above that also fit into this trajectory, such as Dixon (2014), Austin (2013), Walia (2013), and Shragge (2013).

Part of the problem is that much scholarship in social movement studies is incapable of recognizing activist theorizing as equal, as Cox and Nilsen (2007, p. 430) state: "To do so, of course, would raise awkward questions of other kinds. Activist theorising, true, is not always subject to peer review prior to publication. But it is most definitely subject to peer review *after* publication—and peer review that brings together a far broader range of empirical experience and points of view than are found in any academic journal. It is also subject to the test of practice: whether it *works* to bring together an action, a campaign or a network—or to win battles, large and small, against its opponents and convince the as yet unmobilised and unradicalised." Indeed the theorizing in movements can be extremely valuable, and as Bevington and Dixon (2005, p. 190) state, a researcher's connection to the movement can provide "important incentives to produce more accurate information, regardless of whether the researcher is studying a favored movement or its opponents." They are not arguing that movement-relevant scholarship is "uncritical adulation of a favored movement" (p. 191). On the contrary, they write that such an approach neither provides a movement with any useful information nor aids it in identifying and addressing problems that may hinder its effectiveness. Movement-relevant research cannot simply uncritically reiterate pre-existing ideas of a favoured movement—if it "is exploring questions that have relevance to a given movement, it is in the interests of that movement to get the best available information, even if those findings don't fit expectations." Closeness to a movement (or cause) and analytic distance need not be mutually exclusive.

Movements generate new knowledge, questions, and theory. When Robin Kelley (2002) argues that the ideas and visions of movements are important, not just whether they "succeeded" or not, he also emphasizes the need for concrete and critical engagement with the movements confronting the problems of oppressed peoples. He highlights the importance of drawing conceptual resources for contemporary struggles from critical readings of histories of older movements—an approach to which I will return later in this chapter. These kinds of knowledge and theory are often shaped by and for concrete and shifting contours of struggle. We need to retrieve and draw upon ideas and questions generated in the course of activist practice, which engage with dilemmas that may not always be apparent to an outside observer. But this must always be done with a critical eye, not with a nostalgic one. When Bevington and Dixon (2005) studied North American global justice networks to ascertain what intellectual resources they used, they found that many activists not only wrote and conversed about things but also read widely. They often self-consciously analyzed other movements, exchanging ideas and debating directions with them. This happened in meetings, email discussions, conferences, online essays, public talks, zines, study groups, magazine articles, trainings, cultural events, social forums, *encuentros*, and *consultas*, to name some examples. But they noted about these networks that "much of the most current and incisive material is only or mainly available through these media, not books" (p. 191). My own experience confirms that activists are often far more interested in reading critical accounts of past movements and struggles as well as online articles and other materials than academic literature on the sociology of social movements.

What is absent from much social movement scholarship, according to Cox and Nilsen (2007, p. 431), is "a strong sense of process: of how movements develop through the fusion of people's attempts to meet their local needs and organise around their particular issues, collective processes of learning through struggle at many levels." I am also struck by the ways in which much of this literature does not deal with tensions and exclusions related to race, gender, and class—particularly the implications this has for the claims made by movements and activists and the resulting nature of the knowledge produced in and about these struggles.

This is a further argument for knowledge about movements to be produced in a genuine dialogue with activists and the knowledge that they produce themselves. This interchange should be pursued in a way that attends to concerns about race, gender, and class dynamics within organizing contexts. Though this may look different in academic and activist spaces, as Bevington and Dixon (2005, p. 198) observe, movement participants are actively involved in processes of analysis and theorizing. The study of movements should better attend to these activist discussions, which "offer crucial insights into the issues of greatest concern to the movements, and they thus provide an important starting point for developing movement-relevant research topics. From this foundation, researchers can identify the particular questions and issues that may be most pertinent for specific movements or segments of those movements." These authors argue that there are three key questions to explore in examining activist discussions: "What issues concern movement participants? What ideas and theories are activists producing? What academic scholarship is being read and discussed by movement participants? Within these queries, social movement scholarship would, of course, focus on those concerns related directly to the dynamics of the movements themselves, such as questions about structure, effectiveness, strategy, tactics, identity, relations to the state, relations to the media, the dynamics of their opponents, etc. An exploration of these questions should help to identify the areas for social movement research that are of greatest concern to the movements themselves."

Much initial scholarship on the global justice movement may have inspired people to join the larger struggle against capitalism, as well as publicized and garnered sympathy for the movements, as Dawson and Sinwell (2012, p. 2) contend. But there is a disconnect here, they argue, since

> many authors—particularly those rooted in the academy—failed to interrogate, from the point of view of movement activists, what an 'alternative' or 'transformative politics' actually entailed. From scholarly writings, it was clear that an alternative was desirable; some authors suggested that the alternative was decidedly anti-capitalist. But it was not clear whether the millions that made up the movements desired the same and, if so, how they sought to achieve this or a different outcome. Internal documents drawn up by activists themselves may have been clearer about movement ideals, objectives, strategies and tactics, but these were not always reflected in scholarly writing. Relying largely on definitions of transformation that were imposed from the outside rather than those that were generated by activists themselves, scholarship was out of tune with the reality on the ground.

FIGURE 2.2: Members of the community in Rosita, Nicaragua, discuss the illegal logging that was occurring in 1997. Acting on their information and other documentation, activists took action in 1998 at the Nicaraguan Embassy in Washington, DC, to protest the logging of the Bosawas rainforest. That action was widely publicized in Nicaragua and led to the Nicaraguan government cancelling a 150,000-acre illegal logging concession on Indigenous Mayangna land in the Bosawas. (Photograph by Orin Langelle)

Theories *about* movements might learn from theorizing and knowledge *from* movements. While I do not have a neat prescription for the way to do so, this certainly necessitates both a critical eye to history and dialogue with people acting and producing knowledge in activism. An example of knowledge produced in and with migrant and immigrant workers' struggles follows in the next box.

PRODUCING KNOWLEDGE IN MIGRANT AND IMMIGRANT WORKERS' STRUGGLES

Montreal's Immigrant Workers Centre (IWC)* was founded in 2000 as a community-based workers' organization in the diverse, working-class neighbourhood of Côte-des-Neiges by Filipino-Canadian union and former union organizers, other activists, and

* see www.icc-cti.org.

academic allies. The IWC engages in individual rights counselling and casework, as well as popular education and political campaigns that reflect issues facing immigrant and temporary foreign workers: dismissal, problems with employers, wage theft, and sometimes inadequate union representation. Often issues arising from individual cases form the basis for campaigns and demands that are expressed collectively. For community organizations to be part of a broader, longer-term movement for social change, social analysis and political education are vital. DeFilippis, Fisher, and Shragge (2010, p. 177) argue that "[b]oth contribute to understanding that the specific gains made and the struggles organizations undertake are part of something larger, but so is the broader political economy that structures organizational choices." Of major concern to the IWC are working conditions for workers hired by temporary labour agencies.

Besides their own experiences of exploitation, the workers are often positioned to be able to shed light on the identities and (mal) practices of the agencies. Thus, knowledge produced by workers themselves is key to building the organizing, strategy, and broader campaign work on temporary agencies. This emerges during outreach to agency workers at various sites and at meetings of agency workers where they pool their experiences and discuss the conditions and possibilities for action. This knowledge is also particularly key to mapping the sector in Quebec—especially given the "fly-by-night" nature of some agencies, which may shut up shop only to re-emerge under another identity—and informing the direction of campaigns. Another major challenge is the ability to create effective outreach strategies and target sites of companies that use agency workers. The ability to effectively learn and understand the geography of the agencies could happen only through contacts in different immigrant communities and with agency workers, especially through assemblies and organizing meetings. For example, at one meeting an agency worker working for a food-processing company discussed how many agencies operate through financial services offices that handle money transfers, payday loans, and cheque cashing that are clustered in neighbourhoods with sizable immigrant communities. Some agencies did not pay workers directly—instead they received their weekly pay from these businesses. Similarly, in the course of outreach at such locations, through building a wider contact base, agency workers told organizers that one way to find out which employers use agencies is to go to various metro (subway) stations where workers are picked up for work at 6 a.m. This insight has helped locate more businesses that use agency workers, especially in the agricultural sector.

The process of outreach and organizing meetings has enabled the IWC and the new Temporary Agency Workers Association (TAWA), which has emerged through the IWC's support for agency worker self-organizing and leadership, to begin to map the web of temporary labour agencies in multiple sectors, such as health care, food processing, warehouse work, cleaning, and hospitality. Unfortunately, because there is no organized existing body of knowledge that has systematically mapped the political economy of Montreal's agencies (and given the logistical difficulties in doing so, especially for fly-by-night operations), the daily organizing and outreach is a key research resource that allows the TAWA and the IWC to build a clearer picture of the structure of temporary agency work in Montreal. It helps with building a list of abusive and exploitative agencies.

Another aspect of mapping the agency industry involves two other forms of coalition building. The first is a collaboration between the IWC and several unions to discuss agencies and build on the knowledge they have acquired from organizing workplaces which contract out to agencies. It also serves to share resources on broader issues of precarious work, which the unions are currently working on, to put forth a series of demands of agencies in Quebec. The second is an attempt to form an ad hoc agency research committee in collaboration with engaged academics based on the experiences of the organizers. The goal is to build upon the knowledge presented by workers to transform and create a coherent critical narrative. This is an organic attempt to facilitate and develop research relevant to organizing/campaigns by combining the real experiences and knowledge of workers/ organizers with the tools and resources available to academics.

New organizing strategies also emerge from agency workers' knowledge. One issue that the TAWA has taken up is holiday pay.

This demand is a strategic way to achieve a living wage, without going after the employer directly. In Quebec, all workers are entitled to statutory holiday pay for holidays such as Christmas and Thanksgiving. But agency workers do not usually receive this pay. One worker suggested that if the struggle is for agency workers to have equal rights with other workers, they should be entitled to holiday pay. So he put forward a strategy to fight for this by posting complaints and educating workers about what they are entitled to. In turn, the TAWA has produced flyers and framed outreach based on the workers' own strategic demands.

Further demands came from workers and reflected a shift in strategy and political demands. In an open letter to Quebec's minister of labour in 2013, a group of agency workers demanded the right to be made permanent after three months at the same workplace, arguing that merely making agencies and client-companies that use them co-responsible for working conditions was not enough. Drawing from their own experiences and struggles, agency workers have directly put forward proposals about creating fairer labour policies and workplace conditions. It is slow work, but this example shows that coupled with the experience of the IWC organizers, workers' knowledge has been key to mapping the sector and advancing the campaign in an industry notoriously difficult to get to grips with, and to organize in.

My own experiences as an activist and academic reveal that the richness of movement conversations, often in informal spaces and places, is reflected neither in many of the publications, campaign literature, or websites of well-resourced NGOs nor in most academic or journalistic accounts of these activities. Moving from migrant/immigrant worker organizing to "people's summits" and forums that occur during major official meetings on trade and economic issues, I think about the ways in which debates questioning hegemonic NGO and trade union practices, power, knowledge, mandate, and representation are often shut down or avoided. Yet there were moments when such critical ideas were raised from the floor of a meeting and broke through the silences of such events. These ideas were often the ones that attempted to take people from a superficial critique or oppositional position to a deeper understanding that challenged the parameters of the political imagination and moved people from voicing dissent "against" to action and organization that would take us "beyond" those limits. It is partly through recovering, documenting, and validating those literal and metaphorical "voices from the floor"—as well as those who are excluded from or refuse to participate in such settings—that activists can unsettle and challenge professionalized NGO forms of knowledge and programs of action. This also helps them write and talk back to hegemonic positions within NGO/movement milieus. "In their role as gatekeepers, major NGOs may act as brakes on more radical and exceptional ideas emanating from the developing world, and for that reason some important challengers eschew foreign ties," comments Clifford Bob (2005, p. 194). Yet this gatekeeping practice and the replication of dominant hierarchies of knowledge are also challenged by the reassertion of critical perspectives and struggle, sometimes within networks dominated by NGOs and sometimes in entirely separate arenas of struggle. Canadian Union of Postal Workers activist David Bleakney (2012) makes parallel observations of trade union conventions and the parameters of discussion, likening speaking out in convention to speaking out of turn in church.

While activism can work toward emancipatory strategies, it can also be employed to reinforce structures of power and marginalization. Within movement networks purportedly committed to "social justice," "global justice," or "climate justice," there are still major struggles over power and knowledge. Many NGOs replicate dominant approaches to hierarchies of knowledge by favouring academic, professionalized forms of knowledge over praxis developed in social struggles. If in doing so more radical ideas are silenced, erased, contained, or watered down, and tensions and contradictions glossed over, it is one reason why a critical historical lens can be both an important analytical tool and a resource for activism.

Echoes of the Past: The Importance of History

As I suggested earlier, critical engagement with histories of earlier social struggles can be crucial to interpreting contemporary movements; so is the need to uncover histories from below to challenge dominant accounts of social movements. Activists often reflect on how it seems like we're spinning around on or reinventing the same wheel, lurching from crisis to crisis with little time for reflection on strategy, tactics, and vision. Sometimes we think we are facing something new or for the first time, but we are not aware that people who came, struggled, and thought before us might have grappled with similar dilemmas, notwithstanding the learning that we may experience in the moment when it is not apparent that perhaps we are dealing with an older, recurring problem that others have faced. Sometimes seemingly new and innovative activist practices need to be historicized. There is a tendency for so much of academic inquiry about social movements to study them from the top and through a narrow lens, rather than seeking out histories from below. Equally, however, we must be wary of constructing binaries between "top-down" and "bottom-up" approaches to social change, often along an oversimplistic "good/bad" spectrum.

There is a real hazard that histories from below can be treated in ways that lack nuance and are overly romantic and uncritical of "grassroots/bottom-up" struggles, as Dawson and Sinwell (2012) note. D'Souza (2006) urges us to use geo-history as an important concept with which to understand the ways that capitalism and colonialism operate in particular contexts in relation to specific histories. This is echoed by Holst (2002, p. 2) who urges that a "dialectical and materialist concept of history teaches us that even though at any given point in history a particular mode of production (slavery, feudalism, capitalism, etc.) is predominant, due to the constant motion and change of society every mode of production has its time of reckoning, marking a period of social revolution of transformation in which we witness a qualitative change to a new mode of production."

We should not only critically scrutinize academic literature, but also NGO, movement, and independent media accounts. These are often authored by professionalized NGO, academic writers or others who may not necessarily critically engage in movement conversations and debates, and who in some ways mirror the same tendency that Eschle (2001), Sarkar (1983b, 1998), and others charge academic scholarship with: ignoring or misconstruing forms of social action that do not fit within a pre-established theoretical framework. Mathew (2005, p. 203) also argues that to understand contemporary Third World movements means taking history seriously: "Maybe our collective task . . . is to look carefully at the resurgent left social movements all across Africa, Asia, and Latin America and comprehend the ideas of justice that inhere within these movements and the historical memory they are rooted in."

The traditions, trajectories, hopes, visions, and dilemmas of older struggles can offer vital tools for contemporary activism, whether we consider them to have succeeded or failed. As activists, readings of history—and questions about whose version we are reading—can greatly inform our analysis and conceptualization of the conditions we find ourselves in and the political spaces, opportunities, and strategies available to us.

Picking up on a thread that runs throughout this book about connections between the local and global and the knowledge produced through the circulation of ideas across the world, and as South Asian diaspora activists recently organized to oppose US and Canadian visits of India's far-right Hindu nationalist prime minister Narendra Modi, I want to move to thinking further about history and history writing by turning to some debates around Indian history and the broader lessons they offer. History has been hotly debated in India as it grapples with the legacies of freedom movements, global capitalism, "development," the rise of fascist movements, and state repression. I decided to draw upon selected perspectives and arguments from Indian historical debates here as examples of how we can understand history and its contemporary implications.

I believe that these arguments pose questions and have offered us lessons that reach well beyond South Asia. Gramsci's historical analysis of popular mass movements, the failure of the Italian left to achieve radical social change alongside the construction of a unified Italian state, and the rise of fascism resonate deeply with some Indian scholars who explore similar questions, notwithstanding their different geographical and historical contexts. Since the emergence of the Subaltern Studies Group (which borrows its name from the Gramscian concept), many social movement scholars have employed the term *subaltern* in their work to signify marginalized sectors of societies. This scholarship and this term have influenced countless studies of social movements in both the North and the South. In this section I will connect these ideas to literature concerned with history and "global justice/anti-globalization" movements. In doing this I will identify some ways in which these debates can be helpful in advancing a historical understanding of such movements and supporting a critical historical way of thinking about lessons for today.

History is always socially and ideologically constructed. Historiography—or the writing of history—has been key in the justification of colonial rule and how the rights of the colonized to represent or define themselves are systematically excluded in the writing of these histories. History, and therefore historiography, is about power and often blots out insurgent and/or Indigenous views of history. In her critique of the British imperial theorist James Mill's historiography in *The History of British India,* Bannerji (1995, p. 50) sees the role of intellectuals who "interpret the reality to be ruled and inscribe this into suitable categories" as fundamental to providing a conceptual or categorical framework and administrative basis for British colonial rule. This is true not only for India, but also for colonial settler states like Canada and Aotearoa/New Zealand, as Linda Smith (1999) has noted. In critically analyzing historical accounts, we must first always ask whose purpose they serve.

Imagined pasts and selected nationalist histories can be tools to legitimate and popularize violent chauvinistic nationalism and right-wing extremism (Sarkar 1998). As Sarkar demonstrates with reference to twentieth-century India, the far right—in this case, Hindu fascists—can draw upon selective versions of anti-colonial histories of independence struggles for ammunition to fuel communalism and bigotry. This insight also offers important warnings to movements against global capitalism, as groups and movements from many shades of the political spectrum—including the extreme right—mobilize in different ways against economic globalization, including reassertions or recon-figurations of highly racialized and exclusionary nationalism(s) (Krebbers & Schoenmaker, 2002; Monbiot, 2002).

Subaltern, Marxist, and Feminist Historiographies

Subaltern Studies scholars have attempted to understand the consciousness that informs political action by "subaltern" social groups—initially, anti-colonial peasant insurgencies in colonial India. While in his development of the concept of the subaltern Gramsci held that subaltern classes are by definition disor-ganized, often lacking in class consciousness and excluded from the histories of dominant and hegemonic classes of civil society, Indian historian Ranajit Guha (1983) focused on finding signs of consciousness among peasant rebel-lions in colonial India between 1783 and 1900. Guha sought to demonstrate their agency and autonomy, developing an analytical framework and thema-tized reading strategies.

Subaltern Studies initially focused on historical periods and milieus about which scarce data were available and which precluded access to oral histo-ries and ethnographic fieldwork. The main goal was to bring forth a history "from below" and to explore subaltern consciousness from within instead of from above. Sarkar (1983b, p. 1) described the Subaltern school as part of a "worldwide historiographical trend, associated with imaginative use of a wider range of sources, along with a certain distrust or cynicism about more-or-less bureaucratically-organised and outwardly successful political movements." The tension between histories written from above and histories from below continues in both contemporary academic and more popular accounts of present-day social movements.

Although much Subaltern Studies research has focused on peasantry, it has also considered other marginalized people, including the urban poor, Indigenous Peoples, and women as a collective group. Some view Guha's thematic analytical framework as an interesting interpretive tool with which to better under-stand and bring forth voices from movements that have often been ignored, dismissed, or reinterpreted through elite histories because of their marginal location. An initial member, Sarkar (1998) later became a strong critic of the Subaltern school because of its move from social history to cultural history. He writes approvingly of Guha's analytical thematization of peasant move-ments that sought to invert British colonial administration accounts, such as "the role of rumour, the interrelationships and distinctions between crime and insurgency . . ." (p. 86). Thus, for example, peasant and tribal insurgency from below was seen as planned, conscious revolt rather than spontaneous and somehow "natural." The value of different reading techniques to render histories from below more visible remains pertinent for analyzing more recent and contemporary histories. For example, as noted earlier, criminalization of dissent and state repression remains a reality for activists and many targeted communities around the world, as elites often construct them to be criminals or even terrorists (a topic that I will return to in Chapter 3). Marxist historians have frequently been accused of being economistic, deterministic, and reductionist. They have also been accused of failing to address questions of caste, gender, and culture (Sarkar, 1998; Sangari & Vaid, 1989; Smith, 1999) and of sacrificing attention to smaller details and dramas of history to paint a big-picture narrative (Guha, 1982). Some scholars argue that Marxism is ethnocentric and shares similar linear notions of "progress" with capitalist schools of thought, which are undermining Indigenous Peoples' communities and the ecosphere.

Other scholars have responded that many of Marxism's critics overlook extensive debates and discussions about issues of race, ethnicity, and gender. Many Third World Marxists, and others who take a dialectical approach to understanding the world, have highlighted the colonial dimensions of contemporary capitalism. In particular, they consider the importance of national liberation and self-determination as well as class struggle (Biel, 2015). They also note that contemporary capitalism can and does sustain feudalism and the dispossession of peasants—who, along with urban workers, may be a potential revolutionary or transformative force—while locking Third World societies into patterns of underdevelopment through the colonial control of resources by imperial powers. Sarkar (1998, p. 5) reminds us not to overlook "precisely that which had been central to Marxist analysis: the dialectical search for contradictions within structures."

One example is how Sarkar (1998, p. 41) praises Indian feminist scholarship for its attention to nuance and ambiguity in contrast to "a triumphal narrative of unilinear advance in the 'status of women' through male-initiated nineteenth-century social reform, followed by women's participation in Gandhian, revolutionary-terrorist or Left-led movements." Some Indian feminist historians have challenged colonial, nationalist, and Marxist historiographies (Sangari & Vaid, 1989; Kumar, 1993). They question how patriarchy is reconstituted in different forms in different classes, castes, and communities—including within the nationalist movement and post-independence social movements of the left. The attention paid by feminist historians to the private sphere has important lessons for inquiry into the internal dynamics of contemporary social movements, too. There is sometimes a tendency to overlook the importance of interpersonal dynamics and relationships in academic understandings of social movements and activist organizations. This results from a male-dominated view of history that sets parameters for historical inquiry that include only the public sphere. Dominant versions of history, including left-nationalist ones, have frequently tended to focus on charismatic "leaders" and the leadership of movements by local elites. In turn, after independence, ruling groups have claimed legitimacy by identification with these struggles.

The ways in which elite leaders appropriate mass struggles—often aided by sympathetic historical narratives and the processes through which elites legitimate themselves by association with these movements while seeking to limit or undermine militant struggles for radical social change—have long been of interest for historians and activists alike. Sarkar (1983b) notes, for example, "that any leadership, even an avowedly revolutionary one, has a necessarily restrictive aspect" (p. 50) and charges that in India, "Gandhian restraints inhibited the process of mobilization for the anti-imperialist cause of large sections of the poorer peasantry, tribals, and industrial workers" (p. 51). These limitations "inevitably left a considerable variety of movements outside the ambit of mainstream nationalism" (pp. 51–52).

Sarkar (1983b) uses Gramsci's concept of "passive revolution" to analyze how leadership in the Indian anti-imperialist struggle remained with relatively privileged groups in urban and rural areas, and how popular forces failed to build an alternative hegemony. By "passive revolution," he is referring to the process of how "attainment of political independence and unity was successfully detached by the leading bourgeois group . . . from radical social change" (p. 72). In this process, the nationalist bourgeoisie maintains hegemony by incorporating forces that potentially threaten its dominance, while claiming the right to speak for all sectors of society—even those who remain disempowered or marginalized. Smaller or less well-documented movements, or those that do not fit neatly into the typology being applied in standard historical frames, are easily overlooked or defined as contingent on leadership by "charismatic leaders, advanced political organizations or upper classes" (Guha, 1983, p. 4). Thus, besides the categorizations conducted through the application of particular strands of social movement theory, the mode of historical inquiry has a bearing on which movements and struggles are acknowledged as such and how definitional parameters are set in this process.

Some criticize the Subaltern Studies Group for its rejection of or dissatisfaction with Marxist concepts of class as an organizing concept. The group is also criticized for the singular attention that some writers pay to excavating microhistories without adequate attention either to the broader contexts in which they are situated or to Marx's understandings about dialectical relations. Subaltern Studies has been strongly criticized for its tendencies toward essentialism and "over-rigid application of binary categories" (Sarkar, 1998, p. 90). Sarkar (1998, p. 88) argues that "a tendency emerged towards essentializing the categories of 'subaltern' and 'autonomy,' in the sense of assigning them more or less absolute, fixed, decontextualized meanings and qualities." Moreover, some critical historians are concerned that while largely rejecting Marxist class analysis and categories, Subaltern Studies has arguably created a new dualism and new binaries that are heavily based on culturalism. For most Subaltern Studies scholars, a focus on "fragments" or moments of history and studies of "community" and subaltern groups has become delinked from the economy. Sarkar writes that "Colonial-Western" cultural hegemony is set up in stark binary opposition to a kind of valorized "authentic" indigeneity, "subaltern" consciousness, and cultural values. So there is colonial domination on the one hand, and autonomy/resistance on the other. Little attention is paid to internal contradictions within either of these dualistic, homogenized constructs, or to the possibilities that effective resistance to colonial domination might include the subversion of dominant institutions, processes, or discourses. Instead, because of the all-pervasiveness attributed to "Western power-knowledge," it is assumed that autonomy and resistance can take place in fleeting moments of history or in some "community-consciousness" that is "untainted by post-Enlightenment power-knowledge" (Sarkar, 1998, p. 5).

A scholar who holds such a view is Aijaz Ahmad (2000, p. 143), who sees Subaltern Studies as hostile to the left:

> the all-purpose term of "subalternity" is used *conceptually* as an
> alternative to classical Marxist categories of class structure, and *politically*
> as a weapon to attack the organized Left; in its various deployments,
> the term "subalternity" becomes so mobile and indeterminate that
> virtually everyone becomes, in one situation or another, a subaltern.

This is a relevant concern. Indeed, how does one decide who is a subaltern? While acknowledging that domination and exploitation are central to the history of colonial India, Sarkar (1998, p. 43) calls for a more nuanced, self-reflective approach to history, one that recognizes

> variations in the extent of colonial, cultural or other domination across
> times, regions, social spaces, and the possibility of earlier tensions
> (around caste and gender, notably) being reproduced in ways no doubt
> conditioned by the colonial presence, but not uniquely determined by it.

Sarkar (1983a, p. xx) had previously argued that "[s]tudy of the autonomy of popular movements must broaden itself out into more wide-ranging efforts to explore popular perceptions, mentalities, cultures . . . and—above all—a relentless self-questioning of all received categories and frameworks." Triumphalism and romanticism are other tendencies in historiographies of social movements, particularly nationalist ones, that can gloss over important questions. Another danger is posed by totalizing histories that ignore internal tensions, paradoxes, and contradictions within movements, or contradictions and tensions within systems and institutions of domination. The history wars in India are examples where an ultra-conservative Hindu nationalist ideology, drawing upon an imagined history of a precolonial, essentialized, "Hindu" India, asserts that the Hindu scripture, the *Ramayana*, portrays real historical events and characters, that Hindus are the only true and original inhabitants of India, and that Muslims and Christians are foreigners. Such a history is used to legitimate the kinds of anti-Muslim violence that Modi condoned as chief minister of the state of Gujarat in 2002, a period in which up to 2,000 Muslims were killed, many raped and injured, thousands displaced, and their property destroyed.

Democratizing the Production of Critical Histories as a Tool for Analysis and Change

There is a powerful tendency to read what we want to back into history, even to construct imagined pasts. As we saw in the examples above, Sarkar (1983b, 1998), Ahmad (2000), and others suggest ways in which certain historical readings and methodologies can lend themselves, sometimes inadvertently, to support far-right ideologies in broader society. They also show how significant popular movements can be rendered invisible or their importance minimized through being redefined as merely an auxiliary or a forerunner to a more recognized, elite movement, for example, by approaches to history that adhere to certain inflexible typologies. In the Indian context (as elsewhere), feminist historians have challenged historical narratives that perpetuate patriarchal assumptions while they develop new methodological approaches and seek to recapture and make accessible women's voices and experiences.

The project of building a new kind of historical culture and democratizing the production of history is vital. Sarkar (1998, p. 46) writes that "an exploration of the social conditions of production of history cannot afford to remain a merely intellectual project. It needs to become part of wider and far more difficult efforts to change these conditions." In pursuing this, we need to ask how historical writing might enable scholars and activists to better understand the making of contemporary social movements. How are these versions of histories generated? Who writes these histories? What of histories that are not committed to paper, but that circulate orally, perhaps in versions that differ from the written forms, if these exist? While historians and historiography cannot change society, they can contribute to developing conceptual resources for adaptation and use by movements seeking emancipation of societies. Alternative histories can be important foundations for alternative knowledges and ways of thinking about today and tomorrow. Dialogue between movement activists and historians committed to writing social history is crucial.

Big Books, Great Leaders, High Priests, and Superstar Activists

Given the growing number of books and articles written on the histories of movements, there is a large amount of material containing historical perspectives on movements that is key to understanding the twists and turns in how they come to be understood, as well as informing present and future strategies for change today. But there are other problems with how we engage with history. Meyer and Rohlinger (2012) tackle the "big book myth"—the notion, echoed in popular and scholarly narratives, that the origins of several significant social movements (and government action related to causes they were espousing) in the United States during the 1960s lay in four books. This is a form of mystifying movement origins by what Verta Taylor (1989) calls the "immaculate conception" notion of social change. The big book myth makes "mobilization, engagement, and influence appear more accessible, even as they are mystified. Indeed, the actual perquisites of effective action, organization, resources, planning, and strategy are edited out of the story" (Meyer & Rohlinger, 2012, p. 149).

People tend to create heavily edited versions of the past—narrative simplifications—to write accounts of movements and construct coherent stories: "[V]ariant stories are told to different audiences, including both activists and potential activists within a movement, and authorities and broad publics outside. Such narratives make sense of complicated and sometimes confusing events and often reflect activists' strategic efforts to garner public sympathy and support for their cause. Interested parties strategically construct competing narratives about past events to emphasize their preferred vision of causality, and to encourage a particular kind of activity—or inactivity—in the future" (Meyer & Rohlinger 2012, p. 139). Meyer and Rohlinger argue that stories that "draw on resonant themes and speak to the shared experience of larger publics are more likely to gain attention and, therefore, to aid recruitment and mobilization within a movement, and sympathetic recognition from outside. Narratives that make sense of political defeats can sustain participation and commitment by providing a sense of long-term struggle and the prospects for success in the future" (p. 139).

"Immaculate conception" accounts tend to construct movement histories where "apparently spontaneous actions of heroic individuals are cited as a spur for mobilization and political action" (Meyer & Rohlinger, 2012, p. 140). Thus, ideas are seen as being precursors to organizational and political action in a supposedly "open field upon which a good idea, if championed effectively, can prevail by generating collective action and response," including swift government action. This masks the significance of building communities of support for social change and collective struggles, rather than noble heroes with good ideas. As Meyer and Rohlinger (p. 141) contend, the big book myth/model of social change is appealing because of its simplicity: "The notion is that a book, by exposing an injustice or suggesting an idea, reaches masses of people, who then act collectively, generate government response, and affect [sic] social change. This is a common explanation in historical accounts of several movements of the early 1960s."

Meyer and Rohlinger (2012) write that just as some "immaculate conception" myths of social movement origins neglect political organizing in favour of heroic individuals, it is easier to trace the publication dates of books than the start of organizing in creating stories about the past. They suggest that these stories "undermine understandings of the long and complicated process of making social change. Would-be reformers may find themselves waiting for the magic moment or big book, while foregoing efforts to build a context that would allow them to emerge. The innumerable events that don't immediately generate dramatic responses seem to fail—or just fall out of the story. And would-be activists may turn to their computers rather [than] their communities, drafting a text rather than calling for a meeting" (p. 150).

The big book myth is familiar. We need only think of claims sometimes made about contemporary books and films. Naomi Klein's *No Logo* was called the "manifesto" of the anti-globalization movement; a film featuring Al Gore, *An Inconvenient Truth,* was upheld as the bible of climate change/environmental activism by many. This version of social change, like the great leader/radical hero narrative, conforms well to a free market, individualized view of the world. Accounts of movements thus become tales of strong, charismatic individuals, smart authors, and great ideas become the centre of social change rather than the organizing work it takes to build movements.

One of the antidotes to this trend in literature on social movements is scholarship grounded in the micropolitics, tensions, contradictions, and possibilities of movement work and organizing. Once again, I refer to the examples of Shragge (2013) and Dixon (2014), who both, through an engaged analysis developed in dialogue with organizers (and their own experiences as organizers), offer rich insights into the strategy and dynamics of creating and sustaining movements and organizations.

Historiography and the "Global Justice Movement"

In an era of accelerated and deepened global free market capitalism, nationalist histories, both left and right, celebrate the nation-state and contrast it to a vision of a seamless, borderless global economy. These nostalgic, idealized accounts frequently sidestep questions of struggles by Indigenous Peoples, workers, immigrants, and other marginalized communities against injustice and often against the state itself. Academic inquiry, media accounts, and popular histories also often overlook "histories from below," focusing—through "a study from the top downwards" (Sarkar 1983a, p. 43)—on perceived leaders, elites, and efficient mobilizations. Many grassroots struggles are overlooked in this way. This includes radical struggles against capitalism from below in the South that "rarely register on the radar screens in the North" (McNally, 2002, p. 198). This also highlights the importance of understanding neoliberalism and contemporary resistance movements in relation to older processes, especially colonialism and imperialism.

The insights, tensions, dangers, and methodological considerations that arise from the debates on the historiography of social movements in India, as I have discussed above, remain relevant. Global justice movements are affected by several layers of contested histories. Accounts of history in which culture, politics, and the economy are fragmented and detached from each other provide fertile ground for exclusionary and racist cultural nationalisms to develop. So too does the reliance on culturalist lenses, concepts, categories, and meanings that obscure historical and social relations. There are neoliberal versions of history that glorify free market economics and frame its critics as a mixture of Luddites, flat-Earth advocates, self-interested cliques, naive but well-meaning fools, dangerous anarchists (e.g., Friedman, 1999; Moore, 1997, 1999, 2003), and extremists (NZSIS, 1998; CSIS, 2000). Many NGOs and social movements openly contest these versions of history and counter them. But these alternative histories are themselves contested within movement/activist networks, including debates as to when "globalization" and, in turn, "anti-globalization" movements began, as well as different perspectives from people who approach and experience activism from different positions in society and, indeed, the world.

Analytical tools, themes, and debates developed by historians can provide useful lenses through which to understand movements. They also raise warning flags about pitfalls that are easy to fall into when analyzing social movements, as do the debates and tensions among different approaches to studying history or when we seek to learn from history as activists. The importance of historical understanding has not been lost on some activists reflecting on the global justice/anti-globalization movement. Some, especially those writing on movements in the global North, warn of a sense of ahistoricity that often permeates accounts of "anti-globalization" movements and constructs them as recent phenomena. Yuen (2002, p. 7) claims that "the Seattle demonstrations revealed a deep historical amnesia both on the part of the mainstream media, and, unfortunately, many activists themselves." According to this narrative, he continues, "the outbreak of unrest in Seattle was like the reawakening of a mastodon trapped in amber since the days of Kent State." For many academic, media, and activist accounts, the forerunners to Seattle, especially actions against capitalist globalization in the South, do not seem to exist. Katsiaficas (2002, pp. 29–30) notes:

> Such disregard slyly reinforces one of the world system's central ideas: the life of a human being in the United States or Europe is worth more than the life of a Third World person. . . . [P]rogressive and radical history must be qualitatively different than the history of the neoliberalist champions and their corporate masters. Our history must reflect the notion that all human life is of equal value.

This reminds us how important it is to strive to understand history so that we can also grasp how elites have been able to undermine, disarm, and defeat movements from below. Histories of contemporary movements engaged in struggles against capitalist globalization written by and about movement elites, leaders, and notables can marginalize, omit, and silence important debates, dynamics, processes, and events. They can also influence movement dynamics, aspirations, and strategies. Without sustained social analysis and historical understanding, newer movements "can easily find themselves at a variety of dead ends if they fail to understand the nature of the system they oppose and the sorts of social and political strategies necessary to radically challenge it" (McNally, 2002, p. 12).

How history is interpreted, constructed, contested, narrated, or ignored is often central to the campaign advocacy and action work of social movements, activist groups, and NGOs that are also active players in the creation and documentation of this history. The production and popularization of historical understandings of NGOs is an area that deserves more critical attention. Many of the criticisms of NGOs resonate with historical analyses of the role of elites in nationalist social movements and also with some of the critiques of elite forms of historiography discussed earlier. This in turn affects which forms of social action and organization get written about or cited in scholarly literature on social movements.

The way in which many NGOs engaged in campaigns against capitalist globalization tend to conceptualize, categorize, and compartmentalize issues and causes is problematic. This lends itself to decontextualized, fragmentary historical understandings and accounts. Some tend toward a view that sees globalization as an entirely new phenomenon, without regard for analyses that view it as part of a longer historical process. For many NGOs, totalizing histories or ahistoricity go hand in hand with a tendency toward a reductionist, fragmented, single-issue focus. This tends to be quite different from those movement positions that are grounded in and take a longer-term historical perspective on struggles for social change.

Discussing the Seattle anti-WTO mobilizations, Cockburn and St Clair (2002, p. 94) claim that liberal NGOs constructed a "fantasy version of history." They charge that these NGOs concocted a "myth of respectable triumph" in Seattle that downplayed or ignored altogether the role of militant direct action on the streets by thousands in their accounts of the events: "It would no doubt be polite to treat this myth-making as contemptible but harmless self-aggrandisement. But real social movements for change shouldn't be built on illusions, and the self-aggrandisement is far from harmless" (p. 95). Returning to Gramsci's (1971) concept of passive revolution can help us analyze how elites have appropriated popular struggles for their own ends.

How, for example, have particular NGOs, political parties, and trade union leaderships claimed the mantle of "global justice" for their own purposes while detaching it from demands and aspirations for radical social change? The co-optation of some supposed leaders of "global justice" networks by governments and international institutions, their claims to speak and act on behalf of millions, the demobilization of radical struggles, and the appropriation or assimilation of grassroots movements resonate with previous iterations of popular struggles. Further, what lessons can be learned from efforts to resist or oppose these moves? Reactions to recent waves of global capitalism have included retreats into forms of essentialism, cultural chauvinism, nationalism, and movement triumphalism. One can understand how glorifying histories for mobilizing or propaganda purposes and the reasons why valorizing all forms of the "local" and "community" might become a rallying cause against domination by global capital. Yet these can pose the same dangers identified by Sarkar's critiques of the Subaltern Studies Group. As Krebbers and Schoenmaker (2002) and Monbiot (2002) reminded us over a decade ago, and as we have seen since, the far right has in many countries mobilized against international free trade agreements. This is certainly true in India, where some Hindu supremacists and fundamentalists have used anti-colonial and xenophobic ideas to do so. Some

NGOs that claim to be part of the global justice movement, moreover, have forged working relationships and alliances with chauvinist nationalist politicians, parties, and organizations. While finishing this chapter, I have watched exchanges on an email listserv among US trade justice activists about joining forces and combining resources with profoundly racist and xenophobic conservative groups opposed to trade and investment deals such as the Trans-Pacific Partnership. Closer attention to history and political economy might lead to critical understandings that could surely seriously challenge such moves. There are resources that have helped to write back to some of the hegemonic NGO, labour union, and academic accounts of the anti-globalization movements. In the context of documenting movements, for example, the Colours of Resistance website (http://www.coloursofresistance.org) that emerged from the margins of the global justice movement in North America played a useful role in collecting and connecting anti-racist and anti-colonial activists and their writings on struggles against global capitalism and colonialism, and about multiracial organizing, and alliance building. Another resource is the book *The Battle of Seattle: The New Challenge to Capitalist Globalization* (Yuen, Katsiaficas, & Burton Rose, 2002), to which several of the authors cited in this section contributed.

Concluding Thoughts

To fully understand movement and activist networks means grappling with questions emerging from movements and activists themselves. These questions are often based on sophisticated macro (and micro) analyses of social relations and shifting power dynamics. This is certainly not to suggest that evaluation and analysis from the standpoint of being embedded in activism is always rigorous or adequate. Indeed, there are perhaps as many negative lessons to be learned from histories of earlier struggles as there are positive ones. George Smith (2006) and Gary Kinsman (2006) warn of a need to go beyond the "common sense theorizing" that often goes on in these settings, but which does not attend to actual social practices and organization. It can be useful to question and unearth the history of activist practices, processes, and terminology that is used in organizing spaces. Where do they come from? Equally, there are anti-intellectual and ahistorical currents inside some movements and activist groups. Many scholarly, NGO, and activist accounts pay inadequate attention to the significance of low-key, long-haul political education and community organizing work that goes on underneath the radar. It is important to document movement challenges to hegemonic NGO and "civil society" positions—otherwise the latter will prevail unchallenged as the definitive "alternative" discourses and versions of history to be referenced by and to inform future movements and academics (and other authors). Emerging work that engages in dialogue with organizers and activists and combines both micropolitics with macroanalysis of local to global political, economic, and social forces also allows us to see the limitations of social movement theory that produces an outsider perspective on movements based on their objectification and classification. It offers an alternative way to appreciate how learning takes place and knowledge can be produced for movements and social struggles while having a broader significance. Such approaches overcome the split between theory and practice by locating learning/education, knowledge production, and theorizing in the everyday practices of movements/activism and the political and social confrontations they are involved in. This allows us to focus on the pedagogical significance of movement/activist practice and theorizing. In the next chapter I will draw from examples of activist learning and education practice to continue the discussion about how and why these activities are so important to understand.

CHAPTER 3

NON-FORMAL AND INFORMAL LEARNING IN ACTIVISM

Learning Theories and Activist Theorizing

The idea that learning occurs beyond formal institutions and programs is hardly radical. Much writing on adult education, including humanist, experiential, community, feminist, and workplace learning perspectives, agrees that significant learning occurs outside classroom settings. While there are indeed many theoretical perspectives on learning, I will largely focus on one of these in this chapter: Learning is social. Not only can people's everyday practices in struggles contribute to constructing alternative forms of knowledge, but attending to this learning and knowledge production can also help us understand social movements. Without this, we may risk falling back on shorthand understandings of politics and protest, which threatens to do more to obscure than to explain what actually happens in the course of activism—sometimes in the pursuit of trying to prove theories or advocate particular paradigms. Moreover, for those who want to change the world, this kind of knowledge and learning offers important tools for political praxis.

This chapter discusses non-formal and informal learning in activist milieus. In it, I include reflections on popular education and illustrate the dynamics of informal and incidental learning in social action, including contradictions and possibilities. The educational spaces, places, aspects, and moments of organizing for social justice have served and can serve as living laboratories for innovative ways to learn and share knowledge. My discussion here builds on theories about the dynamics of knowledge production and learning in movements/activism and elaborates on processes of knowledge production in campaigns and mobilizations. I also use two extended vignettes drawn from my own activist experience to tease out what this kind of knowledge production and learning looks like in concrete terms. The first of these is an example drawn from reflections on the politics of activist knowledge and learning arising from confrontations with state repression. The second considers some of the tensions and contradictions inherent in the production of such knowledge as well as internal struggles within movement milieus—particularly surrounding notions of expertise, NGOization, and the dominance of professionalized forms of knowledge in many activist settings. This includes attention to forms of pedagogic practice and assumptions about knowledge that underpin educative activities within social movement activism. As suggested earlier, tensions and conflict are often central to much of the critical knowledge produced within movements.

All forms of learning are fraught with tensions and contradictions, but broadly speaking there are two major strands in the evolution of adult education. The first of these has served to domesticate learners, focus on strategies for individual self-improvement, and adjust minds to·conform to a capitalist society. This strand embraces market capitalist ideas on learning as an individual responsibility and, like other forms of education, sees adult education as being geared primarily toward acquiring credentials that benefit economic growth. The second is concerned with emancipation: ways in which learning, education, and knowledge; democratic reflection; and action through a critical identification of issues can be used to help people overcome educational disadvantage, address social exclusion and discrimination, and challenge political and economic injustice.

If we take up the emancipatory theory of adult education, how then can we link it to actual practices of learning? What is the relationship of non-formal programs, activities, and processes of education in movements and activist settings to informal, incidental, daily learning that takes place in the course of organizing and activism? In connecting scholarship on movements to theories of learning and knowledge production, I find the work of critical adult education scholars Griff Foley, John Holst, and Eurig Scandrett helpful. They look at social movement learning and radical adult education through an expansive view of where learning happens and knowledge is produced. I share their analysis that the relationship between education/learning and social change must be understood dialectically. For Scandrett (2012), recent developments in social movement theory emphasize the contribution of theoretical work to movements themselves, the importance of theorists to be accountable to movements, and the theory generated within movements. He argues that this emergent direction entails a dynamic engagement with the research and theorizing already being done by movement participants. He writes that for those working in adult education, "this approach resonates with conceptions of really useful knowledge and popular education in which scholarly knowledge is interrogated by movements of the oppressed for its value in interpreting and promoting their own material interests. Such material interests embedded within knowledge are exposed through dialogical methods such as popular education and lifelong education" (p. 43). By "really useful knowledge" (Johnson, 1979;Thompson, 1997), Scandrett refers to what helps people understand the causes of their conditions and change them. Such knowledge is generated through reflections on their own and other people's experiences of common problems and struggles. It can help build theories and understandings that can inform action for change.

Learning: From Formal to Informal

There have been many attempts to define and compartmentalize formal, non-formal, and informal learning. One helpful way to think about these concepts is to view formality and informality in learning as a continuum. This is particularly relevant today, when there are pressures to informalize aspects of formal education and to formalize informal learning. Elements of formality can be found in informal settings, and elements of informality can be found in formal situations. Four key attributes or aspects to help think through formality and informality in learning situations have been identified by Malcolm, Hodkinson, and Colley (2003). These are *process, location and setting, purpose*, and *content*. Analyzing formality and informality in education has both theoretical and political dimensions, including attention to whether learning is collaborative or individual, the status of the knowledge/learning, teacher–student power relations, the locus of control of learning processes, the location of the learning within broader power relations, and whether the purposes and interests that lie behind the learning/knowledge meet the needs of dominant or marginalized communities. It is worth reviewing each of these four aspects briefly here.

First, by *process* they note the way that more didactic, teacher-controlled pedagogic approaches tend to be seen as formal, whereas more democratic, negotiated, or student-led ones are regarded as informal. Learning processes that are incidental to everyday activities are usually viewed as informal, but engagement in teacher-defined tasks is seen as "formal." Formality/informality is also sometimes gauged by whether the pedagogue is a teacher (formal), industrial trainer, guidance counsellor (less formal), or friend or colleague (informal). Whether or not learning is mainly summative (formal), mainly formative and negotiated (relatively informal), or not assessed at all (informal) is another issue.

Second, *location and setting* refers to the physical location for the learning. Thus a school, college, or university is formal, while the workplace, community, or family is viewed as informal. But the setting of learning matters in other ways, too. Informal learning is often described as open ended with few time restrictions, no specified curriculum, no predetermined learning objectives, no external certification, and so on. Formal learning is seen as the opposite. For those with a radical progressive political perspective, many of the attributes of formal learning may be seen as repressive. On the other hand, more instrumental governmental approaches are seeking ways of introducing these "formal" features to the informal or non-formal learning that they want to enhance and support. From a theoretical perspective, location and setting are key parts of authentic practice. As Malcolm, Hodkinson, and Colley (2003, p. 316) contend, it is "the synergy between practices and setting that ensures successful learning. The assumption is that such synergies are mainly attained in informal settings using informal processes." However, they note that "such synergies [may exist] in more formal learning settings as well . . . and non-educational settings also have strongly formalised dimensions, which should not be overlooked" (p. 316).

Third, the extent to which learning has formal/informal attributes related to its *purposes* depends on the dimension concerned. This means the extent to which learning is intentional, deliberate, and the prime focus of activity, rather than being a largely unintended outcome of another activity or purpose. Learner-determined and -initiated learning is viewed as informal; learning designed to meet the externally determined needs of others with more power—the teacher, an examination board, an employer, the government—is generally regarded as formal.

Finally, in discussing the *content* and nature of what is learned, Malcolm, Hodkinson, and Colley note that acquiring established expert knowledge/ understanding/practices is usually seen as formal, and the development of something new is seen as informal. A focus on vertical or propositional knowledge is formal, whereas everyday practice and workplace competence are informal. Is the focus on high status knowledge or not? Who gets to determine content is also viewed as a manifestation of power relations.

Education is always inherently political, and non-formal learning certainly no less so. Many forms of non-formal learning are connected to and draw upon an often diverse range of struggles and visions of social, political, economic, and environmental justice. Meanwhile, the contribution of non-formal learning to education and society is seemingly recognized, validated, and endorsed by dominant institutions like government ministries in numerous countries as well as major intergovernmental organizations like the OECD, the Asian

Development Bank, and the World Bank. For example, the United Nations Educational, Scientific and Cultural Organization (UNESCO, 1997, p. 41) defines non-formal education as "[a]ny organized and sustained educational activities that do not correspond exactly to the definition of formal education. Non-formal education may therefore take place both within and outside educational institutions, and cater to persons of all ages."

Yet critical educators and scholars suggest that the current celebration of non-formal learning must be understood in the context of widespread cuts to resourcing public education in many countries. In the global South, this squeezing of policy space and resources to provide accessible education and other basic services has often been facilitated through aid conditionalities imposed by international financial institutions such as the International Monetary Fund (IMF) and the World Bank, and pressure from donor governments. In the North, cuts to education and community funding along with broader impositions of market-driven policies have undermined many gains for equitable access to education. Indeed, these concerns are very much at the forefront of popular mobilizations against the current policies and politics of "austerity" in many countries. However, it is to some of the more critical contexts of ideas and practice concerning informal and non-formal learning that I want to return.

Locating Informal and Non-formal Learning: Gramsci and Freire

In 2012 I visited Sardinia, birthplace of Antonio Gramsci, the Italian communist activist and thinker who had a major influence on critical adult education, although he did not explicitly theorize non-formal/informal learning. Gramsci's family home in Ghilarza, a small town in the hills of Sardinia where he spent much of his childhood, is now the Casa Museo di Antonio Gramsci, a museum and centre for documentation and research on his work (see http://casagramscighilarza.org). It commemorates a time when Sardinia was one of the poorest and most isolated parts of Italy. I had long understood Gramsci, who died in 1937, to be a Marxist activist—which indeed he was. Yet often the Gramsci I encountered through others' readings of his ideas and writings seemed quite decontextualized from his actual life. As Phelps and Rudin (1995, p. 54) put it, "Gramsci has become safe, tame, denatured—a wisp of his revolutionary self. Academics seeking to justify their retreat into highly abstruse theories have created fanciful illusions about their 'counterhegemonic' activity." What was most memorable for me that day in Ghilarza—indeed, moving and chilling as I looked into the display case where they rested—were the original court documents from the trial that led to his imprisonment. The sentence he received there was designed, as the prosecutor stated, to prevent his brain from functioning for 20 years. Togliatti (1949, p. 120) observed that "for Gramsci, study could never be something separate from action. Study and life had led him to discover and make contact with a social force which would redeem and renew the world and itself. Study and life would make this contact ever more close." Besides his now classic theorization of hegemony and his explanation of how power relations become the common sense of the social order, one of Gramsci's major contributions is how he theorized learning and praxis.

Gramsci's definition of praxis is crucially important to those of us who work in education—whether in the academy, in community organizing, or in movements. Educators often like to make optimistic claims that education is the key to changing the world. But is it enough? What is the connection between education and action—organizing and building social movements? As Coben (1998, p. 31) reminds us, Gramsci "made it clear that he had no illusions about the power of education *alone* to bring about the revolution. In 1924 he stated that pedagogic methods could not resolve 'the great historical problem of the spiritual emancipation of the working class.'" Gramsci rejected the idealist notion that working-class consciousness could be changed completely before the proletariat had taken over the state, stating that this could only change when the way of living of the class itself changed.

So for Gramsci, political activity was not a chronological outcome of political education, but rather concurrent with it. This is entirely consistent with the notion that learning is integral to all human activity and shaped by interpersonal, institutional, and broader social and political forces. In his work, Foley (1999, p. 64) examines this topic in a way that analyzes and validates the importance of incidental learning in a variety of social struggles. Arguing that this analysis necessitates writing "case studies of learning in struggle, making explanatory connections between the broad political and economic context, micro-politics, ideologies, discourses and learning," he suggests that the "process of critical learning involves people in theorizing their experience: they stand back from it and reorder it, using concepts like power, conflict, structure, values and choice. It is also clear that critical learning is gained informally, through experience, by acting and reflecting on action, rather than in formal courses."

It is crucial to highlight the importance of collective spaces to learn and organize, produce knowledge, and act. These are physical spaces where people come together—social settings, meetings, study groups, marches or demonstrations, and so on. Space, organizing, learning, and knowledge production are deeply interconnected in the course of activism for social change. Gramsci once again is instructive here. In Turin, he and some other young men who were forced to quit school early because of poverty met in a "Club for Moral Life," established by the Italian Socialist Party. They would share their analyses of essays or books for feedback with the aim of achieving the "intellectual and moral communion of everyone" (Gramsci, 1971, p. xxxii). Germino (1990) suggests that the fact that ordinary workers, with only elementary education, could rapidly absorb great ideas of the past must have led Gramsci to see such clubs as possible models for generating revolutionary change. As Holst (2002, p. 92) argues, "education or praxis involves developing a dialectical understanding of the contradictions of social life in order to find avenues of action to overcome the problems facing those with whom we work."

Another thinker who has had a major influence on educational practice and theory is Brazilian educationalist Paolo Freire (1970). Informed by Gramsci's thinking, his work has profoundly impacted formal, informal, and popular education for emancipation. Freire's critique of dominant forms of schooling as a banking model that essentially revolves around teachers dropping knowledge into the supposedly empty vessels of learners' minds is powerful and has been taken up by many educators. Freire's work among Brazil's poor and illiterate aimed to develop education for liberation, not domination or domestication. His literacy work emphasized the idea of reading the word and the world together—that is to say, literacy was intimately connected with an exploration of learners' own realities. He believed that people could develop a critical consciousness through a process of what he called *conscientization* by which they come not only to reflect upon and deeply question their own historical and social conditions but also strategize to take action.

Freire believed that the poor and dispossessed were trapped in a "culture of silence" through which they internalized the negative way in which they were treated by the system of historical, economic, and social power relations that oppressed them. But he also believed that through dialogue they could become both critical thinkers and agents of their own destiny. He saw learning as the joint responsibility of teachers and learners, who come together in a dialectical relationship where both are simultaneously learner and teacher. He theorized that experience and expertise were shared in a process of being able to identify, interpret, criticize, and come up with solutions to injustices. Freire's legacy in popular education throughout the world has been important, and a great deal of theory and practice builds on his work.

Popular Education in Theory and in Practice

What makes popular education "popular"? What assumptions about knowledge underpin popular education? Popular education teaches people to study their own experiences to uncover the analysis and the resources they need to move from where they are to where they want to be, as Australian adult educator Bob Boughton (2013) puts it. Similarly, Bowl and Tobias (2010, p. 282) write that in progressive forms of adult and community-based education "both learner and teacher have personal, social, political, and economic experience and understanding to bring to the learning environment—commonsense experience, which may be explained, explored, and critiqued." With long histories in the struggles of working-class people, peasants, and others who are socially and economically marginalized in societies, popular education encompasses a far greater range of traditions, approaches, and techniques than I can do justice to in this short section. It can be a powerful force for bringing people together, educating and building knowledge for action.

Part of the power of popular education is due to a commitment to starting where people are at, but it generally aims to support them to go beyond that. A Canadian Union of Postal Workers (2009, p. 18) training manual, which draws from US nonviolence trainer George Lakey's Teaching for Change work, describes popular education as the kind of education that seeks "to transform power relations in society, relationships between teacher and learner, and relationships among learners. In this sense it is radically democratic." Many forms of popular education intend for participants to experience, reflect, generalize, and apply learning in their everyday struggles for change. Through reflecting, greater insight and understanding of people's everyday circumstances can enable theories, strategies, and action to develop together for change. It can foster more autonomy for people, give them greater control over their own lives, and work to break isolation.

Popular education is an important link connecting the idea of activism and building collective spaces and movements in which ordinary people can see themselves as knowledge producers and agents of change. European forms of popular education, as Boughton (2013, p. 244) reminds us, date back to eighteenth-century radicalism and became integral to the international socialist movement via nineteenth-century Chartism: "By virtue of this, popular education had already, by the 1860s, become integrally linked to the study of revolutionary Marxist socialism, the 'proletarian science' which occupied radical intellectuals and working-class autodidacts alike, in the discussion clubs, lecture halls and study circles where they mixed."

Learning about injustices, their causes and connections—that is to say, awareness alone—is not enough to bring about change. Reflecting on tensions and possibilities within labour education in Canada and the United States, union educators David Bleakney and Michael Morrill (2010, p. 144) state:

> There are enough unpleasant facts and human squalor that if information transfer was the only thing required (or the banking model, as Freire

put it), we should already have reached a point of widespread rebellion. But in our experience, participants who become mere receivers of unpleasant facts can become disempowered or feel more hopeless about prospects for change than to begin with. Workers not permitted to be participants in critical reflection on their reality are not likely to be agents for change. Resistance is personal and social and requires slipping outside the "quantitative box" into which we so easily, unconsciously, and compliantly fit. The process of using anger and action is valuable in worker-based trainings. However, when workers remain in the anger stage, worker-educators have done no favors to the transformative process. Indeed, resolutions to problems have been contracted out to union advocates, thus reinforcing the model of disempowerment and union paternalism, no matter how well intentioned. Facilitators must aim to assist participants in transforming rage into hope. With hope, action can follow. What is the purpose of worker education if not to assist people to act on their collective wisdom and experience?

The same question can be asked of popular education more broadly. Popular education can work powerfully by using tools that engage people emotionally and move them physically—and in other ways. One of these ways is encouraging people to move past a sense of isolation—a culture of complaint and an enhanced capacity to describe the many problems we face—to one of action and agency. But people also need collective contexts in which to organize for change so that they can connect experience, reflection, and new understandings with action.

TALKING AND LEARNING FROM EACH OTHER

In 2008, La Via Campesina, a global network of small, peasant and Indigenous farmers' organizations, invited me as a resource person to a strategy meeting on free trade agreements, transnational corporations, and food sovereignty. Stepping back and making space for farmer-activists from across continents (and several languages) to talk to each other directly about their perspectives on free trade and how they have been organizing on the ground was a far more useful approach than me holding forth as some kind of transnational expert on the global economy and agriculture. These are the moments that feel most satisfying: You are meant to be a resource person, expert, instructor, or workshop facilitator, but you feel it doesn't matter if you're there or not. It does not hinge on an individual's supposed expertise, or the use of a particular technique or process. People are talking, engaging, sharing what they know, learning from each other, building their analysis and strategy together. Lynd (in Lynd & Grubacic, 2009, p. 75) describes the beginnings of the celebrated Highlander Folk School (now the Highlander Research and Education Center) in Tennessee that supported trade unions and the civil rights struggles through social justice leadership training. Myles Horton, the main founder of Highlander, called a meeting to address community needs and concerns during the Depression in the Appalachian mountains, to which some people walked barefoot: "As the meeting was about to begin, Horton realized that he had nothing consequential to suggest. In panic and desperation he said: 'Let's go around the circle and see what ideas people bring with them.' They did so. A program materialized. The Highlander style of education emerged from this experience." Such experiences happen on a daily basis but are not necessarily documented. Systematizing popular education and movement learning experiences remains a challenge.

Writing about popular education schools in marginalized communities near Cape Town, South Africa, Astrid Von Kotze (2012, p. 104) suggests that "the shift from mere critical to anticipatory consciousness can instill the hope and determination necessary for assuming agency, but it requires a slow process to feed and develop a fertile imagination." The experience of people coming together through powerful popular education activities—sharing moments of opening and sensing alternative ways of doing things, valuing their own roles in producing ideas together—is something difficult to replicate through formal education and curricula. Building the determination and confidence in ordinary people that they can organize to bring about change is crucial.

In my own education practice, in both formal settings and more popular contexts, I am acutely aware of the tensions and contradictions between being directive and dialogical. It is a balancing act to be open about having a political direction, purpose, and principles but at the same time taking seriously the understanding that people can think through their own situations and problems and come up with ways forward. And we are kidding ourselves if we think that asking questions is a less ideological way of educating than lecturing. If we agree that, as Alexander (1990, pp. 66–67) suggests, there is an "unresolved tension between our recognition of the reality that teachers/educators are different from their students by virtue of their theoretical knowledge on the one hand, and our warning on the other hand against the 'demagogy' of pseudo-participatory methods," then how do we navigate this in practice? How do we know what learning takes place? Numerous practitioner manuals, handbooks, and websites catalogue techniques and pedagogic approaches that are used in popular education. We must develop and adapt styles of popular education from and for our particular contexts, and at the same time work on how to turn analysis and learning into action. I do not have a neat resolution here, but I think it can be hard to move away from somehow replicating our own educational experiences and inadvertently ending up with more of a didactic approach than we had intended. Likewise, there can be pushback from participants in the face of attempts to build a space—and learning—around dialogue, as this may be a new way of learning for many people.

Learning and Action

Here I will briefly discuss several examples of non-formal learning in activist milieus. First, in several of the networks I am part of, activists have revived book circles or study groups around particular issues, struggles, and topics. Berger and Dixon (2009, p. 159) write that study groups are a hallmark of the left, intentional spaces for critical and collective education: "Previous periods of crisis, like the 1930s and 1970s, compelled radicals to jointly investigate theoretical and practical models of revolutionary struggle. Often, these investigations led to new organizations or campaigns. Similarly, the current crises have generated several formations that intentionally use study to advance political priorities and explore organizational forms." Indeed, book circles and study groups can provide spaces for conversation, reflection, and analysis in ways that campaign or organizing meetings—especially when crisis driven and reactive—might not. In recent years, I have known activists who have organized reading groups on anarchism and feminism, popular resistance in Palestine and the Middle East, and indeed the latest economic crisis as part of their organizing and learning.

Many movements and activists conduct teach-ins, educational events, conferences, and workshops. While on the one hand these can be useful for connecting people and sharing ideas and analysis, too often the model is the same: experts, panels, discussions, and workshops. How empowering is this? We cannot organize movements through holding events, nor can we build movements by dropping knowledge on people. What is the balance between a focus on the personal qualities and capacity of educators and learning in the struggle? I hear, alarmingly, of instances where concepts from the heart of corporate America, such as having a designated "thought leader," are being used by some environmental activists who plan strategies for change. These concepts are based on a logic that is top-down and relies on a star system, rather than on a commitment to build movements in which all kinds of people can come together, share, learn, and take action. We should be deeply uneasy about merely replicating dominant/hegemonic ideas and practices about learning and teaching. I return to this tension later in the chapter.

Simulation and role-playing games can engage people about power relations and systems that stratify people through unequal distribution of wealth and resources. This can be effective because it works on an emotional level rather than an intellectual one. Often our eyes start to glaze over when listening to another lecture or panel presentation about inequality and power relations, race, class, and capitalism. What is key here is how to build on the insights and feelings people experience and use this open space to reflect and analyze, discuss feelings, and go forward. One commonly used simulation activity uses 10 chairs to dramatize the unequal distribution of wealth. This exercise can create a foundation for deeper learning: how one person representing the 1 per cent (to use the Occupy framework, signifying the massive inequalities associated with the wealthiest 1 per cent of the US population owning a hugely disproportionate portion of economic wealth in the country, against the rest of the population—the 99 per cent) sprawls over seven to eight chairs, while the 99 per cent are crowded on or around the remaining two or three chairs. Kinesthetic learning, and the opportunity to reflect on such an experience and put it into dialogue with theoretical concepts about class, race, and gender inequalities, can remain with someone in ways that other things cannot. Even the most eloquently written, cogently argued article, book, or film, or the most persuasive and engaging talk on the subject might not have the same effect. Workshops on direct action training and working with the media can also be practical spaces to role-play scenarios, build affinity and mutual support, share skills, and rehearse possible responses.

Connected to this is the Theatre of the Oppressed, or forum theatre. Developed by Brazilian Augusto Boal, this is a form of participatory popular theatre that aims to equalize relations between "actors" and audiences. In staging a situation from everyday life, and by bridging the separation between actor (the one who acts) and spectator (the one who observes but is not permitted to intervene in the theatrical situation), the Theatre of the Oppressed is practised by "spect-actors" who are able to both act and observe. They also engage in self-empowering processes of dialogue that help foster critical thinking. The theatrical act is thus experienced as conscious intervention, as a rehearsal for social action rooted in a collective analysis of shared problems. Audience members are urged to intervene by stopping the action, coming on stage to replace actors, and enacting their own ideas. Newman (2006) recalls an example of forum theatre facilitated by an inner-city youth centre in Sydney, while Hsia (2010) describes its use by Taiwanese feminist activists to empower and build leadership among migrant women.

Tensions in Popular Education

None of these different forms of popular education is impervious to the effects of market capitalist perspectives and attributes. When the purposes, principles, methods, and techniques of popular education become detached from each other, for example, and with internal and external pressure on unions and community organizations to cut education programming and to adopt more corporate approaches, we see popular education often invoked but replaced by communications strategy trainings. One tension concerning popular education in some activist contexts is that it can feel like an empty shell when it consists of being talked at by academics, NGO or union staffers, and professional community workers or activists. This can mean panels of "experts" who are activists instead of academics or officials that include a question-and-answer or discussion period where the educator or panelists are deferred to as authorities. Or there can be the semblance of rituals of organizing spaces in a particular way ("let's put the chairs in a circle!"), claims of horizontalism, and participatory approaches that are empty of political content, and which obscure power relations among the participants.

If we claim that what we are doing is participatory, nonhierarchical, learner centred, emancipatory, empowering, and transformative, then it must be . . . right? Ellsworth (1989) wrote about the illusion of equality arising from notions of student/learner empowerment and dialogue that can nonetheless hide the essentially authoritarian teacher–student relationship. She takes issue with vague, abstracted notions and claims about empowering learners and transformative learning in classroom settings. The same market capitalism that so many movements and organizations contest has impacted them (and all of us) deeply. While there remain vibrant popular education practices at work—for example, in migrant and immigrant community organizing—these are often at the margins, say, of labour/women's movements. I have watched the undermining and increasing professionalization and institutionalization of popular education across several sectors and contexts. Some of the trainers, educators, and consultants who draw on adult education practices and techniques as well as the growth of forms of entrepreneurialism are surely an offshoot of the "nonprofit industrial complex" that has adopted business models of funding and evaluation of activities. I think this reflects broader trends of NGOization and the restructuring of the community sector rather than increased funds or resources, and this trend has effects on more critical activist groups that are not funded. With the erasure of histories about organizing and the connections to radical education and informal learning in the struggle, it becomes difficult to push back against these forces. This also restricts the opportunities for new generations of activists—educators among them—to experience popular education and mobilization.

Is there a risk that some better-known popular education stories—and the larger-than-life figures associated with them, like the one about Horton and the Highlander Center—can become myths? While inspirational, this can also detract from the fact that many ordinary people engage in this kind of work all the time. As with the discussion of history above, an overzealous fixation on a certain canon of books, ideas, methods, and the people associated with them can block the recognition of development, innovation, and experimentation in popular education adapted to different contexts, drawing from diverse histories. There is a certain currency in claiming to have known Freire or Horton, to have been to Highlander or a similar institution or program in a different context. This kind of credentialism mimics the very system it is supposed to be critiquing. Equally, popular education can become stylized and can fetishize mastering and using particular techniques, terms, and tools. It can reproduce dogmatism and fall back upon an insistence on claims about emancipation and transformative learning that are held to be self-evident. This in turn can stand in for actual reflection and analysis on practice that is linked to struggling for change. To put it bluntly, popular education involves more than sitting in a circle, invoking Freire, or lambasting banking models of education on the one hand and supposedly vanguardist political education on the other. Similar critiques might be made of the institutionalization of particular processes and practices of organizing meetings (Kauffman, 2015) including the need to understand their historical origins.

We are often conditioned to relate to all forms of education and learning through our own experiences of schooling: a competitive ethos, the passive consumption of education, hierarchies of knowledge and power relations between "teachers" and "students." It is perhaps not surprising how difficult it can be to break from this conditioning. Newman (2006,

p. 10) notes the domestication of the term *critical thinking* in universities and corporate workplace learning contexts, stripped of its connections to and its roots in the pursuit of social justice. Popular education has to be more than a buzzword and not be reduced to semantics and the use of certain terms, techniques, and exercises that can be ritualistic, mechanical, and self-commodifying. It risks becoming disconnected from and disinterested in collective, concrete struggles for change and separated from emancipatory purposes and principles.

The adulation that Freire receives in some community/activist education and academic settings is emblematic of this problem. I first encountered this in community organizations, NGOs, and solidarity activist/popular education contexts in the 1980s, particularly when working alongside some church and other faith-based social justice organizations. Many years later, a few months after taking up my university job, I attended a bizarre academic conference that was more akin to a revival meeting dedicated to Freire's legacy at the education faculty where I work. This event was marked by a cultishness surrounding a version of "critical pedagogy" promoted by North American academics who appropriated images of social movements for their promotional videos while being contemptuous of any actual engagement with concrete social struggles. In practice, I saw that they preferred to give the oppressed and exploited as wide a berth as possible, and with a messianic, self-referential zeal that did not acknowledge that ordinary people can think.

This kind of domestication and faux radical posturing in the North American academy, while hardly unique, seems distant from the inspiration derived from Freire's pedagogic approach for various liberation struggles, such as in South African worker education and conscientization (Vally, wa Bofelo, & Treat, 2013) and community literacy work. Freire's work has been widely disseminated since the 1970s, partly through his association with the World Council of Churches where he was an education adviser. For Youngman (1986, p. 151), "Freire's Third World origins and political-religious radicalism synchronized perfectly with the Zeitgeist of the late 1960s in the West, which was characterized by support for anti-imperialism, the growth of the movement of Blacks, women and students, and the revitalization of the Marxist intellectual tradition. The English language publication of his work in 1970 took place in a moment of crisis in bourgeois hegemony in which many aspects of capitalist society were being brought into question, including education."

Mentions of Freire, and particularly his book *Pedagogy of the Oppressed*, often stand in for or gesture toward claims about various forms of supposedly popular or transformative education. This is why Coben's thoughtful reflection on Gramsci and Freire as "radical heroes" and the politics of adult education resonates with me. She asks whether we should need radical heroes (or heroines) to think through issues of the education of adults in relation to social change. She notes another tension within the Freirian mould of popular education. She writes, "Freire's vision of the oppressed as humanized (civilized? redeemed?) through a process of conscientization initiated and controlled by a born-again leader/educator, motivated by love, may be inspirational for those who identify with the educator/leader/lover, but what of the other, the oppressed, who has not sought—and may not want—the educator's love or leadership?" (Coben, 1998, pp. 187–188). She asks whether "the culture of silence" that Freire evokes when referring to oppressed people might equally well be a culture of deafness on the oppressors' part: "Are the oppressed silent, or are they not being heard? . . . It is as if Freire were saying that the oppressed have no voice rather than that they are forbidden to speak" (p. 110). Further, there is a danger that we credit one person—and mythology surrounding him—with a whole body of practice that dates back over several centuries, with multiple traditions, origins, contexts, and relationships with social movements. Coben notes that Gramsci did not "propose that the liberation of his protagonists will occur as a result of the education process itself, rather as a result of education in the context of a political process which is in itself educative" (p. 123). Freire also acknowledged that his approaches to teaching and education alone could not bring about revolution and the transformation of society (Freire & Shor, 1987). This brings us back to the question of unity of thought and action and learning through struggle.

Another way to think about these questions can be drawn from Boughton (2013, p. 245), who highlights the continuous 200-year history of socialist popular education, arguing the case that we need the collective recovery of this history, which is vital to the popular education movement. He contends that without a documented history and with many of its stories suppressed, the loss of history means losing "the core of popular education's curriculum—the experiences of our movement from which we learn, the experiences which generate 'movement knowledge.'" Through this historical "forgetting," movements become theoretically challenged because earlier movements, especially the international socialist movement, "included some of the most impressive social theorists of their times, people who applied a great deal of intellectual energy to developing concepts which helped them theorise, and thereby reflect on and learn from, the experiences of their movements" (p. 245). Once again, the question of what, who, how, and why

FIGURE 3.1: Blockade during the 16 April 2000 (A16) protests of the World Bank and International Monetary Fund in Washington, DC. (Photograph by Orin Langelle)

we remember—and what we forget—has major implications for how we think things through in contemporary and future contexts. It impacts what we or the generations after us do.

Music, Art, and Political Education

When formal political channels for sharing ideas, analysis, and experiences are not available, and even when they may seem to be, the arts and cultural approaches can provide powerful ways to approach political education work. Creative artists often express this directly, as when Australian singer-songwriter Shane Howard (2010, p. v) states, "Songs hold memory, document history, describe feelings, communicate ideas and are one of the most potent, portable and transmissible vehicles of thought and feeling in the human experience." Reflecting on South African worker education during the struggle against apartheid, Vally, wa Bofelo, and Treat (2013, p. 470) concur when they write that informal education efforts included "a dizzying range of cultural and

mass-media forms, including the writing and production of plays, poetry readings, songs and musical choirs, and dozens of community-based and trade
union newsletters. These efforts aimed to provide everything from general literacy and technical work-related skills to running democratic and accountable
union structures, organizing, political consciousness and social mobilization." Large and small, movements and mobilizations across the world have
been rich in places where politics, art, and education meet. These forms not
only sustain movements but also connect across time and space with other
moments, other struggles.

Like so many others, music and the arts have played a major role in my
own politicization and political education. For me, Dykstra and Law's (1994,
p. 122) insights are key to thinking about movements and the creative arts
in that "the full life of a social movement—poetry, music, petitions, pickets,
and so forth—brings culture and politics together in an inherently educative way." Robin Kelley (2002, p. 10) takes this even further when he writes,
"In the poetics of struggle and lived experience, in the utterances of ordinary folk, in the cultural products of social movements, in the reflections of
activists, we discover the many different cognitive maps of the future, of the
world not yet born."

But these poetics of struggle can be so politically powerful that some
artists have been banned or assassinated. Miriam Makeba's citizenship was
revoked by the apartheid South African state while overseas. Argentinian
singer Mercedes Sosa was arrested, banned, and exiled by the military junta
in her country. Pakistani revolutionary poets Faiz Ahmed Faiz and Habib
Jalib were jailed. Nigerian musician and songwriter Fela Kuti was beaten and
jailed for his music's trenchant social commentary and criticism of the military. Argentinian singer-songwriter Atahualpa Yupanqui was jailed under Juan
Perón in the late 1940s and early 1950s for his Communist Party affiliation.
Québécoise feminist/independence activist and singer Pauline Julien was
one of many people attacked by police and jailed for several days during the
1970 October Crisis. The RCMP's Security Service spied on Canadian singer
Rita MacNeil while surveilling feminist organizations in the 1970s: "She's the
one who composes and sings women's lib songs," reported an RCMP memo
(Hewitt & Sethna, 2012, p. 139). Some artists have been assassinated. Chilean
folk singer and activist Victor Jara was tortured and murdered in the early days
of Augusto Pinochet's military regime in September 1973. Forty years later,
Greek rapper and leftist activist Pavlos Fyssas (Killah P) was stabbed to death
in Athens by neo-Nazi Golden Dawn supporters. The list goes on.

The power of radical artistry clearly troubles the powerful. Once again
Robin Kelley's (2002, p. 11) words are instructive: "[T]he most radical art is

not protest art but works that take us to another place, envision a different way of seeing, perhaps a different way of feeling." Richard Iton (2008, pp. 8–9) deepens this analysis:

> The suggestion that art and politics should be divorced . . . depend[s] on a notion of the aesthetic as a realm that by definition should not be implicated with the political. . . . Political communication is not divorced from the same kinds of considerations that determine our responses to artistic work: imagine Malcolm X, for instance, without his comic timing and his sense of humor. There are aesthetic grammars that determine the relative success of political interactions and the impact of political communication in the cultural realm: signs, styles and performances whose qualities transcend the political and artistic realms.

Music and the arts affirm our sense of the world in ways that are emotional, intellectual, and educational—they offer hope and inspire action. On a personal level, they can become vehicles for ideas, as well as ways to bring people together and build a sense of solidarity and connection. They not only nourish hope and possibility, but affirm ideas and feelings as well as educate. Sometimes we downplay the educational and mobilizing role that music and the arts can play because we compartmentalize them as being somehow qualitatively different from other forms of education or knowledge production.

Similarly, educating for social justice needs humour. The educative and communicative role of comedy and laughter, sometimes through parody, satire, and ridicule of economic and political elites and prevailing ideologies of racism, sexism, and homophobia, for example—as well as laughing at ourselves—should not be forgotten. Some of the most memorable actions that I have organized or participated in have been firmly tongue-in-cheek. For example, in the course of campaigning against state surveillance of political activists in Aotearoa/New Zealand, we created and publicly launched a booklet of fairy tales to lampoon and debunk claims made by politicians and officials about the operations of the New Zealand Security Intelligence Service. Women comrades also created an ad hoc "Witches against APEC" guerrilla theatre act that placed a "hex" on the official APEC meetings with a humorous "spell" full of critiques of free trade. In 1999, when the US Secret Service mistakenly sent top-secret faxes to a bewildered chicken farmer just before former president Bill Clinton arrived in Auckland, the witches were able to claim that their spell had worked! In both cases, the media duly obliged with extensive coverage of these actions.

Those in power are usually not too keen on being publicly caricatured or ridiculed. Sometimes earnest activists are not too keen on using humour as a weapon and educative tool either. Burgmann (1995, p. 42), describing the educational efforts of the Australian Industrial Workers of the World (the union), writes that this "was conducted not just in study circles but also in humour, denunciation, (and) iconoclasm." In *Electoral Guerrilla Theatre: Radical Ridicule and Social Movements,* Larry Bogad (2005) analyzes the international campaigns of performance artists who run for public office as a radical prank. English comedians Mark Thomas and Alexei Sayle combine left politics with genuine comic genius, as did the Australian stand-up comedy duo Nazeem Hussain and Aamer Rahman, whose "Legally Brown" and "Fear of a Brown Planet" shows address immigration, racism, and other social and political issues with withering wit. Humour is an extremely underrated tool for activist-educators—and should be used more often. Indeed, some say that it's their perverse sense of humour that keeps them alive.

Informal/Non-formal Learning in Social Movements and Popular Education

Building on the earlier discussion of informality/formality and learning, some people talk about education and learning in social movements by trying to break it down into categories of informal/incidental and non-formal/popular education. Scandrett (2012, p. 48) describes this as a dialectic between structured educational processes sometimes used within movements, community organizing, and consensus decision-making techniques, and "informal and incidental learning and knowledge generation within social movements through political practice, repertoires of contestation and collective reflection: in short between what may be called *popular education* and *incidental learning.*" Discussing education and strategic learning in a successful anti-privatization campaign by a union in Colombia and its supporters, Novelli (2010, p. 124) contends that "'popular education' needs to be seen as not only involving formal educational events, but is part of much bigger processes which, though appearing 'informal' and 'arbitrary,' are very deliberate. In this definition, both the 'popular education' events that take place, and the actual practice of 'strategy development' and 'protest actions' can be seen as examples of popular education whereby the 'school' (the social movement) learns." These analyses show us that the categories of learning/education are not as firm as we might wish to make them and that much learning takes place in the spaces that overlap.

Indeed, much education within activism is not intentional. Church, Shragge, Fontan, and Ng (2008) suggest that solidarity learning happens not according to an explicit curriculum but spontaneously and unpredictably through social interaction in situations that foster people's participation. Some people have thought about this, drawing on Lave and Wenger's (1991) situated learning theory. This holds that learning is a social process based on participation in a community of practice rather than the acquisition of knowledge by individuals. Lave and Wenger wrote that we learn through participating in the activities of a given community—that is, the set of relations that create the context for learning—the people, the practices, and the broader social world. Thus, learning is a process of becoming part of a community and being able to fully function within it. These insights also recall Holst's (2002, p. 81) reminder that much educational work occurs inside movements "in which organizational skills, ideology, and lifestyle choices are passed from one member to the next informally through mentoring and modelling or formally through workshops, seminars, lectures, and so forth." He uses the concept of "pedagogy of mobilization" to describe the learning inherent in building and maintaining a movement and its organizations: "Through participation in a social movement, people learn numerous skills and ways of thinking analytically and strategically as they struggle to understand their movement in motion. . . . Moreover, as coalitions are formed people's understanding of the interconnectedness of relations within a social totality become increasingly sophisticated" (pp. 87–88).

All of this supports my argument that in practice there is a much more dynamic interrelation—indeed a dialectical one—between non-formal, intentional education such as workshops, discussions, and popular education activities and the incidental learning and reflections of people's everyday lives. Other theorists also acknowledge this, like Scandrett (2012, p. 44), who observes that incidental learning can sometimes "have the character of dialogical interrogation of knowledge which leads to the process of critical analysis which Freire calls conscientization. This form of incidental learning in social movements . . . has the dialectical character of popular education but without its structure (i.e., the 'methodology' as distinct from the 'method' of popular education)." Relying solely on informal, incidental learning in social activist contexts for political education is not enough.

Learning to adapt and to resist is also not a dichotomous process. Allman (2010, p. 157) contends that "revolutionary critical education must offer an 'abbreviated experience' or 'glimpse' of the type of social relations that we are working toward establishing through revolutionary social transformation. This idea is based on the recognition that authentic and lasting transformations in consciousness can occur only when alternative under-standings and values are actually experienced 'in depth'—that is, when they are experienced sensuously and subjectively as well as cognitively, or intel-lectually." Allman suggests that this education can occur through dialogue. *Dialogue* in this context means more than the sharing of monologues, as in a "discussion"; here it is a creative exchange in which new understandings are generated. Previous ideas and knowledge can be brought in but only offered as tools and not as ends in themselves. Newman (2006, pp. 110–111) builds on this, claiming that "[t]rue dialogue can transform us by transform-ing our understanding of ourselves in relation to our social, cultural and political worlds. It can transform our conception of knowledge. It can alter our consciousness." Dialogic process forms and re-forms activists' views and their collective actions in relation to what they are fighting against and how to succeed in that struggle.

All of these theories echo the way in which Gramsci (1985, p. 25) concep-tualized education and praxis, as an activity that entailed "the detailed work of discussing and investigating problems, work in which everybody participates, to which everybody contributes, in which everybody is both master [*sic*] and disciple." People can learn from contradictions, have epiphanies—those "light bulb moments"—but they need space to reflect as individuals and with others. Praxis is the theoretical reflection that is based on action and tested in further action. There is a kind of learning that happens in encounters between groups and movements—how people learn to frame and reframe their stories in shar-ing their experiences, knowledge, and perspectives with others outside of their circles or networks. We see this in coalition-building contexts, campaign work, and at forums bringing different groups and movements together, whether or not education or learning is "officially" on the agenda.

This does not mean that all learning is easy. Learning through involve-ment in social struggles can be contradictory and constraining. Foley (1999) acknowledges this. His reflections on how such contradictions and tensions were managed in the context of political education in Zimbabwe's liberation struggle resonate with Petras and Veltmeyer's (2001, p. 137) critique of NGOs' intellectual policing roles. They charge that "control of intellectual fashion, publications, conferences and research funds provides post-Marxists with an important power base, but one ultimately dependent on avoiding conflict with their external funding patrons." Because of this, Foley (1999, p. 140) empha-sizes the importance of "developing an understanding of learning in popular struggle." His attention to documenting, making explicit, and valuing incidental forms of learning and knowledge production in social action is consistent with the notion that critical consciousness and theory emerge from engagement in action and organizing contexts, rather than being ideas developed elsewhere dropped down on "the people" from movement elites.

To return to the question of learning informally and incidentally, we must consider the place of learning through deliberation and collective decision making at meetings. In her study of direct action protest tactics in two North American cities, Lesley Wood (2012, p. 12) highlights the importance of deliberative processes within activist organizing spaces: "Such talk is more than a mechanical evaluation of alternatives; it is a collaborative process through which people tell stories, make arguments, and define and redefine their identities and strategies. In the midst of such conversations, an activist may explain who they admire, who they refuse to work with, and where and when a particular tactic emerged." Wood sees such conversations and a level of reflexivity therein as being particularly powerful for changing political and social knowledge and "not simply about talking politics and wrestling with ideas. Deliberation is about action" (pp. 12–13). In tandem with this, people may also learn to question and critically assess the ways in which activist spaces are organized, including the adoption of specific processes, practices, and terminology.

In what follows in the rest of this chapter, I will reflect on and discuss examples of informal learning and knowledge production that do not follow a curriculum but are instances of the critical learning that, as Newman (2006, p. 240) puts it, "can occur suddenly, by chance, and as a part of another activity altogether." The first section addresses learning through experience by confronting the national security state in the course of activism. The second section discusses the notion of expertise and knowledge politics in the global justice movement.

State Repression, Learning, and Knowledge Production

While activists have written and campaigned about state repression and surveillance of social movements for decades, the significance and micropolitics of the activist learning and knowledge arising from these experiences are not often discussed, least of all from the perspective of those targeted. George Smith (2006) reminds us that the potential for activists to explore the social organization of power is revealed through moments of confrontation. I believe that we can learn much about the social relations of struggles in which we are engaged through conflict and confrontation. This can happen when the state's repressive structures are laid bare when we come up against its forces, as Thompson (2006, p. 104) suggests that "in swallowing us, they expose their squishy insides, their ineptitudes and the causes of their indigestion." He notes, for example, that many activists emerge with a better understanding of how the system works through their actual experience of being arrested and thus become wiser to its mysti-fications. Material experience forms our learning and consciousness. I am not advocating that people should actively seek arrest or infiltration by state secu-rity agents to learn about the contours of political repression and the limits of dissent in the liberal democratic state. Indeed, these experiences and the under-standings and knowledge they produce are likely to also reflect people's race, gender, and class locations. Experiences of state repression—arrests, violence, harassment, intimidation, surveillance, and sometimes entrapment—however, can help analyze state power and the interests of capital from the standpoint of those targeted. But as Sunaina Maira (2014) and others note, forms of state surveillance and violence are racialized, which influences the intimacy of surveil-lance and its regularization in people's everyday lives.

For its targets, state repression can be a topic fraught with challenges about how, whether, with whom, when, and for what purpose to talk about it. All the more so in a world that is still dominated by a geography of colonial violence, where old and new forms of racism operate to justify and work through rapidly expanding forms of state surveillance. While accounts of its actual practices may read like spy fiction or paranoid fantasy to some, people targeted by the state in this way can find themselves stigmatized or carry a burden of suspicion of being guilty even if proven innocent—if indeed that is even an option—when such practices are shrouded in secrecy. But these experiences can also lead to rich forms of activist knowledge and learning being produced. A corollary of polit-ical policing, the surveillance of activists, and the use of informants and *agents provocateurs* can have a chilling effect on dissent. Yet the breadth and the sheer ordinariness of most of the people (and what they actually do) whom states deem to be threats and then surveil and harass—along with growing concerns about ever-expanding capacities for intelligence agencies to routinely read what is on our computers and monitor emails, phone calls, social media, text messages, and other forms of communication—can give wider publics cause to question the legitimacy of such practices and perhaps to think about larger questions about liberal democracy, society, and freedom. Indeed, as Maira (2014) notes, one reaction among primarily South Asian-, Arab-, and Afghan-American youth has been to normalize surveillance in their everyday lives in the United States rather than to bear a burden of private shame.

There are risks in going public about state surveillance, harassment, and repression, not least for racialized immigrants, people with precarious status, and those of us with First World passports who are not white and are more likely to be targeted today because of our origins and names. Nonetheless, some have chosen to go public in an effort to turn the gaze back on the watchers and also to question the repressive nature of liberal democracy and to engage in political education and organizing around these issues. While the expansion and reinforcement of the security state is often treated as a post-9/11 phenomenon, such a view risks decontextualizing both the "War on Terror" and the violence of the security state from history. I offer this section of the chapter as a personal example of how we bounce experiential learning off of more theoretical forms of knowledge, as well as dialectically learn through engagement with other activists. Moreover, rather than viewing such cases as "exceptional," both the historical and contemporary breadth of state repression could—and should—encourage us to reflect on how and why such state security practices play a central role in the societies in which we live.

Visiting La Casa de la Memoria in Resistencia, the capital of Argentina's Chaco province, in 2013, what struck me was the ordinariness of the building. Situated on the main plaza, it was a clandestine centre for detention, torture, and extermination during the military junta. It now commemorates the lives, deaths, and disappearances of many people from the region perceived to be political dissidents—the students, journalists, members of the agrarian leagues, and others who were victims of state terrorism. Walking through its rooms reinforced for me both the ordinariness of the regime's victims and the banal nature of evil, as Hannah Arendt vividly argued in her work on the Nuremberg trials of Nazi war criminals (Arendt, 2006). But I also view practices of state repression along a continuum, rather than as being qualitatively different between "democratic" and "undemocratic" states. Indeed, what can experiences of state repression, political policing, and the criminalization of dissent tell us about the nature of democracy and freedom in liberal democracies—and the nation-state itself?

Writing on the Canadian context, Kinsman, Buse, and Steedman (2000, p. 278) note, "The fundamental issues underlying secret police surveillance and systems of collaboration and informing on other people are rooted in the context of power relationships in contemporary capitalist and bureaucratic states and societies." The concepts of national security and subversion, write these authors, are social constructions developed to protect those in power; the definition of "national security" is flexible and elastic enough to expand and contract at will, depending on the ruling ideology of the day.

The kind of activist knowledge about state repression of dissent, political policing, and the national security state that can emerge through the experience of being targeted is constructed through dialogue and in dialectical relation to state security practices—the dialectical relationship between the development of consciousness and what Allman (2010, p. 165) calls "the sensuous experiencing of reality from within the social relations in which we exist." But first I need to share some details. Like others, over many years I have had very personal experiences with political policing and repressive actions of state security. I have been told that parts of my life sound like a spy TV show, although it often feels rather mundane to me. Here is one of the episodes.

In 1999, the New Zealand government brought a British woman, on whom actress Judi Dench's portrayal of "M" in the James Bond films was based, down to the capital, Wellington, to speak as an expert witness at a parliamentary intelligence and security committee hearing where submissions on an amendment to give the New Zealand Security Intelligence Service (NZSIS) explicit power to enter private property were being heard. This bill was in response to a landmark legal case that I brought against the New Zealand government following a bungled NZSIS operation at my house and which New Zealand's Court of Appeal had ruled to be illegal. The woman, now a spy thriller writer herself, was Stella Rimington, former director general of the British intelligence agency MI5. She dutifully supported the amendment.

To back up a little, just before an APEC trade ministers' meeting in Christchurch in July 1996, two men—NZSIS agents—were caught fleeing my home. The friend who disturbed them realized that these were no opportunistic burglars, gave chase, noted their licence plate number, and from there the plate was traced to a fictitious company in Wellington. The break-in occurred while I was at a forum on free trade held by GATT Watchdog. Days later, while I was away on a speaking tour about APEC, NAFTA, and free trade with an academic/activist from Red Mexicana de Acción Frente al Libre Comercio (the Mexican Action Network on Free Trade), a hoax device was found outside city council offices and my house was raided by police supposedly looking for bomb-making equipment. Nothing was there, and nothing was found. My friends and comrades and I were immediately suspicious of the connection between the two incidents and were concerned that others might be targeted in this way by the state, so we went to the media.

GATT Watchdog had long argued that human rights violations and the suppression of dissent go hand in hand with free market capitalism. Contrary to those who see states as no longer relevant or powerful in an era of global capitalism and notwithstanding the growth of private security services often working for corporate clients, it is primarily governments that continue to repress movements and activists. After the Cold War ended, the New Zealand state continued surveillance of left activists and organizing among Indigenous Peoples, as in Australia, Canada, and the United States. As a concept employed by states, "subversion" has notoriously flexible parameters. Thus, the NZSIS break-in could be seen as a logical action for a government so zealously wedded to free market capitalism, so invested in vigorous international promotion of the "New Zealand experiment" (Kelsey, 1995) that it would not tolerate dissent. In the three years leading up to an eventual out-of-court settlement with the government, the aftermath of this break-in was a Kafka-esque period of official stonewalling, a news media frenzy (which sometimes opened up more opportunities to communicate with broader publics about a range of issues, including our critique of global capitalism), time wasting with toothless and sham official oversight mechanisms, and official "neither confirm nor deny" statements and national security mantras, the latter of which ultimately trumped my legal arguments for the courts to access secret documents needed for me to fully prosecute my case. While this is a story from a small country in the South Pacific, many of the experiences and the learning done within it have strong parallels and resonances in other countries.

In addition to the NZSIS, the experience also confirmed a mindset and operational culture within the New Zealand Police that, like many other police forces, frequently equates challenges to prevailing political and economic orthodoxies with criminal activity. At that time, the police's Criminal Intelligence Service (CIS) monitored political activities that it considered might involve a breach of the criminal law, although how such activities were assessed was anybody's guess. Police and NZSIS documents obtained through legal actions and witness statements in a related court case against the police revealed ongoing, long-standing, broad spying operations on me and a range of individuals and groups in my activist networks, some of which clearly involved the use of informers. Unsurprisingly, the police and other state authorities had collaborated with the NZSIS in relation to this 1996 operation, as confirmed in some of the documents released.

Using informers in political policing, Steve Hewitt (2010, p. 159) asserts, allows governments to "direct, disrupt and even destroy individuals, groups and movements it does not like or finds threatening." Writing about the use of informers, he argues that this "can be managed more unobtrusively in 'open' societies where it is not anticipated, as opposed to closed societies where the hand is expected to be heavier." I think this is important to consider in societies such as Aotearoa/New Zealand and Canada. As elsewhere, we noted several dubious characters in our midst lurking around taking photos, sometimes seemingly wanting to be noticed and sometimes sitting more discreetly in unmarked cars or vans at the end of driveways or across the street from where I and other activists worked or met—and various *agents provocateurs*, informers, and undercover police (or other agency) types. During the years of intense organizing against APEC, there was the fake journalist claiming to be reporting for a (fictitious) student paper at the local university, wanting to know when the "heavy stuff" was "going to go down"; the person with unwanted offers to help break into buildings, monitor police radio, and to instigate various illegal things, and who years later was publicly revealed to be a police informant; there was the frail old man who was always just . . . around . . . who sought and gained sympathy from activists, seemed to give $5 to every cause going, and freely told people he used to be a paid spy on left-wing activists but had changed sides . . . but clearly hadn't broken with his spying past. And so the list goes on. Hewitt (2010, p. 133) has observed that "[b]etrayal is and remains a powerful human force. . . . The presence of informers, either real or imagined, sows division and paranoia and can have a direct impact on operations. It is a force of disruption and discontinuity that divides instead of unites." Arguably, this is an intended consequence. Lesley Wood (2012) echoes this in her description of how police and intelligence agency infiltration and surveillance of global justice activists in North America discouraged emulation and identification of broader publics to join protests and direct actions after the 1999 WTO protests in Seattle.

When informers are deployed by intelligence services and police forces, "they are directed against specific communities, groups and individuals. It is within these same categories that controversy arises over the practices. However, because those targeted are frequently on the margins, their perspectives and understandings receive little attention within dominant discourses. Only when the wider population in liberal democracies feels threatened by informing, and here the parallel exists with certain types of electronic surveillance, does widespread opposition, particularly within societal elites, emerge" (Hewitt, 2010, p. 158). The stigma attached to being targeted by state security forces can have major human impacts on people who have suspicion cast on them even if there is no evidence to support their treatment. This is arguably an intended effect of state practices—there is a pedagogical component that seeks to deter others from dissenting and/or a racialized frame that feeds into existing racism against certain communities.

As with counterparts in other countries (see, for example, Austin, 2013, and Hewitt and Sethna, 2012, on Royal Canadian Mounted Police [RCMP] and political policing in Canada), in Aotearoa/New Zealand, my experience confirmed that the CIS conducted similar surveillance operations to the NZSIS, and the two agencies enjoyed a strong relationship. For many years, the CIS clearly granted itself a broad mandate to collect information on people on the basis of their political beliefs and sympathies and views formed by police intelligence officers and informants. Their work in this area had much in common with political elements in other police forces that routinely monitor, harass, and criminalize organizers and activists. Innuendo and guilt by association, whether based on accurate or erroneous assumptions, are a stock-in-trade for police intelligence work dealing with activists. By deeming many groups and individuals to have a sufficient propensity to commit criminal offences on the basis of their perceived or actual political views and affiliations, such political policing contributed to the criminalization of dissent in Aotearoa/New Zealand. In turn, this encourages front-line police to exercise contempt and a cavalier disregard toward rights to freedom of expression, association, and peaceful assembly. A New Zealand Police training video about the 1995 Commonwealth Heads of Government meeting in Auckland that was circulated among activist networks disingenuously intermixed peaceful demonstrations with bomb blasts and showed a senior police intelligence officer with a pile of local social justice/activist publications, mischievously conflating political activism with violence and terrorism. Such conflation is politically useful to governments wishing to depict themselves as protectors of society from internal or external threats.

My case confirmed this close relationship between the NZSIS and the police, as well as challenging the official claim, backed by both major political parties in the New Zealand Parliament, that a former High Court judge who was newly appointed as inspector-general of intelligence and security would provide some independent accountability. It revealed a security service that relied on informants, collated news media clippings, and cross-referenced documents on the files of individuals and groups of interest to them. In early 1996, NZSIS powers were amended by expanding the definition of security to include "the making of a contribution to New Zealand's international well-being or economic well-being," wording adapted from Canadian legislation. Several of us warned the public that the government would use these powers against critics of free market policies and free trade. And although it turned out that the interception warrant the NZSIS used in my case was issued before the new definition took effect, the break-in incident and the events surrounding it were symptomatic of a growing intolerance of dissent about the country's economic direction. When, in a submission on the new legislation, we raised the possibility that the new definition of "security" in the bill might be used to monitor organizations engaged in legitimate critique, we were told by the then-leader of the (Labour) opposition that we were "naive and paranoid."

The NZSIS file note (classified "secret") reproduced in Figure 3.2 on the next page justified using an informer to spy on the annual general meeting of a small organization opposing transnational corporate power and monitoring overseas investment which I addressed two years after the botched break in. The group that I spoke on behalf of was dubbed "extremist," one whose "activities pose, or have the potential to pose a threat to security." This file note very much proves the analysis of Kinsman and Gentile (2010, p. 269), where they demonstrate how police/intelligence reports show a standard feature in how they are socially organized; they "produce external organizational accounts that focus on surveying and managing local forms of protest. The standpoint of external organizational observation is central to the social character of these reports and to their construction as 'objective.'" This can be seen in the context of how I came to have access to the note as well.

In a cover letter accompanying the release of the NZSIS document pictured in Figure 3.2, a former NZSIS director wrote that the documents were "of a pedestrian nature." This begs the question: Is it ordinary or "pedestrian" to

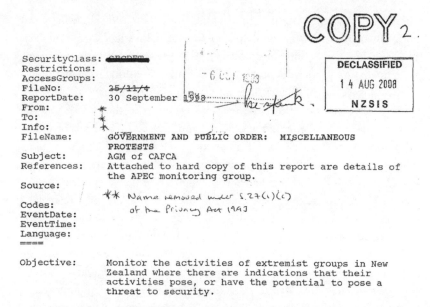

FIGURE 3.2: Excerpt from a New Zealand Security Intelligence
Service declassified document: "GOVERNMENT AND PUBLIC ORDER:
MISCELLANEOUS PROTESTS: AGM of CAFCA" (30 September 1998/
declassified 14 August 2008).

construct lawful activism—and the specific groups monitored and targeted
as evidenced by the declassified document—as "extremist" in a society that
the New Zealand government (see below) claimed to be an open, liberal,
participatory democracy that can "accommodate debate and dissent"? What
criteria did the NZSIS use to determine what constitutes "extremist"? And
what exactly constitutes "indications that their activities pose, or have the
potential to pose a threat to security"? What standards of evidence or proof
are at play here?

Another example of this can be found in Canada. Security documents made
public during the Commission for Public Complaints Against the RCMP
into controversial policing of protests at the 1997 APEC Summit in Vancouver
identified "long-standing native issues in British Columbia such as gaming,
self-government, land claims, fishing rights and resource control over claimed
lands, along with a collection of ad hoc groups opposed to APEC" as "a potential security risk" (CSIS, 1997). In a 2000 report on the "anti-globalization"
movement after the Seattle mobilizations, the Canadian Security Intelligence

Service warned against the "tyranny of small groups, minorities, or even major-ities, to prevent the exercise of such rights by trying to shut down meetings as unacceptable in a democracy." Not unlike the kinds of pathologizing, psychol-ogistic views of movements outlined by early social movement theory in the previous chapter, protesters are deemed to be a security threat since they are organized and can "identify and publicize targets, solicit and encourage support, establish dates, recruit, raise funds, share experiences, accept respon-sibilities, arrange logistics, and promote goals," and because they "share a mutual antipathy for multinational corporate power. Large corporations with international undertakings stand accused of social injustice and unfair labour practices, as well as a lack of concern for the environment, management of natural resources and ecological damage"; "underlying the anti-globalization theme is criticism of the capitalist philosophy, a stance promoted again by left-of-centre activists and militant anarchists," states the report (CSIS, 2000). As Kinsman and Gentile (2010, p. 440) note, "simply opposing capitalist social relations is enough to make one a risk to national security." All the while, such state practices seek to deflect attention away from state violence carried out by the police or other state security agencies.

Analysis of official texts was a key aspect of practice that informed the strategy of the campaign we mounted against the hosting of APEC 1999 in Aotearoa/New Zealand. In 1998, in the middle of my legal case against the NZSIS, I obtained a New Zealand Cabinet Strategy Committee paper entitled "APEC 1999—Engagement with NGOs" for GATT Watchdog under New Zealand's Official Information Act. This document showed that government intentions were to co-opt "responsive" NGOs and harness them to promote APEC domestically, and also to project to international audiences an image of a democratic government that valued differing opinions. My experience of being targeted by New Zealand state security forces in 1996, my involve-ment in previous years' anti-APEC mobilizations in several countries, and my interactions with police at demonstrations and the noticeably increased surveillance a number of us were subject to provided a context for reading these documents and our activist education strategy. The cabinet paper was a clear example of a document that operates in the state's interest in drawing up a plan to contain dissent and manage the government's image, rather than supporting substantive dialogue. The government clearly sought to divide and rule NGOs and others into supposedly constructive and disruptive elements.

Drawing from these documents, a key part of our anti-APEC strategy was to publicly denounce the New Zealand government communications strat-egy and to politicize attempts to co-opt or silence critics through "dialogue."

Through media work and dissemination through NGO and community group mailings and meetings, we publicly revealed the government strategy of containment and propaganda through limited dialogue and state surveillance and harassment of the more radical critics. Our strategy involved politicizing the disjuncture between stated intentions for dialogue, the calculated rationale expressed in the official documents, and the actual, lived experiences of criminalization of lawful dissent. After circulating the cabinet papers to a wide range of NGOs and trade unions, the government's plan to co-opt NGOs and harness them to sell APEC to "middle" New Zealand failed, with few attending NGO consultation sessions.

During this period of challenging the NZSIS, in contrast to the shock and surprise that many expressed, I recall the unsurprised reaction of friends who had experienced state repression elsewhere only to find similar happenings in Aotearoa/New Zealand. One example is a dinner conversation I had with a visiting Mapuche activist about the criminalization of dissent in the so-called democratic, post-dictatorship era in Chile, which used a Pinochet-era anti-terrorism law against him and other Mapuche asserting their Indigenous rights to their territory and against the encroachment of forestry corporations. A New Zealand–owned company, Carter Holt Harvey, had invested in Pinochet's Chile. At the time of our conversation, its Chilean subsidiary, Bosques Arauco, used former Pinochet goons as armed security guards against Mapuche who were trying to stop logging that was in violation of a court order not to fell the forest. Fundamental claims about the socially progressive nature of liberal democracy are thrown into stark relief by political policing and state repression, revealing its borders and foundations. Such practices should cause us to question national myth-making that tries to exaggerate the distance to distinguish "our" democracies from "those other countries"—while brazenly ignoring their own colonial injustices and roles in imperialism.

Moments where the state reveals its politically repressive side—to some, at least—are key opportunities to dig deeper and unsettle the powerful image-making of liberal democratic national narratives. But unless grasped, if not swept under the carpet altogether, they can quickly slip away in a sea of liberal outrage that misunderstands the state as being as open and democratic as it claims. As an ironic postscript, while I was finishing writing this book I was reminded again of the disjuncture between the knowledge that arises from experiences of normalization of living under surveillance and expressions of surprise when Canadian media released a government report obtained by an opposition Member of Parliament noting RCMP surveillance of a panel on colonialism in Quebec that I co-organized and chaired at Concordia University in Montreal in the fall of 2013. Details of hundreds of events and protest actions monitored by federal agencies and law enforcement agencies, including this panel, were collected by the Government Operations Centre, an agency that prepares the federal government's response to emergencies. While social media outpourings of disbelief flowed from some activists and academics, many of them avowedly anti-colonial/left thinkers, I wondered what it meant to hold forth an anti-colonial analysis of the Canadian state—with a critical historical perspective at an intellectual/political level—and to still manage to feel surprised by such surveillance. This incident once again demonstrates Gramsci's argument: History is crucial to understanding power relations in the present and can help think through action to challenge power. More recently, amid controversy over Bill C-51 (The Anti-terrorism Act 2015), an RCMP internal document surfaced in the Canadian media entitled "Criminal threats to the Canadian petroleum industry," dated 24 January 2014, that dubbed the "anti-petroleum" movement a growing threat to Canada's national security. Journalists and a range of organizations noted that the report's highly charged and pro-industry language reflected government hostility toward "foreign-funded" environmentalists and Indigenous activists (McCarthy, 2015). Perhaps there should be fewer surprises if we stop and think for a moment about the history of the construction of national security in Canada.

As this section has shown, such knowledge and learning is largely experiential—forged through specific confrontations with the sharp edge of state power and the blunt tools of political repression. I have underlined the importance of both incidental learning and more theoretical knowledge in trying to unravel the practices of state repression and expose the myth-making narratives of democracy. This is also affirmed and extended by interactions with people and ideas with experiences that come from other contexts of state repression. My own analysis is inevitably also shaped by geographies of violence that connect racial profiling, police brutality, unjust immigration regimes, "random checks" at airports, and advances in new mass surveillance technologies to the drone attacks and never-ending wars and occupations. At both the micro and macro levels, systems of surveillance and state repression impact and shape the lives and politics of many of those who must encounter them or are made aware of them. Besides the understandable fear and stress it engenders, the organized resistance, not least in racialized Muslim/Arab/South Asian, Indigenous, and Black communities targeted by these agencies, is instructive and inspiring. This is not to be naive, since history is replete with examples of people whose lives and livelihoods have been destroyed or severely disrupted by encounters with state security agencies because of their (real or imagined) political views, commitments, and associations, as well as the practices of profiling. Yet when people can be open about their everyday lived realities of state

FIGURE 3.3: Mapuche men walk through a newly planted monoculture plantation of eucalyptus seedlings near Chol Chol, Mapuche Territory (Chile), 2005. The man on the left steps on the seedlings. In Chile, plantations are concentrated on former farmland in the traditional territory of the Mapuche people in the Lumaco region. (Photograph by Orin Langelle)

surveillance and normalize talking about this out loud, we have an avenue to really analyze and theorize the nature of the state we're in, to educate, and to organize resistance.

Informal Learning about Knowledge Politics: "Experts," "Leaders," and Constraining Movement Critiques

The second example here is related to the first but focuses on the informal learning that takes place *about* the politics of knowledge and learning in activist networks. During and since the 1990s, I have participated in, addressed, chaired, and facilitated numerous NGO conferences, community and "civil society" forums, and activist teach-ins in what later became known as the global justice movement. As an organizer, activist researcher, and educator on APEC, the WTO, and the global free market economy who has been involved in local and transnational campaigns and struggles, I wondered increasingly about the ways in which these activities, the documents produced, and the discourses employed have served to create and reify "experts" and "leaders"—particularly through writing, speeches, and other narratives. These writers, spokespeople, and "leaders" are frequently academics, journalists, or NGO professional analysts and researchers, rather than organizers or people working in grassroots struggles. NGO professionals and scholar-activists tend to produce texts prolifically. They are able to claim power to speak for and represent movements and mobilizations, with a ring of credibility and authority. In doing so, they sometimes contribute to the misrepresentation, silencing, and marginalization of ideas and perspectives from grassroots movements and organizations. Indeed, in part it was my own first-hand experience of these power struggles that led me to try out university after having "dropped out" during the second year of an undergraduate program in Aotearoa/New Zealand two decades earlier.

The importance of alternative knowledges and voices from below is often talked up in these networks. However, there is often a deep reticence among both scholar-activists and professionalized NGO staff to meaningfully support marginalized and excluded perspectives and ideas if indeed they are aware of these. Among other things, this would include stepping back to allow space for others to speak and act. Arguably, militant mass movements are needed to create political spaces to concretely challenge power relations—rather than ungrounded appeals for "alternatives" in conference declarations, NGO charters, and media interviews.

This dynamic is reconfirmed in the scholarship. Clark and Ivanic (1997, p. 5) note that there is unequal distribution of access to "socially prestigious and socially shaping" forms of writing, and that this has its roots in a society's economic, political, ideological, and social structures. Kress (1982, p. 3) has argued that this has economic, political, and ideological effects: "[T]hose able to produce meanings and messages are few by comparison with those who consume meanings and messages. Hence the control of messages and meanings is in the hands of a relatively small number of people." Vast numbers of people and social groups are excluded "from contributing to the collective store of knowledge, cultural and ideological activity; from the production and projection of ideas that fundamentally shape society" (Clark and Ivanic, 1997, p. 55).

The capacity to be able to produce and distribute publications deemed credible and authoritative, the priority given to generating such texts, time and access to media and other outlets for communicating information and opinions tends to favour specific kinds of research-oriented and advocacy NGOs and academics. In turn, these publications reinforce the expert status of those who write in them. Perspectives from mass movements or community organizers whose priority was local organizing and mobilizing against capitalist globalization were often only heard if they spoke from the floor in such "civil society" meetings—regardless of the critical analysis and knowledge produced in such struggles, reinforcing notions about separation between the brain and brawn of movement activism.

The status accorded to academics and NGO policy analysts and researchers, and their interpretations pose challenges for any movement or network that espouses democracy and community. Why would these professionalized "experts" be best placed to propose a program of action? Once again, organizations tend to reproduce the same hierarchies that structure broader societal relations. In their efforts to uncover the meanings and implications contained in the text of trade and investment agreements, for example, do policy analysts not also frequently create their own elitist discourse? Or, indeed, internalize a frame and a language from the agreement itself? Narrow textual analysis of trade agreements by NGO policy analysts frequently fails to take into account questions of broader social and political context(s), and underlying ideologies that underpin these texts. Rather than adopting a popular education approach to reach broader publics, they assume a particular kind of literacy that includes understanding the technical jargon of trade and economic policy.

For those committed to putting democratic forms of organization and nonhierarchical values into practice when building social movements, the emergence of a class of "high priests" of global justice or climate justice movement networks, and the weight given to policy analysis, is worthy of further critical reflection. Does the mastery of specialized technical discourse—in written texts, public forums, and teach-ins—empower others and amplify critical ideas and voices coming from below? Or does it merely reify the power, status, and ideas of professional "experts" in the context of these movements?

Activities in many NGO/activist circles can be highly formalized and institutionalized—from internal meetings, membership meetings, and training sessions; to conferences, teach-ins, media events, and speeches at rallies; to reporting and other relationships with funders. For all of the claims that such conferences were democratically organized "people's" spaces, NGO summits, forums, and teach-ins that I have participated in have usually been tightly controlled and quite hierarchical, even the ones claiming to be horizontally structured. It was clear that tensions existed between creating a space for critical reflection and the possibilities for transformation and action, and vested interests in maintaining order, authority, and the institution itself. A particular aspect of this hierarchical structuring in relation to knowledge, order, and power is illustrated by the preponderance of academic and NGO professionals who addressed the meetings. Similar critiques have been made of the dynamics of social forums. Their relevance and usefulness to movement-building and daily organizing continue to be debated.

FIGURE 3.4: An Indigenous man watches decision makers from the balcony at the UN Convention on Biological Diversity in Bonn, Germany, May 2008. (Photograph by Orin Langelle)

Concluding Thoughts: Broader Lessons

> That's a mistake committed before, that education should come just exclusively after organizing. Education is *before,* is *during,* and is *after.* It's a process, a permanent process. It has to do with human existence and curiosity.
>
> —Paulo Freire (Horton & Freire, 1990, p. 119)

This chapter has shown how building a social analysis that informs and is informed by grounded practice often draws on informal and non-formal learning that occurs in the process of doing and acting. I have found the work of Scandrett (2012), whose characterization of the common terrains and dynamics of learning within social movements to be insightful. He captures well the dynamic relations between more structured forms and processes of popular education in movements and the informal and incidental learning and knowledge production that take place. He writes that learning may take place

> as a dialectical interrogation of knowledge from the perspective of struggle, and may occur through structured popular education or

incidental learning, and in a complex relationship between the two
as values and knowledge interact. Incidental learning occurs prior to
and as a result of structured popular education, but is affected by such
experience through dialogue with knowledge to discern what is "really
useful." At the same time, incidental learning, even in the absence
of structured popular (or indeed didactic) education, can take place
through alternative processes, such as in discursive encounters with
other movements, in which the methodology, if not the method of
popular education occurs. (p. 52)

Notwithstanding the sheer urgency for action and change, tenacity is crucial
in long-haul organizing, education, and learning for social change. Chris Dixon
(2012, p. 47) writes that activism is "based on mobilizing individuals around
particular issues and events, and frequently involves demonstrating opposition to specific policies and institutions. Organising has a more sustained and
constructive focus." To put it another way, in building movements we need the
"patient, often discouraging, long-distance running required of a local organizer" (Lynd & Grubacic, 2009, p. 107). Many of the efforts of social movements
are protracted struggles, sometimes with unclear results, setbacks, losses, and
disappointments. But there are also the steps forward and the victories—we
should acknowledge this more.

My own politicization and political education can best be characterized as
a jigsaw of events; moments of revelatory disjuncture; exposure to radical ideas
through music, poetry, and other artistic forms; conversations; and learning by
doing. This kind of process has no obvious beginning or end point. It involves
connecting experience, understanding, and reflecting with taking action to
try to change things. Many of us have been inspired and even educated by
some of the music we listen(ed) to rather than what we read in books. This
process also frequently involves appreciating that social conflict at the micro
and macro levels can fuel learning, and that learning in the struggle takes place
across a spectrum of formality/informality. So in writing this chapter about a
somewhat eclectic set of experiences, sites, and modes of learning and education, I have presented a constellation of analysis and experiences rather than a
linear account. The world in which we live and struggle is complex. So too is
non-formal and informal learning in social movements, which is resistant to
simplistic systematized explanations, however tempting it may be to formulate
them. Allman (2010, p. 157) suggests that "the revolutionary transformations
in self . . . can only come about through a unitary and coherent *deep transformation,* or a transformation through which, as Gramsci suggests, knowledge
becomes so well 'integrated' and 'assimilated' that it becomes located within

our subjectivities, and thus, in addition to being known, it is felt, or subjectively experienced, as a type of 'lived' compassion and commitment." Further, by standing back—but not detaching and reflecting—we can sometimes gain greater insight and understanding to help theories take shape. This in turn can support strategies for change.

We must continue to think through how different forms and moments of learning relate to each other and lead to, nourish, or sustain action. What are the connections between the learning that takes place and the modes and structures of organizing/organizations? There is no neat answer. One challenge we surely face is that for so many of us, the social groupings, networks, and organizations, both formal and informal—"the infrastructures of dissent" (Sears, 2005b)—no longer exist with the depth and breadth that they did throughout parts of the twentieth century when social movements made significant gains. Can we rebuild these infrastructures of dissent—and if so, how?

Reflecting on the rich legacy of education and learning in South Africa's labour movement, Vally, wa Bofelo, and Treat (2013, p. 486) contend that scholarly research and analysis "can provide evidence and conceptual resources for use by working people who are engaged in struggle—not merely for improved working conditions but for deeper collective self-consciousness and greater self-determination—but in the absence of such grounding and accountability such scholarship can quickly become irrelevant or even distracting." With this in mind, in the next chapter I turn to explore activist research conducted in and with movements outside of academic institutional settings and frameworks, and its relationship to education and action.

CHAPTER 4

ACTIVIST RESEARCH

Broadly interpreted, one could argue that some kind of research is intrinsic to most decisions that activists and organizers make and the foundations on which they act. For example, there is research involved in figuring out whether, where, and when to have a demonstration, picket, blockade, meeting, workshop, or other activities; what is effective and what is not; whether to take part in a campaign; who to seek support from or offer solidarity to; or how to build a campaign or reach more people. Within movements and different activist contexts, there are also more deliberate forms of research, although defining the lines between such intentional activity and the implicit kinds is not an easy task since they are often tightly interconnected. This chapter looks at the relation between activist research and theorizing rooted in activism as well as how both inform effective activist practice. It delves into the processes, tensions, and forms of production, dissemination, and mobilization of research that occur in several activist contexts. To do this it draws connections between knowledge production, questions of political economy, and micropolitics. Building upon my earlier discussions of the politics of knowledge production in activism, I will look closely and in depth at the articulation and analysis of methodologies and theorizing that emerge from research activist practice among formal and informal networks of activist researchers working directly with community activists and social movements at local, regional, and global levels. What follows draws on interviews I have conducted with a range of activist researchers and places their own words in dialogue with the other ideas I am presenting here.

A common underlying assumption in much writing on activist research, research for social change, and community-based research is that professional researchers with specialist academic training must conduct or facilitate it. Scholarly literature on this subject often tends to focus on university faculty or graduate students researching in collaboration or partnership with communities, community organizations, or activist groups. Even in many critical versions of participatory action research and community-based action research, the (at least) facilitative involvement of outside academic research professionals is presumed. These research strategies attempt to democratize interpersonal relations among outside researchers and the communities researched with the intention that power be shifted to insiders during the project. Much of the academic writing on activist research tends to be more concerned with the implications of such work on academic careers, scholarly credibility, and contributions to academic disciplines than on engaging with the substantial research and intellectual work generated from within activist/community organizations (Cancian, 1993; Naples, 1998; Routledge, 1996; Hale, 2008). There is a considerable academic focus on the involvement of university-based scholars in forms of popular/community education, activist research, academic activism, engaged scholarship, and research partnerships. There are some useful accounts of the politics of knowledge in community environmental struggles that have collaborated with scientists. Such "people's science" or "civic science" mobilizes and makes accessible scientific knowledge that is co-produced by community members through the strategic use of scientific tools deployed along with the systematization of lay knowledge and experience, as in struggles against industrial pollution by villagers in Tamil Nadu, India (Narayan & Scandrett, 2014) and by the South Durban Community Environmental Alliance in South Durban, South Africa (Scott & Barnett, 2009). Besides a more established body of work on participatory action research (PAR), other scholars have articulated different politically committed approaches to doing research with and for movements, such as Scheper-Hughes's (1995) militant anthropology and Juris's (2007) militant ethnography, as well as political activist ethnography (Frampton, Kinsman, Thompson, & Tilleczek, 2006). However, relatively little work documents, explicates, or theorizes actual research practices of activist researchers located outside of the academy—let alone takes the perspectives of these activist researchers' everyday worlds as its point of departure.

Forms of investigation and research undertaken within activism are sometimes overlooked or unrecognized. Nonetheless this work is inextricably linked to action and analysis in many movements and mobilizations. This unequal relationship between activist and academic forms of movement theorizing must be dealt with more directly, as Cox and Nilsen (2007, p. 430) do, charging that academic social movements literature "may *exploit* activist theorising (while claiming the credit for itself), *suppress* it (when it challenges the definition of the 'field' that the literature ultimately seeks to assert), or *stigmatise* it as 'ideology' (rather than analysis grounded in practical experience)." Part of what I have been trying to challenge throughout this book is the false distinction made between these different locations of theorizing and to suggest that we more seriously engage with analysis coming from within movements while not ignoring useful contributions from academic theorizing.

The kinds of tensions that exist in activist research indeed exist in all research. Speed (2006, p. 74) contends that there is a great deal of tension in activist research in particular "between political–ethical commitment and critical analysis"; those of universalism, relativism, or particularism; power relations between researcher and researched; and between short-term prag-matics and longer-term implications. For her, "[t]he benefit of explicitly activist research is precisely that it draws a focus on those tensions and maintains them as central to the work." I agree with this and, in extending her observation to work taking place outside of academia, would under-line again here the point emphasized in the introduction to this book that research and theorizing are a broader part of the life of activism and social movements, whether explicitly recognized or not. I have emphasized the importance of engaging with knowledge being produced by, and the internal debates within, social movements and activist networks to more fully under-stand movements. Claims are sometimes made in scholarship on research for social change that there are implicit connections between social justice, activism, and certain methodological approaches. Alternatively, Naples (1998, p. 7) suggests that "the questions we ask and the purpose to which we put the analysis are much greater indicators of what constitutes activist research than our specific methodologies." The demands and goals for academic and activist writing are often different. Thus activist research is not just about a researcher's political credentials or using a self-proclaimed "engaged" or "emancipatory" method or methodology, but also about the reasons the research is produced and how it can be used.

To explore the question of activist research and theorizing more deeply, this chapter foregrounds activist researchers' reflections upon their own processes of research and knowledge production. By analyzing in-depth interviews, it explores the practices of several activist researchers working in social move-ments, NGOs, and people's organizations in the Philippines, North America, Britain, South Africa, and transnationally. It shares their understandings of the theoretical frameworks and methodologies they engage with and use. Analyzing problems, systems, and structures as well as proposing alternatives is central to many movements. While many of the people I spoke with noted differ-ences between their work and academic research, theoretical frameworks and methodology still mattered to them. They articulated these in different ways, sometimes making explicit reference to categories of analysis and theoretical traditions that might be quickly recognized in academic circles, and other times using language more grounded in everyday worlds of activism. Some offered critiques of both academic and dominant NGO research approaches, which they believed to be disconnected from—and of questionable relevance and utility to—affected communities. These researchers emphasized the centrality of relationships of trust with organizations, movements, and struggles that their work supports as resources for developing the frame of analysis and methodology of the research itself.

Movement research is produced in diverse ways. In some contexts, this includes the establishment and maintenance of specialized research and education institutions by social struggles to support social movements. Some movement organizations and NGOs combine grassroots work with research, publication, and knowledge generation. The case for specialized research NGOs is often made, as Bazán et al. (2008, p. 191) argue, "to become a counter-discourse with teeth . . . everyday knowledge [of social movement actors] needs to be synthesized, systematized and given coherence. It also has to be linked with analytical knowledge of the contexts within which everyday practices occur—contexts which, while they impinge on people's life, are in many cases analytically inaccessible to them." While this may not be the research model appropriate to every situation, it is important for us to recognize the diversity of ways that research is organized and takes place within movements, and validate this as intellectual work that itself is theorizing, whether or not it is immediately recognizable to us as such in our locations.

To examine these issues very concretely, the first part of this chapter explores how activist researchers in the Philippines understand, practise, and validate research. It looks at how such research relates dialectically to organizing in social movements. For many social movements, people's organizations (POs), and NGOs, research is a fundamental component of local, national, and transnational social struggles. First, I introduce activist research and foreground the discussion with the social relations of this knowledge production. I not only discuss how this knowledge is constructed and mobilized as a tool for effective social action by and for movements, but I also discuss the relations of the production of the research itself to collective struggles. After giving a brief background to the Philippines and introducing the movements/POs/NGOs discussed, I outline a theoretical framework of analysis that, through dialectics, suggests that research and organizing/action are mutually constitutive. Following on from the focus on movement research in the Philippines, the second part of this chapter engages activist researchers from North America, South Africa, and Europe about research strategy, theoretical frameworks, and methods.

NGOs, Mass Movements, and People's Organizations in the Philippines

The Philippines remains a semi-feudal neocolony compliant with US neoliberal economic and geopolitical prescriptions. Robyn Rodriguez (2010) writes that the economic, political, and social structures established in the Philippines under US colonial domination laid the basis for neocolonial conditions post-"independence." The Philippines boasts a large NGO sector and many social movements and trade unions divided into several ideological tendencies. A comprehensive account of the country's historical and socioeconomic context, including the ideological movement splits after the ousting of the Marcos dictatorship in 1986, are outside the scope of this discussion, but it must be noted here that mass-based left movements and organizations have remained strong. The ways in which NGOs in the Philippines have engaged with this context is expressed by Sonny Africa (2013, p. 118), who writes that the

> Philippine experience highlights the possibilities but also the practical limits of NGOs as opposition to prevailing hegemonies. In the country's specific conditions and historical context the general tendency has been for NGOs to operate in accordance with prevailing political and economic arrangements rather than in sustained opposition to these. Whether consciously or inadvertently, they have aligned with the conservative political program of the established State rather than with that of progressive social movements challenging inequitable structures.

The people I spoke with are from POs and movements in the broader anti-imperialist Philippines national democratic movement, as well as progressive-research NGOs that conduct research and education work with and for social movements. Activists from these left social movements, along with journalists, human rights advocates, and others, continue to be targets of extrajudicial political killings and disappearances. This means that the stakes of political engagement of this kind are high, and there are real risks for researchers from these movements.

Those interviewed for this chapter included two staff of human rights organization KARAPATAN (Alliance for the Advancement of People's Rights); two researchers with labour rights education and research organization EILER (Ecumenical Institute for Labor Education and Research); a senior researcher at the IBON Foundation, an independent research institute and databank, and another researcher from its international division, IBON International. From mass movement organizations I spoke with two staff members from Pamalakaya

(Pambansang Lakas ng Kilusang Mamamalakaya ng Pilipinas/National Federation of Small Fisherfolks Organizations in the Philippines), which claims over 80,000 individual members and 43 provincial chapters. I also interviewed two staff of Kilusang Magbubukid ng Pilipinas (KMP), which describes itself as a democratic and militant movement of landless peasants, small farmers, farm workers, rural youth, and peasant women, claiming 65 provincial chapters and 15 regional chapters nationwide; and a researcher for the umbrella alliance of mass movement POs BAYAN (Bagong Alyansang Makabayan/New Patriotic Alliance). In the Philippine context, POs are "membership-based organizations of citizens coming together to advance their common/collective interests and welfare and are sometimes referred to as grassroots organizations or community-based organizations. Politically active POs are generally organized along class/sectoral lines" (Africa, 2013, p. 124). Researchers with POs and mass movements such as KMP and BAYAN explained that their research role is just one of many—they "double up" in multiple roles as organizer and media/public information/communications person—and so are not professionalized and specialized in the way that many researchers in NGOs tend to be.

The most high-profile and clearly identifiable "research" organization in these interviews, the IBON Foundation, has supported domestic and international movements contesting social and economic injustice for over three decades in ways that Bazán et al. (2008) highlight. Founded in 1978 during the Marcos dictatorship, IBON studies socioeconomic issues confronting Philippine society and the world. It provides research, education, information work, and advocacy support, including non-formal education to people's organizations and all sectors of society. Yet only a handful of its small staff are primarily researchers. IBON International provides capacity development for people's movements and "civil society" organizations outside of the Philippines. A common feature of the research discussed here is its production within movement contexts themselves with little or no input from academic researchers or institutions. Indeed, as noted below, those involved with the research work are active participants in social movement networks, have seldom completed any formal academic research training, and their roles and social functions do not fit neatly into the usual understandings of research professionals.

Mapping the Contours of Praxis, Research, and Action

My understanding of activist research once again is dialectical. By this I mean that it draws on Marx and Engels's (1976, p. 42) dialectical materialist approach to understanding existence and consciousness. For them, forms of consciousness "have no history, no development; but men [*sic*], developing their material production and their material intercourse, alter, along with this their actual world, also their thinking and the products of their thinking. It is not consciousness that determines life, but life that determines consciousness." A Marxist theory of praxis that insists upon the unity of thought and action, therefore, necessitates a dialectical theory of consciousness in which thought, action, and social relations are inseparable. This is why I agree with Kinsman (2006, p. 153), who contends that sometimes academic discussions about research and activism can replicate "distinctions around notions of consciousness and activity that are detrimental to our objectives. We can fall back on research as being an analysis, or a particular form of consciousness, and activism as about doing things 'out there,' which leads to a divorce between consciousness and practice." Arguably, different forms of intellectual rigour, conceptual resources, and theoretical contributions emerge from concrete engagement in social struggles which themselves often challenge scholarly understandings of social change and knowledge production.

The people I interviewed all specialize in research as a major activity within these Philippine social movements and NGOs. Their profiles— including educational backgrounds—varied. While some had undergraduate degrees, none had undertaken what would generally be conceived as formal academic training in research. Broadly speaking, those organizations with a stronger "research" role or focus, such as IBON and EILER, do internal training and train other social movement/NGO activists on data collection and analysis. For organizers in social movements—BAYAN, KMP, and Pamalakaya, as noted below—research is a key first step in effective organizing at the grassroots, conducting basic "social investigation and class analysis."

All of those interviewed emphasized how peasants, workers, and fisherfolk, among others at the grassroots, are fundamental to producing activist research in the Philippines. The place-based nature of such movement knowledge offers a counterpoint to conventional academic and scientific modes of knowledge production, according to Casas-Cortés, Osterweil, and Powell (2008, p. 43): "The latter tend to be predicated on an authority that often lies precisely in being unattached, removed from 'place,' to gain the necessary status of generalizability; whereas the knowledges produced by movements are enriched by their spatial and temporal proximity and accountability to the places which they affect, and from which they come." Movement researchers I spoke with clearly articulated the relationship between the concrete locations of struggles, material conditions, and the knowledge produced.

Research for What—By Whom (and at What Cost)?

As some activist researchers themselves suggest, boundaries between research and organizing are sometimes blurred to the point of nonexistence. Such understandings challenge binary thinking that separates, fragments, and compartmentalizes activities into categories of "research" and "organizing," and actors into "researchers" and "organizers." I point out above that much of the theory produced by participants in social movements may not be recognizable to conventional social movement studies since it is produced by activists. As Bevington and Dixon (2005, p. 195) note, "[t]his kind of theory both ranges and traverses through multiple levels of abstraction, from everyday organizing to broad analysis." In theorizing "collective ethnography" conducted in organizing/political spaces, Mathew (2010, p. 169) observes that

> Organizers formalize the knowledge that is emergent through these multiple levels, repackage and force each short cycle of knowledge production back into circulation, and facilitate the evaluation of the knowledge produced through external agents/allies. Thus, organizers facilitate the expansion of knowledge, and each round of knowledge is quite immediately returned to other levels for engagement. . . . It forces a short cycle of theorizations—and ensures that each round of theorization is immediately engaged with the materiality of the domain of organizing.

Mathew's point is relevant to the discussion here in pointing to both the theorization that takes place in organizing spaces and movements and also how it works.

This process speaks directly to the experiences of the people I interviewed, as will become clear in the discussion and specific examples that follow here. George Smith (2006) suggests that, for activist researchers, a wealth of research material and signposts can be derived from moments of confrontation to explore how power in our world is socially organized. Being interrogated by insiders to a ruling regime, like a public prosecutor, brings one into direct contact with the conceptual relevancies and organizing principles of such regimes, according to him. Thus, as mentioned earlier, confrontations with the state can be rich entry points from which to map out the ways that governments, along with domestic and transnational capital, socially organize power. Perhaps this helps to explain why organizers and activists with first-hand experiences and knowledge can be so effective and skilled as researchers—because of their direct way of generating analyses from everyday material experiences.

The costs of such confrontation in the course of activist research and organizing in the Philippines can be high. Jim Fernando, KMP's campaign officer, stated that a major challenge to research is the security of their researchers. He noted that KMP's organizers are also their researchers, "and being involved in land campaigns you have to deal with state security forces, private armies of big landlords, so that's another challenge for not only the research—for the researchers themselves" (personal interview, 13 December 2012). Cristina Palabay, KARAPATAN's secretary general, corroborated this from her organization's experience in investigating and exposing human rights violations. She explained that the greatest challenge to research is the attacks on human rights workers themselves, noting that under the previous administration 35 KARAPATAN workers were killed in the course of gathering information and providing paralegal support. Many more have been subjects of threats, harassment, and trumped-up charges. She said, "I think those are state-sponsored violations on these human rights workers ourselves. This is the time when defenders become victims themselves, so the kind of counterinsurgency policy that also brings its guns on those doing documentation and research work on the ground—so it really costs lives on the part of KARAPATAN. That remains the biggest challenge for us, especially now under [current president Benigno] Aquino that many areas are being increasingly militarized because of the economic projects that the current administration is conducting with international corporations in far-flung areas" (personal interview, 13 December 2012).

Research for Movement-Building

For Paul Quintos, an IBON International researcher based in Manila, the ultimate arbiter or indicator of the relevance of research is if it helps to unite people toward certain positions and mobilize people to advocate for or to advance that position—"and sometimes it doesn't. It's not that it doesn't matter whether you actually win the concrete gains or not, but sometimes you can't win because the balance of forces is against you. [It] doesn't mean your analysis and your research is incorrect. But if it's framed for movement-building, it's about whether it helps build the movement, not so much whether it actually wins certain concrete gains in the short term. Nevertheless those are also important, so it's essential to have sharp analysis that actually would help win concrete gains that are meaningful and important to people and inspire more action" (personal interview, 12 December 2012).

A Pamalakaya activist said that research should not be divorced from practice, as something that only intellectuals with academic credentials do: "Research should be done for and with the people" (personal interview, 12 December 2012). Cristina Palabay differentiated KARAPATAN's approach to doing democratic and participatory research from what mainstream NGOs claim as participatory research. She explained, "It's easy to be 'participatory' doing your research. You know, you will just go into an area and ask for a focus group discussion—you co-sponsor this with a certain organization, it's easy! It's easy to claim that your research has this participatory character but I think our advocacy is the kind of research that is democratic in the sense that the actors do not only participate, they themselves are knowledge formators [sic]." She emphasized that people at the grassroots generate knowledge, do the data analysis, and "claim these analyses as their own analyses and the actions that they put forward are the people themselves . . . even in the process of doing forensic work and investigation" (personal interview, 13 December 2012).

IBON's Sonny Africa addressed the primary importance of the question "research for whom?" in discussing how to orient and advise new researchers who intend to do research for social change. He suggested that by conducting research closely with people's organizations like a trade union or a peasant group, new researchers will come to appreciate and practise research that is relevant for people's struggles:

> That's important because you will be able to check yourself in the course of working with these groups and from immersing yourself in their specific nature and dynamics . . . I mean it's very easy when you're doing research to let your mind fly, to go for all these novel ideas, and to generate data to couch some technically rigorous but fantasy argument. But in the end, two things are important. One, is it data from the perspective of the organization of workers, for instance, and so will be relevant for them? That won't be ensured just by getting written guidelines from them or after a short meeting with them—rather it comes from going to them, discussing your research design with them, spending time on the picket line, and talking to workers. And when you actually volunteer to do research just have them ask you, "so, how is it going to help us?" (personal interview, 16 December 2012)

Africa highlighted the importance of researchers maintaining an organic link with mass organizations while doing the research. This includes "really looking at your research from other people's, someone else's perspective, from the end-user's perspective . . . there really is no substitute to spending time with an organization and working through your research question with them" (personal interview, 16 December 2012).

EILER head researcher Carlos Maningat said that his main advice to those wanting to do research to support labour movements in the Philippines would be to answer the question "research for whom?" If research is for the workers, he suggested, this orientation is key to establishing a framework, choosing the methods, and determining the approach to data interpretation and synthesis. "And on the capacity side . . . practice is the best teacher in research for social movements" (personal interview, 16 December 2012). Analea Escresa, another EILER researcher, urged that people who want to do research for social movements "should first be part of that social movement because . . . that will guide you on the needs of the social movement. You will know what are the needs and you know that what you're doing will contribute to something and . . . it will not just be on paper but it will be used for social action, for social change . . . visit a factory or a picket line or just immerse themselves in the workers—without that they cannot, they won't, have a grasp of what we really do" (personal interview, 12 December 2012).

While some of the research practices described here seem to echo some of the more politically engaged traditions of participatory action research (e.g., Fals-Borda, 1979; Jordan, 2003; Kapoor, 2009), and while PAR as a methodology is known in many activist/NGO networks in the Philippines, none of the researchers I interviewed used this terminology to describe their research. I think we should be careful not to conflate such activist research practice with notions of PAR or community-based action research from academic literature, or try to "analyze social movement experience as grist for the testing of hypotheses as the illustration of concepts" (Flacks, 2005, p. 8). I am less concerned with fitting the research practices and processes discussed into existing research typology than with making visible the dialectical relationship between "research" and "organizing." This relationship is central to understanding activist research practice within movement and organizing spaces.

The Dialectic of the Research Process and Organizing

The dialectical relations of "research" and "organizing" are a major strand of the reflections of activist researchers interviewed in Manila. So too is the relationship between knowledge produced in struggles at the grassroots and the material conditions experienced and contested by workers, peasants, and others often key to producing "research." As the interviews illustrate, knowledge production/research and organizing/action are mutually constitutive and are seen in this way by the people producing it.

For Quintos of IBON International, who has a background in labour research with EILER and as a union organizer, research is

> very integral to organizing and mobilizing so it's definitely not a stand-alone or distinct category of activity . . . you can't really put boundaries in terms of "am I doing research now, or am I doing education, or am I doing organizing?" The lines are blurred, and . . . that struck me more when I was in organizing as opposed to when I was in a research institution. In the NGO research institution that's the daily work that we did in support of organizing. We were indirectly involved, so the boundaries were clearer. Picking relevant issues and distilling lessons from the experience of grassroots communities and social movements toward guiding collective actions for social change, that would be my definition [of] research. (personal interview, 12 December, 2012)

Africa from IBON highlighted this "blurred" relationship by explaining that the sort of skills that the researcher has are also skills useful for other aspects of political work. He said that a good researcher has skills that will be useful to an organizer, a media liaison, a propagandist, or to be a good manager for whatever work is involved. "So when talking about research skills there's a sort of a tension between using these for research or for other things. They're so useful for other lines of work in the mass movement that there's a tendency for the research work to be downgraded" (personal interview, 16 December 2012).

Reflecting on past experience in labour research at EILER, Quintos described the work of setting research priorities as a dialectical process. He said that in tactical campaigns or struggles this means starting with what workers are complaining about—their grievances. But alongside this empirical work,

> we also do a more trending kind of scoping of general trends, and these are not necessarily trends that were based on what . . . workers actually say or perceive, so we also do that kind of research. So for instance, we did research on labour flexibilization in the Philippines: Workers weren't yet talking about labour flexibilization as such. There were certain expressions of it, or examples of it, but it wasn't yet appreciated as a structural trend, let alone the dynamics behind it. So that was more informed by a combination of theoretical framework and then the empirical evidence in terms of trends, but not literally

what workers were saying or asking for. But it's always a combination of that because eventually even that kind of research would ultimately be validated by concrete examples of how it plays out in different industries and different sectors, and how workers actually respond to recommendations that you initially drafted. (personal interview, 12 December 2012)

This process in KARAPATAN is also integrated with organizing. KARAPATAN researchers often return to organizers who made an initial analysis to check, verify, and validate the analysis, bringing in additional information on trends and patterns of human rights violations that are connected to local issues in the community. In turn, organizers add more analysis and trends to the initial information produced that is returned to them. Cristina Palabay explained the relationship between activist research, mobilization, and popular education in KARAPATAN's work. She said that "in the case of an engagement with people in authority . . . this analysis and crystallized information is a tool in their actions. So it becomes part of [the affected community's] education program, even among other members of their community and outside of their community. For us in the national office [in Manila] it becomes a tool to generate support for the local communities. So we give this information also to international agencies, we give this information to Malacañang [the government], to the diplomatic community, to anybody!" (personal interview, 13 December 2012) This process of reflection and working back through information echoes Mathew's (2010) collective ethnography, as research, organizing—and education—are explicitly and organically tied back to each other in practice.

These interviews about activist research practice and processes often emphasized the importance of knowledge production and organization at the grassroots. Carlos Maningat (EILER) said that trade unions are "actually standby research machineries, so we just have to maximize them and they should be able to realize or be enabled to conduct data gathering on issues affecting them, like contractualization, two-tiered wage system, and so on" (personal interview, 12 December 2012). For Palabay (KARAPATAN), "the analysis and conclusion often comes from the grassroots. We just synthesize this data in an organized and more concise manner, but the local community are the ones saying 'yes this is true, yes this is factual, yes this is our experience.' It cannot come from us because we are from Manila! So it has to come from them" (personal interview, 13 December 2012). A Pamalakaya researcher shared that the process of movement research has to happen alongside organizing, "because you cannot talk to those small fisherfolk if they're not organized. For a scientific collation of the data we need to have an organization for a specific and holistic approach on all of the data coming in, what's happening with them through the economic status and regarding also the environmental impact from those years up to the present and how this is done by the supplement or the new policy that the government wanted to change specifically in [the] Laguna[8] area, so our research work [involves] accompanying and organizing" (personal interview, 12 December 2012).

Another Pamalakaya staffer described their research process as "experience-based science . . . the day-to-day experience and struggle of the people and how the people from the grassroots collect this data, interpret these data at the grassroots level. And then we collectively discuss it with the people on how to affirm it, concretize it, making sure that it is the real data arising from those interviews, so there's a process also of scrutinizing further and going deeply to this data at hand" (personal interview, 12 December 2012). Pamalakaya researchers described their work as a continuous process:

> First we go to the grassroots, discuss with the people, obtain data, and then these data are processed by the organization, including those at the grassroots to separate the chaff from the grain, to underscore the real issue regarding issues and concerns of the communities. And these are further validated by continuing check-up and monitoring, and at the same time we also seek the assistance . . . of other people who understand the plight and struggles of the small fisherfolks. So the validation of data and the reaffirmation of data is primarily done by the organization, by Pamalakaya and their leaders and members at the grassroots level, and these data are further affirmed and validated by other concerned groups who used to work with or support the advocacy, issues, and struggles of the ordinary people at the grassroots. So that process is a never-ending process: It is a continuous process that goes on and on, so there's always this process of reality check, because things change most of the time, and monitoring and check-up are necessary to make sure that we'll not be blind on the chains of events that confront us in our day-to-day world. (personal interview, 12 December 2012)

Social investigation by organizers at the grassroots is crucial for research, education, and organizing for Arnold Padilla, who was BAYAN's public

....

8 Laguna Lake, the Philippines's largest freshwater lake, and the communities dependent upon it for their livelihoods and food have suffered from overfishing by large commercial operators and serious contamination through industrial pollution, and face a public–private partnership reclamation and development project that some fear will displace about 82,000 fishing families—or 500,000 people (see Quijano, 2012).

information officer and researcher when I interviewed him: "[T]hat is the first step, actually, when you're involved in the organizations of BAYAN that are doing community organizing work." This means that organizers must understand the community; identify relationships within that community, including people's class background and source of livelihood, because this guides them in their organizing work and in terms of whom to approach; and they must work out the most pressing issues impacting people and the issues that will mobilize them to action. "So the mass movement and its growth and its strength actually depends on effective organizing, and effective organizing is impossible without social investigation because it gives you the guide—when conducted properly and effectively—it gives you vital information that will help you in your organizing work," he observed (personal interview, 15 December 2012). This continuous, mutually constitutive process of research and organizing blurs the boundaries of those often categorized as "organizers" and "researchers," and it carries into all phases of the cycle of such activist research.

.   The ongoing process of work involved in research, including appraisal and validation, entails collaboration between those taking a lead on research and documentation and those organizing at the grassroots. This process further illustrates the dialectic between organizing and this kind of research/knowledge production. One Pamalakaya staffer explained their "hierarchy of appraisal" in this way:

> There's always data coming in, coming out, from researchers, from fraternal organizations and other grassroots organizations that we are with, and government-backed data sources and others. We appraise this data through what we think is more important to the people we advocate [for]. First of all, we believe that research is partisan and you can never have a research that is for everyone, that would benefit everyone, and that would draw into conclusions that would be for everyone, so we appraise this data through what is important to the people. For example, we have this data from government, there's this high GDP and other stuff like that, and according to how we do our research, well, the people doesn't [*sic*] feel that. So basically our type of research, yes, it concerns itself with empirical data, but also it gives more importance to what is really felt by the people, what really affects them, how these theories, how these conclusions will affect their lives. So that's how we do our research, and we validate this research when we go back to the grassroots areas, when we're together with the organizers. (personal interview, 12 December 2012)

Sylvia Mallari, KMP's training and research coordinator, emphasized how validation of research connected research findings with action in the context of ongoing relationships with grassroots communities. She explained that research studies are given back to people at the base of their organizations, and one form of validation happens if they "embrace the findings of the research and transform it into a program of action which can be carried out in an annual or a two-year program. . . . And then from one year or another two years in adapting a general program of action, that's another form of validation" (personal interview, 13 December 2012).

Reflections on Research and Organizing in the Philippines

As noted earlier, many people see activism as practice, and education, theory, and research as something generated elsewhere. Yet through their practices, activists actually generate various forms of sophisticated knowledge, and through their activism engage in significant learning and research. Focusing on movement researchers and organizers in the national democratic movement of the Philippines, the first part of this chapter has illustrated the dialectical relationship between research and organizing, consciousness and the material conditions that shape it, and in turn—through praxis—are acted upon.

In the cases and contexts discussed here, decisions about framing research and strategy were influenced by explicit political positions, sets of understandings and relationships with and within social movements. Those engaged in this work make decisions in dialogue with others in the best way they can, based on experiential knowledge and analysis that emerge from people's active involvement in the struggles on the ground as they attempt to change their material conditions and overcome exploitation and oppression. Taking the time to "get the research right" is crucial. If done poorly, it can be easily—and publicly—discredited by better-resourced protagonists and media. This in turn can undermine efforts to build a campaign through reaching and mobilizing a broader base of people. BAYAN's Arnold Padilla stated that without solid research launching a campaign and mobilizing people, "getting the attention of the people that you are targeting would be much more difficult because they could easily have dismissed activist groups [like] us as propaganda. But if you are able to back it up with solid research, you're able to cite experiences and macro data that can support your advocacy; then they will be forced to engage with you and you will be able to influence public opinion" (personal interview, 15 December 2012). Further, as already discussed, there are also more serious threats to activist researchers and organizers in the Philippines. As seen in the examples here, processes of validation and fact-checking are often in practice inseparable from organizing and education.

Reflections on doing activist research, as well as research for activism itself, often emerge from collective and collaborative relations, discussions, and exchanges with a wide range of actors. While some activist research targets policymakers and international institutions, the main goal in the cases discussed here has been to support and inform social change through popular organizing and mass movement building. Implicit within this work is an understanding of the importance of building counterpower against domination by the interests of capital and states.

The activist research processes described here are embedded in relations of trust with other activists and organizations that develop through constant effort to work together in formal and informal networks and collaborations. These networks are spaces for the ongoing sharing of information and analysis. They allow for the identification of research that is most relevant to particular struggles and communication of that research in ways that are meaningful and useful for movement-building. They are invaluable in the production, validation, vetting, or "getting the research right" in the applications, strategic considerations, and dissemination of the research.

But research spaces can also be spaces of organizing. As those interviewed in the Philippines noted, the research process itself can be a form of organizing, building, and strengthening communities, movements, and alliances. This in turn needs an organized grassroots to foster and develop research for struggles. This is an ongoing process that informs action—it is not a process that ends, for example, when research is "written up" and a report published. It continues to be produced and used strategically, drawing upon new knowledge and challenges that arise in the course of confrontation, whether this is with transnational corporations, government agencies, state policies, impositions by international financial institutions, or others. The organizations and movements discussed here are good examples of this because they are engaged in long-haul struggles for the transformation of Philippine society. So it should not be at all surprising that those interviewed emphasized the links between short-term campaigns or crisis-driven research for mobilization as well as longer-term processes of research for and in the context of strategies and tactics for movement-building.

The people interviewed here include those who are primarily researchers within an organization that has a major research focus (with rather modest resources by comparison with many NGOs) as well as movement activists who conduct research as one among several other roles. Rather than attempting to categorize activist research processes into (falsely) neat, finite models, I think it is important to capture and understand the dynamic interplay between

FIGURE 4.1: Protesters tear down sections of wire barricades at the World Trade Organization (WTO) meeting in Cancún, Mexico, September 2003. (Photograph by Orin Langelle)

activist research and organizing. Further study of methodologies and theoretical frameworks at use in activist research practice in relation to approaches in academic inquiry claimed as "activist" methodologies has the potential to develop powerful tools for critique of capitalism—different ways and new intellectual spaces not only to understand the world but to change it. As Mathew (2010, p. 170) suggests, such praxis can challenge us to "think through the urgent need to return to the project of active public knowledge production from deep within political spaces." Insights from activist researchers—in the Philippines and beyond—have great potential to enrich, broaden, and challenge understandings of how, where, and when education, learning, research, and other kinds of knowledge production occur.

Lessons about Theory from Other Activist Researchers

For the next part of this chapter, I draw on insights of other activist researchers about the theoretical frameworks informing their work. This material comes from interviews with people working in three organizations: Maquila Solidarity Network (MSN), a Toronto-based labour and women's rights organization that operated between 1994 and 2014 and supported efforts of workers in global supply chains, mainly in the global South, to win improved wages and working conditions and a better quality of life; GRAIN, a small international organization that supports small farmers and social movements in struggles for community-controlled and biodiversity-based food systems; and the (now defunct) Anti-Privatisation Forum, which brought together community organizations, workers' groups, activist groups, and individuals to oppose privatization in South Africa.

The activist researchers interviewed spoke at length about the question of the theoretical frameworks they used and developed in activism. Kevin Thomas, a researcher at MSN at the time of our interview, explained that a research framework is important so that people understand you did not just draw the facts and ideas out of a hat. But the process doesn't usually *start* from that idea of a hypothesis—it starts with gathering the facts and building from there:

> That is, you don't go in with a theory you're trying to prove and develop a way of testing that theory on the ground. You usually start from a relationship either directly with workers or with a particular organization, with a trade union, with a women's organization, one that has come to you with a particular issue, a problem. They talk with us mostly because there's an ongoing relationship between us, because they know we have some capacity to assist in what they're doing. . . . That also means that the way the research gets done is divided up based on that relationship. They'll have already done a lot of groundwork, they'll have documented what's occurred—not necessarily everything that needs to be documented, but they'll have started the process. They start with "we know what the problem is, here is how we found it out" and sometimes what we do is a research test: "What have you been able to get, how are you able to link that to a global company, have you found labels, do we know that those labels are not pirated, [that] we can trace them in some way that's credible? And what are our options for action here?" (personal interview, 20 April 2013)

Relationships and dialogue are also central to GRAIN's research process. GRAIN researchers suggested that the organization can produce research relatively quickly because it has "an analytical framework which probably we haven't articulated as a theory. . . . But there is an internal culture in GRAIN where there is a common understanding of how these things work, so we don't need to put that on some pedestal, to say this is our methodology or theory" (personal interview, 13 December 2011). Another GRAIN researcher said that this frame is grounded in the organization's mandate of biodiversity, which places people—especially Indigenous Peoples, rural people, and small farmers—as the source of agricultural biodiversity that is sustained by local markets:

> Our organization struggles against a really genocidal trend right now to wipe out those kinds of food systems . . . and the people who are supportive of them, the basis of them. That's the frame where we start from, so if you look at it that way and say "what is really at the source of this and how do we explain it in that way? How do we connect it in that way?" . . . and sometimes you might leap from that just to give more traction to an issue that you are working on where you see the connection and maybe you are not so much making it the focus of what you write, but when you realize that connection is important. (personal interview, 14 February 2012)

GRAIN's research process is always ongoing:

> You are always connected with people that you are going to be working on the issue with and in developing the analysis and bringing in whatever information you see as important. . . . So it's a matter of, early on, learning from what is happening there and also trying to [highlight] that experience . . . for others to use. Of course there is the publication of the research, but what is happening all the time throughout that whole process is dialogue with other groups . . . together trying to figure out what are the processes that we need to be a part of . . . what can we do next and what is possible, and then that will probably stimulate other research at a certain point because things will be identified. (personal interview, 14 February 2012)

When talking about his own process, Dale McKinley, who was an activist/researcher with South Africa's Anti-Privatisation Forum (APF), also references a Marxist, anti-capitalist theoretical framework that borrows from a range of theorists. In 2000, the APF emerged as a response to the social and economic impacts of the South African government's adoption of the free market Growth, Employment and Redistribution (GEAR) macroeconomic policy—which included privatization. He recalled that in the APF's early days, a research committee was formed partly out of a commitment to building a cadre through basic skill-building so that activists could learn to do participatory research in their communities, conduct surveys, and document findings. Three large-scale research projects were established and run from within the APF with full participation of all its constituent community organizations and those who had more formal experience, perhaps undergraduate or graduate degrees, but who were not located within the academic world.

McKinley noted that the APF included over 20 different community organizations within the movement, and that at the time they saw very little research being done that connected HIV/AIDS and basic services. But, as he explained, because a lot of the struggles in the communities were around water, electricity, housing, education, and access to basic services, the APF wanted to try to highlight the link between access to water and having an HIV/ AIDS–positive status and show how the experience of not having access to water affected people's quality of life and daily existence. McKinley recalled that South Africa has had the highest prevalence of HIV in the world, and massive amounts of money have been channelled into huge research agendas. Yet, according to McKinley,

> most HIV-positive people, at least in the Gauteng[9] where we were
> working, had no clue of any of this. [There was a] complete gap
> between what was going on there and people's own experiences and
> actually a reticence on the part of formal researchers to make links
> with socioeconomic and political-economy issues, in terms of their
> understanding of this epidemic and how it affected people's lives. So
> we were trying to bridge this gap with . . . a research product, so to
> speak, that was accessible and understandable to ordinary people. It
> wasn't in "academ-ese," it wasn't in journals, it wasn't about those
> publications. It was about getting it around and having policy impact,
> partially, but also fundamentally [about] being able to have a sense
> that people are our goal in this. We did another [research project] on
> prepaid water meters . . . and one on housing. The whole point was
> to hook into a component of people's struggles—research can be one
> component of that. So it's not just about marching and picketing and
> doing all the other kinds of direct actions and writing good analyses
> and critiques of government policy, but countering what was out there
> with research from the ground. . . . We tried as much as possible within
> that committee to have input, for example . . . we actually got people
> to make the survey up themselves. . . . We wanted to try to make
> this so that people in the community felt very comfortable because it
> was people from their own communities doing the work, asking the
> questions, because they themselves experience these things. So it is

....
9 South Africa's most populous province, of which Johannesburg is the capital.

participatory much more than just simply methodologically, but in human and experiential terms. . . . I think that lent itself to a much richer response and engagement with [the] interviewees. (personal interview, 3 December 2012)

The process through which APF members collectively conceptualized, carried out, and validated research meant that all the reports and updates, as the research was happening, were fed back into democratic structures and discussed. So the research was not just kept within a small group that then presented their findings at some point; instead, everything was taken into the more democratic, larger structures of the APF and debated. In this way, as McKinley put it, "research becomes just like we would talk about what we're going to do on a march of 5,000 people, and how we're going to confront the authorities and the different tactics one uses, and you need to fight that out, you debate it. It's the same approach to research: trying to pull that into a collective democratic process was one of the best ways that we found. It always had to be brought back—this took place in a democratic structure of an organization, so everything was referred back into that organization." In this context, "participatory" did not simply mean that members would participate in the research, but that the research process was participatory of the membership of this group, of community organizations themselves, including people who lived in those communities where the research was taking place. So, McKinley suggested that it was "community participation, not simply individual participation. The entire research project from the very beginning of the conceptualization to each of its stages went through a democratic debate and discussion and that made it participatory beyond simply the researchers and those participating in the research project to those who were in the organization themselves. This was an organizational project." Every two months the coordinating committee, comprising 10 members of every APF member organization (which might mean 150–200 people), would sit all weekend long discussing these things. He remembered that "when the research came, there were massive fights and debates about 'no, now you're asking the wrong question, why aren't you doing this . . . ?' And *that* is participatory—it's constant feedback, constant shifting of the research project and the way you're doing [it] as a result of the participation of those in that organization. That was our understanding of participatory research in its fullest organic sense, as opposed to just saying, 'we choose 10 of you to participate in this research because you're from there,' which is a more functional relationship" (personal interview, 3 December 2012).

In his reflections, Thomas outlined how MSN and local activists, organizations, and unions worked together to contest working conditions and other abuses in the global supply chain. He explained that the people with whom MSN worked on the ground had developed a methodology of how they document cases: "They have experience of having done this time and time again—unfortunately, of *having* to do it time and time again. That's not a good thing, but it does mean you develop the skills and tools to do it well. You know that if you put forward a case and make allegations about abuses at a particular factory, you're going to have to back those up with X, Y, and Z, and that's where the research has to focus." Thomas explained that MSN tended to document the power relationships and locate the points of influence. Local groups may know about local labour tribunals or other local tools available, about the local factory management and the dynamics of the movement and actors in their own country. But he said that they do not always know how to link international buyers, Northern consumers, or other institutions to that local reality. Yet, as he explained, in many cases those outside links can be a real force to reckon with in a factory because they are part of global supply chains based on decentralized and contracted production. Foreign buyers' influence may have a significant impact on factories that depend entirely on them for their orders. Thus MSN always looked into the buying relationships first because buyers can push the factory in a way that even the local government often cannot. He continued by explaining,

> A local or national government may say, "OK, this is what you have to do, these are the standards you have to meet," but the reality is that some of these factory owners can shift production to the next country over or somewhere else entirely, almost overnight. They can't necessarily do that with their customers. They don't necessarily need the government, the locale, or the workers in that factory. They can find workers elsewhere. But they do need the customers. So we focus on finding and acting on those connections, and on finding and acting on the forces that in turn can influence those buyers. That's a type of research that we're getting quite good at. (personal interview, 20 April 2013)

As touched upon earlier by several Philippine activist researchers, "getting the research right" is crucial. A central aspect of activist research is the relationship of trust and engagement built up with social struggles and movements, and this is easily damaged by shoddy research. Although much emphasis is placed on the value of academic peer review, and it is often pointed out that activist research is not always subject to the same kinds of procedures, several activist researchers described formal and informal peer-review processes in their work. Indeed, while activist theorizing is not always subject to peer review before publication, through being tested in practice, it arguably undergoes a form of peer review afterwards: Does it work on the ground, in campaigns, and in movements? Is the research relevant?

For Thomas, such review processes are key to validating research. MSN was "part of a movement in which there are many actors and many moving pieces. There's a type of peer-review process in that field, although we don't tend to label it as such. Before we publish anything, we send it to other people engaged in the same work to make sure that we've answered the questions that they would have about the issue—that our findings, conclusions, and recommendations hold water with people who know the field really well" (personal interview, 20 April 2013). He explained that MSN would often share research with experts on both sides: for example, companies and labour rights experts. This is not only a process of fact-checking, but also to gauge reaction from opponents: "When you're trying to write something, you always think about the potential counterarguments, of course. And you try to anticipate those arguments and answer them as best you can because that makes your research more effective as a weapon. But when you actually test the research with outside reviewers, sometimes they come back with things you didn't anticipate and probably couldn't anticipate, because we don't all think the same way—which is partly why we're on opposite sides of an issue in the first place. So there's a sort of peer-review process which we engage in for written work" (personal interview, 20 April 2013).

Before this stage, he said that MSN and its partner groups would begin to develop research to address an issue that had come up for the movement in general in informal conversations. Indeed, he attributed much of the research and writing work to that ongoing conversation among groups where a problem had arisen that they have not collectively been able to answer:

> So the research process itself is based on a collective exchange where priorities get identified and mapped out, rather than just based on the interests of one person or organization. I'm talking here about research that's at a broader level than just a specific factory struggle, that's not just about getting a set of facts documented. There's research which is more about keeping our movement informed about changes in power relationships, for example. We do a lot of research around trade patterns, where the industry is moving, where sourcing is going, changes in wages, battles around wages in different countries. This isn't just information for information's sake: It's part of the process of developing strategy. (personal interview, 20 April 2013)

GRAIN researchers emphasized the collaborative, dialogical nature of their research through interactions with movement activists, farmers, and others. They underlined forms of validation that occur through checking, testing, and sharing material within the organization and in networks throughout the research process, including a kind of peer-review process. A central question for GRAIN is to understand how people take what the organization writes and use it in the battles that they are fighting and the issues they are dealing with at the local level. As one GRAIN researcher told me, "you can't just put anything [out] there; our goal is not to be sensationalist, the goal is to provide solid material. The reputation of the organization depends on it, too, and our relationships with our partners" (personal interview, 14 February 2012).

GRAIN's research practice sometimes involves analyzing information from industry and official sources, much of which is available online. Interviews are also important for their research:

> The validation is [that] we test it and we share it with people, always. In GRAIN we never had [individual GRAIN researchers'] names in our publications—it is always collective material. It is an ideological thing, but it also reflects that there is a lot of bouncing back and [constant] checking. There is a lot of that kind of circulation of material, within GRAIN and also with friends and [other] groups. So you will call that a peer review, I think . . . because in a way that is exactly how it works . . . you want to be challenged and you want to get serious feedback. So that's a way of validating. But the real validation lies in what happens when we put it out. (personal interview, 13 December 2011)

The self-reflection presented by GRAIN researchers very much validates the ideas laid out previously about what makes activist research. Here we see that GRAIN feels that the research they put out that is used and useful to people on the ground is the validation of it, echoing Naples's (1998) words that it is not so much the research methodologies employed, but rather how it gets used that makes it activist research.

Disseminating Research for Education and Action

How activist research is integrated with education and mobilization is certainly not always connected to the idea of a final "research report" for dissemination. Platform is a London-based organization that combines activism, education, research, and the arts in projects that promote social and ecological justice.

Founded in 1983 and based in one of the global centres of the oil industry, much of its focus over the past 20 years has been on British oil companies and their human rights impacts around the world. Platform argues that oil companies use the city to extract a combination of financial, political, legal and technological services that enable them to produce, pump, transport, refine, and sell oil and gas. "By looking closely at corporations, trying to get to know their 'texture,' their 'life story,' we can see the possibility of change. The focus of our work is to look closely at BP and Shell, the two giants of the global oil industry that have head offices in London, our city," explains Platform's Unravelling the Carbon Web website.[10] Platform's research on the oil industry and its relationship to London is often shared through arts-based educational strategies.

In 2012, for example, to expose and oppose oil industry sponsorship of the arts—and in particular BP's funding of the Tate Gallery—Platform launched "Tate à Tate," a collaboration with sound artists to try and present information and research through a three-part audio tour from the different Tate spaces, which can be downloaded onto a portable mp3 player, an iPod, or a mobile phone on which the mp3 audio files can be played.[11] Kevin Smith, who was a campaigner with Platform when I spoke with him, said that arts-based approaches make it possible to speak to people who "feel alienated or are left a bit cold by the idea of reading an NGO report. . . . Sometimes, as long as you can validate the topline message with what's there in the rest of the research, you can repackage that in more interesting or innovative forms that might provoke more people to engage in it" (personal interview, 7 March 2013). For example, Platform also ran a program in the form of a performance promenade and site-specific theatre that involves leading groups of people to various locations in London that are related to the network of financial and political interests of the oil industry, and small performative deliveries of information or reportage among participants.[12]

Kevin Thomas of MSN echoed this in his reflections upon the external pressures on research NGOs to produce research in ways that are not necessarily the most conducive to supporting wider dissemination, education, and action. He observed that there is sometimes a bias toward written research materials in the activist world, and that while some audiences really like this, others do not make effective use of it at all. For him,

> the best dissemination tends to be in terms of a workshop format,
> or speaking format, even one on one, but in some way where you're

....

10 See www.carbonweb.org
11 See http://tateatate.org
12 See http://platformlondon.org/p-eventnew/oil-city-site-specific-theatre-by-platform-10th-21st-june-2013/

working with the group, going over the findings and the outcomes and the strategies that come out of it. The problem with that [for most NGOs] is that the funders like written, published materials that they can link to on their websites. [There is] a bias in terms of funding towards written material, documentation, and there's a bias in terms of actual effectiveness, in my opinion, in terms of the group work where you are actually thinking about and discussing what the research means. So the written document is, I find, fairly dry—I work very well with written word, I can take that and think about it and disseminate it. I think in terms of activist stuff, the best stuff happens in groups, and the best kind of strategy happens in groups, and so research that feeds into that process is usually better. (personal interview, 20 April 2013)

Much of the research described here is part of a continuous process, where information and analysis is shared and processed constantly with others—from beginning to end. Some of the most important products of this research may come from email exchanges, meetings, and time spent on picket lines, in affected communities, or in workshops that happen before anything is formally written down. This process strengthens the research, as collaboration brings out more information, deepens the analysis, and connects it with others working on the issue. The research process itself is often critical to building networks, long-term relationships, and organizing. It also helps enable the research to have a greater impact since the groups and individuals involved will be more connected to the work. This means that there will be more reason for them to use it and share it within their networks. It informs and shapes—and is in turn informed and shaped by—other forms of incremental, informal, and non-formal learning and knowledge production that take place in social movements.

The final person whose reflections I include here is Bobby Marie from South Africa, who discussed his work in the Community Monitors Project with me. This project was established by the Bench Marks Foundation in Johannesburg, an NGO mandated by South African churches to support local communities to act to stop the destruction of their environment and community by transnational corporations (especially the mining sector) and omissions of the government in relation to this. This program emerged from Bench Marks coming to understand that the direct involvement of communities most impacted in the mining areas was crucial. A key part of this has been the creation of Community Monitoring Schools, which are set up in collaboration with local community organizations, where community activists develop their skills in information gathering, writing, research, communications, and community action (Bench Marks Foundation, 2012).

Marie emphasized the importance of creating a space where especially younger people from these communities could come together and reflect on what they do, observe, write, and how they communicate their concerns. This was about building community members' confidence, analysis, and collective action—building knowledge and a process for communities to come into their own in ways that do not impose outside structures on them from above. He noted that this was a different process from generating NGO research reports (which Bench Marks Foundation does) and exists in tension with notions of research that are backed up with statistics and are scientifically referenced. Yet, he contends, in many research reports generated by NGOs "the little voices of people are really good, but they get added on in a decorative way . . . and it also struck me that that's how I've seen lots of reports being written. That's called 'the community voice': You do the research, and then you add on people's voices to illustrate your point, the whole structure of it" (personal interview, 2 December 2012). Starting with the experiences and ideas of community members, and viewing writing as a powerful organizing tool, this program develops skills needed in information gathering, analysis, and strategies and tactics for community action. In addition, the program gathers information and documents events through photographs and video taken on mobile phones, and uses social media and the Internet (e.g., blogging, webcasting radio programs[13]) to disseminate campaign demands, help organize community campaigns, and connect with others nationally and internationally.

Concluding Thoughts

The activist researchers whose reflections animate this chapter clearly take knowledge emerging from movements seriously. This does not mean, however, that they do so uncritically. All of the researchers interviewed discussed their deep concerns with and reflections upon both methodologies and theoretical frameworks. They underlined their serious commitment to the notion that research should be useful for social change. There are strategic considerations in how information is pulled together and released that are rarely central to academic research. Decisions about framing research and strategy are shaped and influenced by explicit political positions, sets of understandings, and relationships to social movements. Many activist/movement researchers make

13 Go to http://communitymonitors.net.

decisions and develop research in dialogue with others based on experiential knowledge and analysis arising from active involvement in and relationships with struggles on the ground. We see this clearly in the approaches articulated by the researchers interviewed here. As Dale McKinley notes, taking movement knowledge and a commitment to democracy and the participatory process seriously may necessitate that all aspects of the research be subject to intense scrutiny, vigorous debate, and challenge within a movement, as it was within the APF.

This chapter validates the notion that being receptive to arguments and analysis of people in movements is crucial to understanding their work and how they function. This strongly echoes the ways in which the researchers I interviewed work. Listening to people on the ground is a vital component of GRAIN's research practice, for example, which is built on a critical political, economic, social, and ecological analysis developed over years of this work. For GRAIN, it is important to listen to people because part of research is just learning: "So when you talk to people you have to listen to them and you have to integrate what they say" (personal interview, 13 December 2011).

As many activist researchers have said, it is not knowledge itself that challenges power structures, but how it is used. For example, this is affirmed by insights from GRAIN in reflecting on their own research practices:

> We know there are movements, people on the ground, either part of movements or NGOs or whatever, who need to take our material and translate it, transform it in a way, so that it becomes much more relevant at the local level. It is not only about translating it to a certain language because of giving it a different shape or a different form or whatever . . . but that happens a lot. Much more than with more traditional academics with traditional research . . . I think our stuff is more relevant from their perspective than whatever I see coming out of academia. That's the big problem with what is being produced on our issues in the academic world. It is not connected; some good researchers come up with good theories and good materials, but it stays out there in its corner of being scientifically, theoretically correct perhaps, but not very useful. (personal interview, 13 December 2011)

Some scholars engaged in thinking about these questions have increasingly heeded the same kinds of analysis, as where Bevington and Dixon (2005) argue that a test of the quality of activist research is whether it is taken up by activists in struggles. That may happen quickly, or it may take some time for its relevance to become apparent. Social movement scholars located in academic institutions stand to extend their understandings about theory and methodology—as well as about the movements themselves—from the actual practices of activist researchers. For activists and organizers, it is important to demystify "research" and restate that it is inseparable from struggles to build and sustain movements.

In drawing this book to a close, there is much to think about concerning the hard work of building strong movements and the role of learning and knowledge production that contests the prevailing dominant ideology. The next and final chapter revisits the book's key insights to discuss lessons, challenges, and implications for activists, academics, students, and educators interested in social movements.

LESSONS FROM ACTIVIST LEARNING, EDUCATION, AND RESEARCH

Throughout this book, I have suggested that we need to engage with, value, and take seriously the ideas, visions, and actions of ordinary people who are learning, organizing, and acting in struggles for social change. This does not mean romanticizing or viewing them through rose-coloured glasses. Indeed, as I have discussed here, it is often from dissident and marginalized perspectives within, or perhaps at the edges of, larger struggles for change, that we see positions and demands that name, confront, and challenge both broader power relations in society or the world *and* hegemonic positions within movements. Thus, engaging with the learning and knowledge produced in activism requires reflexivity and a willingness to debate ideas, learn from the past, organize, and take action. This includes questioning and re-evaluating practices and processes within activist and organizing spaces, however heretical that may sometimes seem. I have argued for an expansive understanding of what theory is, recognizing that theorizing happens in many different places. Likewise, as argued throughout the book and particularly in Chapter 4, we need to think about research as encompassing a much broader set of activities than is often described by the word *research* itself. A critical understanding of history will deepen our analysis of power relations and remind us that organizing and building collective struggle changes things, but there are also pitfalls. This will help us move forward with the desperate optimism that is surely needed to challenge power relations and address the causes of ecological, social, and economic crises. In this concluding epilogue I pick up some threads, topics, and questions that run throughout the book to connect them back to concerns about the politics of knowledge, academic research, teaching, and learning.

FIGURE 5.1: At a week-long forest activist training camp in northeast
Vermont, an activist ascends a tripod that is used in forest defence.
(Photograph by Orin Langelle)

Digging for Knowledge, Mapping Relations

In late 2007, I was sitting in a restaurant by a river near Ayutthaya, Thailand,
with friends and colleagues from two small organizations that support people's
control over biodiversity and small farmers' rights. We were taking a dinner
break from our intense work writing and editing a publication called "Fighting
FTAs," which documents movement struggles against bilateral free trade and
investment agreements.[14] This work stemmed from our collective involvement

14 Available for download in English, Spanish, and French from www.bilaterals.org.

in organizing a strategy workshop on the issue a year earlier, and several years of working together in and with movements against free trade agreements. In a lighthearted moment, we convulsed with laughter as a Thai activist friend read through the menu and drily informed us which dishes would probably contain products produced by Thailand's largest agricultural conglomerate, the powerful Charoen Pokphand (CP), which Thai activists and small farmers had been battling for years. This is activist knowledge and research in action.

While writing this book, an activist contact in Ecuador emailed me, asking for help in tracing connections between Conservation International (a controversial US-headquartered conservation organization), several transnational corporations, and the US administration. In a couple of minutes I found what he needed with Internet searches. Then I scratched my head, wondering whether there is something different that I know or do to discover this information from anyone else searching the Internet. This pushed me to think about how it is that my years of doing activist research on corporations, international financial, and economic institutions and processes means that these search strategies come as second nature to me now. But I realize that this is knowledge built up incrementally before and after the advent of the Internet, including the work of tracking funding, "partnerships" of various kinds, and other relationships with governments and NGOs. I learned how to do this largely because it is what I did for many years, often in collaboration and conversation with others doing similar kinds of work. At times, articulating how to do it seems harder than carrying out the actual research itself. What seems obvious to some activist researchers about the processes of knowledge production in which they engage may not be so obvious to others—until you actually do it. Indeed, in the course of the interviews that I drew upon in the previous chapter, many activist researchers said that the experience of being interviewed was a rare opportunity to consciously reflect on their practice and articulate what it is that they do and how they do it.

How do we learn what we learn and come to know what we know? These questions are often left unexplored in social movement and activist spaces, especially when the learning that takes place—and even the fact that it takes place at all—is not always immediately apparent. My own experiences and conversations over the years with other organizers, popular educators, and activist researchers have reinforced this to me. It is often difficult to discern when experience becomes something that we can label as "learning" or "knowledge." The answers to these kinds of questions are not always straightforward and linear. How do we make these processes visible so that we can understand them better? The ways in which activists create knowledge, social movement learning, and informal and non-formal learning comprise relatively diverse collections of practices. Students and scholars interested in social movements stand to learn from the informal and non-formal learning that takes place within them as well as through the practices of activist researchers who work outside of university/academic institutional contexts and partnerships. If people are able to pause and stand back for a moment, they can often, on reflection, think of different learning that has taken place in their lives across this continuum of formality and informality, sometimes all at once. Writing out case studies of learning and knowledge production in action (as Griff Foley suggests) can help to render visible learning and knowledge that is perhaps not obvious. But this should not be just an academic exercise.

I have suggested that there are severe limitations to trying to understand movements and activism at a level that is too abstracted from the very real differences, contradictions, and particularities on the ground. This is particularly true of the risk of overlooking geo-historical contexts. Bannerji (2011, p. 4) reminds us not to disconnect people from history, and that "all meaningful, useful generalizations need to be shown as having a material, a social/existential and an historical ontology. To think otherwise is to indulge in the absurdity of separating human consciousness from existing human beings and detaching both from lived time. Thus micro-histories are part of history or history's mode of existence, they are inconceivable without each other, and subjugated knowledges are the pedestals of the dominant knowledge." Theory and analysis about movements and activism thus require a concrete grounding in people's everyday activities in the world—the activity of actual people working to produce their own existence in concrete conditions. To do this seriously means critically engaging with dominant accounts of past and present social movements, whether produced by university scholars or generated by movements themselves.

All of this means that understanding movements and activism necessitates paying careful attention to the political, historical, cultural, and economic forces at play in any one place and moment (and sometimes in or across multiple locations and times). We must work out how activists and movements relate to the state, to capital, and to each other. Some scholarship about activism can be reductionist, Eurocentric, perhaps focused only on men's activities, and disconnected from the movements and organizations that are the objects of study—even if it has otherwise made contributions to knowledge in the formal sense through which academic production is understood. Some movements are overlooked or ignored because they do not conform to a model or typology that the researcher wants to employ. Other accounts—activist and academic—may minimize or erase critical challenges arising within movements, such as currents confronting racism and the sexual harassment and violence that occurs in some supposedly progressive/activist political spaces.

These struggles and the forms of knowledge and analysis that they produce are often pushed aside in the interests of a neater defensive or perhaps more celebratory narrative. Yet some of yesterday's marginal and excluded voices and demands sometimes have greater resonance today. For example, many migrant and immigrant workers' organizations have been formed to address marginalization and exploitation not only because of workers' race/class/immigration status in broader society, but also because of the failure of some trade unions to adequately represent and organize these workers and take up their demands. The knowledge and learning that takes place within migrant and immigrant worker organizations is not only important in its own right, as the example of the Immigrant Workers Centre in Montreal in Chapter 2 suggests, but it also critically engages with the knowledge and action that other, more dominant parts of the labour movement often produce and helps to build a sharper understanding of social conditions.

Speaking recently at a critical conference on extraction in Vancouver, in the context of today's urgent struggles against accelerated resource colonialism, environmental devastation and irreparable climate change, I recalled Cree lawyer Sharon Venne's (2001) accurate words from about a decade and a half ago and her clear view that not only are these processes not new, but that Indigenous Peoples have been raising these concerns for a long time: "Colonizers believe that they can use our lands and resources without acknowledging those resources and lands belong to others. Now, the colonizers are being used and consumed by their own corporations and companies. Their governments cannot protect them. There is an assumption that this is a new process. Rather, it is colonization continued. It is a beast who knows no limits. When it cannot consume the Indigenous Peoples' lands and resources, it has turned on its own people. In an attempt to understand, the colonizers have called it 'globalization.' For Indigenous Peoples, it is not a new concept. It is just the continuation of the colonization that began in 1492." Elsewhere, Venne (2004) reflects on how Indigenous Peoples' perspectives about "development," drawing from traditional knowledge about the land and the environment and calls for a collective commitment to care for them for future generations, have often been dismissed or ignored as being "radical." Like her, we should ask "what is radical?" as we confront the global ecological and social consequences of failure to listen seriously to such challenges and understandings.

Part of my argument in this book has been to suggest that a sounder analytical framework not only engages with knowledge and theory arising from movements themselves about the social, political, and economic power relations that they strive to challenge, but that this work can be messy. Such work needs to identify and critically engage with internal debates. It recognizes the importance of engaging with "history from below," "struggle knowledge," and "learning from the ground up" rather than seeking to interpret movements and mobilizations only through an imposed interpretative framework or set of variables. At the same time, however, this framework would understand that these spaces, including some of the most apparently oppositional and radical ones, can be places where the same kinds of dominant forms of social relations of class, race, and gender operate. It would be attentive to the ways in which state and capital work together to create ideas about what forms of dissent—including ideas and perspectives—are "acceptable" or not. Such an analytical approach would also be sensitive to how particular forms of movements, organizations, and modes of activism are rewarded by prevailing political and economic systems, and within this, what the conditions for learning and creating knowledge are. One of the important contributions that Frantz Fanon made in his writing was his prescient warning of the pitfalls of national liberation struggles at a time when there was great excitement at the prospects of decolonization in many parts of the world where there were huge popular movements for independence and liberation. So too should we pay heed to the contradictions and tensions within today's struggles. As David Austin (in Hudson, 2014, p. 231) succinctly puts it, "The point is not to avoid contradictions but to engage them, understand them, and to think about what they mean in terms of the challenges and possibilities of confronting similar circumstances in the here and now."

Everything leading up to this point should make clear that I do not think of theory as a grand body of canonical knowledge that is somehow created in space by particularly clever thinkers and then imposed on concrete conditions of struggle to explain it. Meaning-making, explanation, prediction, and problem-solving are not the monopoly of university-based theorists. When we abstract and decontextualize ideas and thinkers from their contexts, we can run into problems, as we can do when we overextend their ideas in the process of theorizing and divorce theory from the material and social world in which people live and struggle. The theories of learning and knowledge that make the most sense to me and that I have used throughout this book owe much to dialectical Marxist analysis grounded in material concrete social relations—especially those that are also informed by and grounded in geographies and histories that connect resistance against colonial violence and imperialism. These theoretical insights can usefully help to map social relations, envision horizons of political possibilities, and inform a framework of analysis with which to understand the structural conditions of social life to change them.

One way in which to think about the links between theory and practice is to think about how people in concrete situations, at particular moments, understand and act to change them. This issue is close to the heart of my own involvement in movement activism—the importance of identifying and engaging in key movement discussions. Such ideas and reflections can generate understandings and theoretical thinking. In my experience, some important ideas and issues are worked out in practice long before they are theorized or even documented (if at all) in academic literature. To bring the discussion back to the study of movements, I strongly agree with Flacks (2004) and Bevington and Dixon (2005) that research about movements should be "movement relevant." Yet it can sometimes be hard to know at the time what may be relevant to current or future movements. People may only realize the significance of an issue, question, debate, aspect, or dynamic in a movement much later—and this indeed is one of the points of thinking historically. Kinsman (2006) also suggests that we need theory that is connected to and constantly transformed and enriched by practice that can help map social relations of struggle, identify sites where progress can be made, and develop strategies for fighting to win these struggles. Theory can offer potentially powerful analytical tools and resources to think about the quandaries of practice and to deepen our understanding of our context and about how power operates. There is fertile ground for learning in struggle through practical experience to develop in creative tension with more powerful generalizations—theory—to map and build effective strategies. But this does not necessarily hinge on engagement with university academics, since deeper theoretical thinking circulates more widely than academia. Nor does it preclude such engagement. Boron (2005, p. 20) urges that emancipatory struggles require "an adequate social cartography to describe precisely the theatre of operations, and the social nature of the enemy and its mechanisms of domination and exploitation."

To sum up, organizers and activists need ways to think about experiences in larger and abstract terms while remaining grounded in these material experiences. People need maps—not ones that are faded and rendered illegible with age, but rather those kept updated with new developments and directions. Today's maps must deal with connecting what is immediate with the bigger picture. They must be useful in plotting power relations to make them visible and for plotting against them. History is important, but it is not enough to help movements move forward, and there are dangers in trying to recreate past real or imagined "glory days" through nostalgia, which erases the ways in which so many people have also been excluded from and felt alienated within movements—if they have been recognized at all for their roles. This kind of mapping and attention to the micropolitics, context, and the relationship of organizing to the knowledge being produced seems pertinent to consider when so much emphasis is sometimes placed on the idea of "scaling up" local activism to have national or international impact. Is it as straightforward as working to "scale up" such actions to achieve broader impact without being cognizant of the differences across organizing in different contexts? It is not likely that models of organizing and building movements can simply be trans-posed from one context to another without looking at the bigger picture and micropolitics of each place and time. Here I am also reminded of Lenin's (1977, p.185) observation when he wrote, "Too often has it happened that, when history has taken a sharp turn, even progressive parties" [for these were the popular forces which concerned Lenin] "have for some time been unable to adapt themselves to the new situation and have repeated slogans which had formerly been correct but had now lost all meaning—lost it as 'suddenly' as the sharp turn in history was 'sudden.'"

Mapping and documenting struggles, debates, and challenges brought at the margins of social movements that confront practices and power relations within activist contexts is both difficult and vital. Internal tensions and friction within movements and tensions between NGOs and popular movements over the professionalization/domestication of activism, and over class, race, gender, and colonial relations, are not only vitally important struggles, but ones that produce valuable knowledge, learning, and theory. For example, anti-racist, anti-colonial currents driven by racialized people within many movements, across many feminist struggles, labour organizing spaces inside and outside of trade unions, the global justice movement, and the recent Quebec student strike have been significant, but these struggles are rarely centre stage. They are too often ignored or silenced in the dominant narrations of these move-ments, and the conflicts are sometimes papered over at a later date to present a kind of celebratory history of imagined consensus and inclusivity. Attention to these internal struggles and the terms of fragile or nonexistent solidarities among different people can challenge received opinions about activism and draw out rich but often ignored perspectives on power and social change.

Academia and Activism

What role can and do those studying, working, or affiliated with academic institutions play in relation to all of this? The focus of this book is on learning and knowledge that takes place largely outside of classrooms and in activist and social movement settings. My criticisms and caution about academic scholar-ship should not be mistaken, however, for a dismissal or devaluing of formal education or all academic research. Highlighting the significance of knowl-edge produced experientially in struggles, and noting the tendency of much academic scholarship to dismiss or overlook activist knowledge and learning, does not undermine all academic knowledge. Indeed, if we think critically, we should question all ideas, claims of expertise, and the value placed on different forms and sources of knowledge regardless of where they originate from. And, as we have seen, there is a long history of bringing different forms of knowledge alongside each other, in conversations arising from and related to people's actual lives and struggles, whether or not these practices have been documented. Besides claims about whose knowledge matters most, this process can also raise uncomfortable questions that can sometimes lead to productive exchanges.

To feel deeply ambivalent about academia—as I often do—is not the same as rejecting all things academic. People interact with, or come through the doors of institutions of higher education for a variety of reasons. When I enrolled in university, halfway across the world from where I had been living, I had to pull back from the all-consuming intensity of organizing and activist work that had been my life for many years, but I did not retreat from it. Many of my activist networks were transnational, and through various movement and community/ activist connections it was not difficult to be plugged into Montreal's vibrant activist scene upon arrival. While one eye was focused on navigating my way around the expectations and protocols of graduate school and the codes of academic writing, the other was finding ways to continue to maintain, build, and support activist networks. This connected to my long-standing interest in seeing what kinds of resources within the academic world are useful or relevant to movements. It was also connected to my interest in how informal, non-formal, and formal learning and knowledge can contribute to struggles against exploitation, oppression, and inequality.

Thinking about these questions necessitates collaboration and maintaining relationships of trust and dialogue with activists and movements, particularly when you move between these spaces. When you are not there, you cannot presume to know what others need. This work takes time, patience, and humility. These things are not always in abundant supply in an academic world that encourages a scholar's "achievement"—measured and evaluated in specific ways that reinforce individualism and competition. Academic spaces are often locations in which people are highly invested and rewarded for their supposed detachment from the rest of the world. Academia frequently operates on a kind of "star system," where individuals rise and fall based on the quantity of publications they have in refereed scientific journals, their ability to win large grants, to prove their "research impact" in scientifically measurable terms, and to show how well they play institutional politics in particular ways and appear in the media as experts. Collaborations with community partners are usually expected to conform to certain parameters through research funding criteria. This in turn can cause academics to calculate that it's easier to build a CV with nominal engagements and positions in "the community" and to claim relationships on paper (to show to funding agencies should they require evidence of community "partnership") than it is to put time and resources into building and maintaining relationships that are mutually defined and beneficial. On the other hand, academia is not monolithic, and is a space that can be inhabited, occupied, and its resources used for valuable work. Academia and academics can and should be held accountable by the communities and societies that they are supposed to serve. And while it is true that funding agencies can place constraints on research, much research, both on and off campus, is conducted without significant funding, if any at all, and therefore with less requirement to navigate funding conditions. All of this work requires reflection, confidence, and organizing with others.

Reflection is indeed one of the things that I appreciated about my entry into academic life after so many years working outside of academia. During my doctoral program, I was able to think more deeply and systematically about the movements and activism of which I had been part. I appreciated being able to bring my experiential prior learning into dialogue with what others have thought, read, and written. Co-authoring and co-designing research between academics and organizers can be one way to leverage the perceived legitimacy and credibility of academic activity to valorize knowledge and ideas from activist spaces. In their academic and extracurricular activities, there are many possibilities for people who work in or pass through universities to work with movements to systematize knowledge; to work on popular education practices and experiences; to document, reflect upon, and evaluate learning; to bring their own experiences and practical knowledge into dialogue with different kinds of "theory"; to build analyses of power; and to study forgotten histories. Together people can better tap into the considerable resources of universities such as libraries, databases, and other materials that are not publicly accessible. Indeed, the privatization and commercialization of the knowledge that comes from those of us who work in public universities through for-profit models of publishing in journals and books (including this one) need to be resisted through concerted projects of democratizing such knowledge.

Universities—not least through important waves of student struggles across many continents and eras—remain contested spaces. It is important that the histories of the roles played by those in universities in movements for social change are not forgotten—from Black and Indigenous liberation struggles in North America, to working-class struggles for equal rights to education in numerous countries, through to the anti-apartheid movement in South Africa and today's growing boycott, divestment, and sanctions movement to pressure Israel to end the occupation and colonization of Palestinian land. At its most potent, campus activism has gone hand in hand with organizing with communities and movements both inside and outside of universities to bring about social change. We need to keep these efforts and achievements in clear view, especially at a time when universities—and indeed all levels of education and learning—have been increasingly hitched to narrow business models of evaluation, economic goals, and profit margins.

Maintaining relationships with movements, organizations, and activist groups involves considerable work, which often goes unrewarded and unrecognized in terms of pressures to win research funding and the ways in which academics are evaluated. Moreover, there is a transformation of work within higher education, especially regarding the pressure to do individual work rather than collaborative projects unless they are constructed in particular ways which meet funding criteria or institutional priorities. Even in the short time I have been in a university position, I have experienced the equivalent of speed-up in the academic industrial complex, which sometimes feels more and more like an assembly line of production. There are cuts across the board, causing more responsibility to be downloaded onto (especially junior) faculty, students, and a shrinking administrative workforce who are the lifeblood of any university. As education becomes further commodified—delivered by providers to clients—campuses are also becoming more heavily reliant on the labour of a growing number of precarious workers while at the same time becoming spaces that are more securitized. Despite this, there are ways to remain engaged and accountable to social movement activism from within academia. In the face of these very real pressures, recent years have also yielded some powerful moments where students, faculty, and non-academic staff have come together in mutual support—for example, during a labour strike and the Quebec student strike at the university where I work.

Unfortunately, it has not been my experience to see many academics take action and participate in movements. Besides the conservatism that pervades many universities, there is a tendency for many academics to excuse themselves by saying they are "not activists," that they "did their bit" as students, or, alternatively, that their scholarship or teaching is their political work. Others are given to self-censorship whether or not any external censure for participation in political events or activities is based in reality. Although many academics are unwilling to deviate from activities that do not translate into professional career advancement, and although there is a great deal of fear and insecurity built into academic competition for grants, publications, and constant peer-review processes of various sorts, there are academics who aren't afraid to learn from and with activists, and there are those who are also activists. This includes those academics who work with movements and engage with activist knowledge and learning.

As I unexpectedly moved into a position teaching at a university, I consciously followed in the footsteps of scholars with whom I had worked in movements and community organizing and who have continued to do so unapologetically. For example, Sunera Thobani (2002, p. 5) eloquently states her position, which I strongly identify with: "I place my work within the tradition of radical, politically engaged scholarship. I have always rejected the politics of academic elitism which insist that academics should remain above the fray of political activism and use only disembodied, objectified language and a 'properly' dispassionate professorial demeanor to establish our intellectual credentials. My work is grounded in the politics, practices and languages of the various communities I come from, and the social justice movements to which I am committed."

Intellectual rigour and the capacity for reflection, abstraction, and theorizing are not the monopoly of those who claim neutral, scientific distance from the subject of their inquiry or the content of what they teach. So while indeed the university is becoming more corporate, it is important to keep finding the ways in which and the places where progressive thinking and action can be nourished on campus.

One such location is the Centre for Education Rights and Transformation (CERT), housed in the Faculty of Education at the University of Johannesburg. CERT brings together scholars and activists with a long history of involvement in educational, labour, and other struggles in South Africa, including researchers who bring experiences of trade union and workers' education during the anti-apartheid struggle together with education rights struggles post-transition. CERT works closely with social movements, community organizations, trade unions, and several marginalized communities across South Africa to develop research capacity and implement education initiatives through building long-term relationships. For example, one of these projects, focused on community literacy and numeracy, uses participatory action research to understand community problems and design activities that support literacy education. Its research is published in both academic and popular mediums. Among other activities, CERT produces accessible booklets on education rights, broadcasts through community radio, and draws upon and employs popular education methods that serve as an educational and organizing tool.

There is a fine line between students being exploited through internships to do unpaid labour and when these placements allow for the exploration of possibilities for work with community organizations and activist groups to mutual benefit. When students get credit in their courses for such internships and organizations are required to put time and energy into supervising or training students, it can go several ways. But I have seen academia and activism sometimes come together productively through student practicums at the Immigrant Workers Centre (IWC) in Montreal. The IWC has encountered many social work, law, and other students who, through their practicums, research, case work, campaigning, translation, and other tasks, have become activists who have sometimes moved on to other organizing work in trade unions or elsewhere.

Students, academics, and wider communities can and still do march together, discuss ideas, learn from each other, and share resources in movements for change. In the face of open and veiled hostilities towards progressive activism on campus, important solidarities can sometimes be forged. This might involve forming informal networks of racialized/Indigenous students, professors, and non-academic workers to discuss and strategize against institutional racism at their university, or a group of working-class students coming together to support each other. During the student strike and in today's campus Palestine solidarity, anti-racist, climate justice, and anti-war activist groups, to name a few, we can often see parallel learning happening on the streets, in classrooms, in corridors, and in organizing meetings. Students and all who work on campuses have to contend with hierarchies of formal education that are reinforced by the ascendancy of managerial culture in these institutions that further cement barriers to forming solidarities within and beyond the university. Where official university bodies and processes have failed, informal learning and organizing outside of formal associations and committees have often played an important role in countering institutional racism and sexual violence on campuses and the communities in which they exist.

Buried Treasure: Building the Archive

Time pressures and the need to prioritize different kinds of work mean that movements are rarely able to focus on how best to pass on knowledge about visions of social change, stories of their struggles, and their histories. Yet documenting vanishing histories, excavating and archiving them, is crucial for educative and knowledge production work in today's movements and activist groups. Writing on independent Black British community archives, Flinn and Stevens (2009, p. 8) note that documenting histories, especially marginalized and subordinated ones, can be subversive and political. They write that centres and archives dedicated to this work "are not seen as alternatives to struggles but as part of them, a resource for continuing and renewing the fight. Sometimes this has developed into a more definitively historical project but even in these cases the history represented by the archive and created by those who research in the archives is frequently connected to an agenda of education for social change—either as a resource to inform present and future actions, or as a corrective to the absences and misrepresentations of mainstream and dominant accounts."

It is vital that we find ways to support this kind of work before losing more of what was learned in the past, the knowledge from earlier eras of struggle. One contribution that those of us based in academic institutions can make is to consciously access and deploy resources to support the documentation of struggles, movements, and perspectives that are unrecorded, misrepresented, or otherwise rendered invisible or inaccessible.

I can give an example of this from a project I have recently been involved with in Montreal. Through a Ministère de l'Enseignement supérieur, de la Science et de la Technologie (MESRST) Fonds des services aux collectivite's grant in partnership with le Centre international de documentation et d'information Haïtienne, Caraïbéenne et Afro-canadienne (CIDIHCA), a Quebec Haitian community organization, I was able to support the mobilizing of its archives for popular education resources for dissemination to Caribbean youth in Quebec.[15] We produced a bilingual pictorial history of Caribbean community life in Quebec, a series of workshops and activities, and a website from organizational and personal archives.[16]

Other academics with commitments to activism have collaborated to digitize or otherwise preserve and make accessible publications of organizations that do not have the material resources—or for whom it is not a priority—to create an archive. Like Flinn and Stevens, I do not believe that such initiatives are luxuries or exercises in intellectual vanity, but see them as useful and necessary sites for learning and knowledge production. Many archival initiatives are built on people trying to make sense of relevant ways to preserve their collective histories. Within that work, people are forced to learn to think creatively about the meaning and process of building archives, which are relevant to communities and struggles for preservation, dissemination, education, and mobilization purposes.

This is very much in line with how Diana Coben (1998, pp. 6–7) writes about adult education, when she cautions us of the dangers of

> privileging the written, published form over the spoken and unspoken lived experience of adult educators and students. Often, exciting, innovative practice remains unknown to anyone outside the immediate circle of those engaged in it. Innovative interpretations of Gramsci's and Freire's ideas may be being worked out every day in different areas of adult education practice, but if they are not recorded they are not available for others to share insights and debate ends and means. The work that is researched, written up, presented at conferences or submitted for assessment toward a degree, and the even smaller amount of writing that is published, is a small and not necessarily representative sample of a much larger enterprise.

The photographs that illustrate this book are another important example of preserving movement histories. These photos by US activist and

---

15 "Histoire et culture de la diaspora Caraïbéenne au Québec: Préparation d'outils éducatifs pour les intervenants jeunesses communautaires." Most of the credit for envisioning and completing this project lies with community educator and PhD student Désirée Rochat.

16 Quebec's Caribbean (Hi)stories website; http://caribbeanquebec.com/

photojournalist Orin Langelle transcend the sometimes clichéd "protest" images that we often see. Integrating photography into organizing/education initiatives, especially around climate justice, anti-globalization, food sovereignty, and Indigenous resistance struggles, his work is a historically informed look at social movements, struggle, and everyday life. In Langelle's words, his photographic work aims to "counter the societal amnesia from which we collectively suffer—especially with regard to the history of social and ecological struggles. This is not merely a chronicling of history, but a call out to inspire new generations to participate in the making of a new history."[17] Langelle writes that he strives "not just to document and expose the harsh reality of injustice—much of which is linked with the struggle for the land—but to inspire viewers to participate in changing the world, while helping empower those striving for justice because they know that photographs of their struggle are revealed to a larger audience." As Langelle says, in contemporary struggles for change, we cannot afford societal amnesia.

Who Is an Expert and What Is Expertise?

If the personal is political and experiential learning in our own lives and struggles may be very powerful, how then do we avoid the pitfalls of self-absorption? Biju Mathew (2003, n.p.) is worth quoting at length here. While acknowledging personal experience as a fundamental building block in learning and understanding our relationship to the larger landscapes of history, he writes that if we

> are to locate ourselves in political dialogs as people or collectives with a historical consciousness, we leave behind the space of the personal—the space that we do not share with anybody else except with our very own—and build instead a situation where we not only create some distance from questions of personal hurt and anger on the one hand but also a space where a common historical understanding of a situation emerges—something multiple peoples can feel empowered to act from within. In the anti-globalization movement, it is only the historical perspective that gives me a sense of how small an actor I am. . . . In the anti-war movement, it is a history of resistance to imperialist wars and occupations that gives us a perspective of how long term a struggle this is and how long people from across the world have already been committed to it. History is a perfect antidote to the self-absorption of experience.

17 Go to http://photolangelle.org to see more of Langelle's photos.

Here, Mathew is not denying that people can learn and be motivated to act through anger and personal hurt, and indeed emotion can be an important aspect of how and what we learn. But he points out that there are limits to this, and that to move forward collectively a dialectical relationship between individual experiential knowledge and group learning is important to develop.

One concrete way that I have worked on this issue in a movement-learning context was in 2013 when I was invited to run a one-week intensive course at the Labour College of Canada with around 30 participants drawn from public- and private-sector unions from across the country. In designing and teaching this course, selecting the readings and films to be used, I suggested that we look at a variety of social change movements along with personal stories/histories to try to come to a better understanding of some of the current challenges faced when working within unions and in solidarity across differences. By discussing these movements, I hoped that we would learn more about the intricacies and complexities of social change itself—be it challenging power structures, understanding power and oppression or "divide and conquer" tactics, and so on. I also emphasized, as this book has done, the need to learn from history and to ask what conceptual resources from earlier struggles or different movements can provide tools for contemporary activism. What tools can help us effectively reflect on, analyze, and act in our world today? What struck me once again, in this context, was the wealth of knowledge and experiences accumulated in people's daily interactions with their worlds, both as workers and as people engaged in their communities, which forms the basis for analyzing and changing the world.

One powerful example from this course has stayed with me. At the beginning of the week, few people in the group knew much about hydraulic fracking. Having space to talk about other forms of organizing that people were engaged in outside of their union enabled one participant from a rural area of Newfoundland to passionately and effectively lay out the impressive grassroots education and action campaign that he and his community had been engaged in—a story that nobody in the room had heard or read about previously, but an issue that was on everyone's minds by the time we parted company. Such knowledge and learning is embedded in action for social change.

These examples lead us back to two important questions: Who are the experts? Why is it so hard to put into practice what many claim to believe: that ordinary people can think, act, and take control over their destinies? A partial answer takes us back to the professionalization of social change and the internal power relations of activist spaces that are themselves tied to broader systems of domination. The effects of NGOization, internal ways of disciplining dissent, defusing resistance, and silencing some people within activist spaces, and the ways in which some "alternative" spaces replicate the very structures of economic and political power that they exist to struggle against has had major impacts on what—and whose—learning and knowledge is valued. This should not be understood in a deterministic fashion, nor should all NGOs be lumped in together as agents of containing more critical opposition, but the ascendancy of NGOs and the "nonprofit industrial complex" has greatly changed the terrain of political struggles in many locations around the world.

After an NGO-dominated meeting on the WTO some years ago, involving teach-ins that were supposedly participatory and forms of "popular education," I recalled the words of Frantz Fanon, leading me to reread this particularly apt passage from *The Wretched of the Earth* (Fanon, 1968, p. 152):

> If care is taken to use only a language that is understood by graduates in law and economics, you can easily prove that the masses have to be managed from above. But if you speak the language of every day; if you are not obsessed by the perverse desire to spread confusion and to rid yourself of the people, then you will realize that the masses are quick to seize every shade of meaning and to learn all the tricks of the trade. . . . The business of obscuring language is a mask behind which stands out the much greater business of plunder. The people's property and the people's sovereignty are to be stripped from them at one and the same time. Everything can be explained to the people, on the single condition that you really want them to understand.

Perhaps the language is a little stiff and awkward in places some 50 years after it was published in English translation from French, but these words ring true in many activist and social movement spaces today. Jargon, overspecialization, and setting narrow, compartmentalized parameters for "issues" and campaigns echo in the way in which knowledge is divided up into "disciplines," reinforcing colonial power dynamics and obscuring capitalist social relations even where they are meant to be undermined. Elsewhere, Jill Hanley, Eric Shragge, and I (Choudry, Hanley, & Shragge, 2012) discuss how forms of activism that insist on framing discussions and statements that rigidly adhere to the invocation of certain stock phrases and terms at the beginnings of meetings run the risk of getting caught in ritualized assertions of a kind of stylized militancy that do not work toward building a broader base. They also exclude or dismiss those unfamiliar with the rituals and the "right way" to talk instead of trying to build a critical analysis in accessible language that draws upon people's knowledge and brings in more people. The framing of issues in this language, like narrow campaigns, focuses on technical aspects of texts and official processes and "party lines" that must not be questioned, and therefore is hardly conducive to popular education for mobilization and indeed shuts out the majority of our societies. Many in the activist networks that I have been a part of—especially in struggles against capitalist globalization—unfortunately use language that obscures rather than advances popular understandings of processes and institutions that impact our lives. Some groups insist on dogmatic adherence to particular processes and practices which, in the name of democracy and addressing dominant power dynamics, can serve to alienate those outside the ranks of the initiated. Without being connected to broader political, economic, and ecological questions—and struggles for justice and dignity—both activities and analyses can seem as disconnected from on-the-ground reality as the heady world of trade bureaucrats. This is indicative of the larger question of a split between what is seen as intellectual work and what is seen as manual work.

Troubling the Expertise and Status of Academic-Activists and NGO Professionals

In some ways, the "institutional self" of many prominent NGO activists and spokespeople strongly parallels academia. In Chapter 3, I discussed the way in which these people frequently form an elite of movement experts, celebrities, and civil society "leaders." At an international level, some work in what Carroll (2013, p. 706) terms "transnational alternative policy groups":

> the activists who animate these groups are not themselves deeply
> placed within subalternity. They are, like many movement activists,
> well-educated and comparatively resource rich; typically they are
> members of . . . the cadre stratum—a diverse formation of professionals
> and administrators to whom a good deal of capitalist authority is
> delegated, who may align themselves either with the capitalist bloc
> or against it. To the extent that activist intellectuals are "organic,"
> their close relation to the subordinate class may be more a political
> accomplishment than an existential fact preceding activist careers.

Notwithstanding the important role that socially engaged academics can and do play in social activism, the emergence, existence, and reification of such a stratum is problematic. This is particularly true in movement and NGO networks that purportedly support social and economic transformation, equitable social relations, participatory democracy, and the rights and aspirations of the most marginalized. This is especially contradictory when we experience the silencing—or total absence—of grassroots organizers from marginalized communities at such meetings or their relegation to providing testimony about their "plight."

Often this kind of expert status is derived from an underlying assumption that NGOs can convince officials, politicians, and businesspeople with their powers of rational persuasion if they draw upon people seen as "credible researchers."

Yet in doing so, organizations not only obscure asymmetries of power between themselves, states, and capital, but they also reproduce these asymmetries, placing their faith in "rational debate" as the means of social change.

As in academia, a "star system" operates in the professionalized NGO world, at international and national levels, as indeed it also exists in many social movement and activist networks. Such a system establishes certain people as authorities through conference addresses, publications, or media profile, while often contributing to the silence of those with most at stake—and perhaps with the most effective strategies—in struggles for change. It also often reflects dominant intellectual and political trends in terms of which issue or struggle is prioritized and when. I believe that it is crucial to question the social status of "civil society" speakers and writers. We must ask whether or not they are accountable to a social base, if they have a mandate, how and with whom they are connected, and what their relations with political and economic elites are.

For example, it is unclear why a university professor (or someone who has written a book—or both!) should be considered the best person to formulate or articulate strategies and alternatives for the future rather than a landless peasant farmer or an Indigenous person who may not be formally educated and yet may have a greater grasp of what is at stake and the possibilities for change. Yet more often than not, people in the latter kinds of positions, if they do speak, will be pigeonholed into talking about their "sector" or their "plight." Many NGO conferences and networking are often dominated by academic-activists—whether these people are based in universities or NGOs (or both). They take up space talking to each other and more often than not move discussions and interactions onto an elite plane. Much of the learning done in such milieus, however, occurs through participation and networking at a very different level from that of those playing the "experts." This knowledge is produced in the informal ways characterized above as learning in social action.

As suggested in Chapter 1, activism—even anti-capitalist activism—is not impervious to the influence of capitalistic pressures. With the ascendancy of NGOs and the institutionalization of many community organizations, forms of entrepreneurial social change and the emphasis on individual action have become more and more prominent. These kinds of organizations and ideologies are focused neither on mass movement-building nor on harnessing people's knowledge and insights to change things. If notions of victory or success are framed in what is essentially a capitalist, competitive marketplace of ideas—evaluated in terms of access to funding, the media coverage received, or other ways of "making it" in the mainstream—this should perhaps give us pause to reflect.

This brings us back once again to the issue of which voices are valued and which are pushed aside. Histories of contemporary social movements written by and about movement elites, leaders, and notables have often marginalized, omitted, and silenced important perspectives, processes, ideas, and actions. They also influence our movement dynamics—the setting of our parameters, aspirations, and strategies. This is one reason why we should rethink where the power lies and why learning through action is important. Perhaps there is also a need for movement activists to develop "a comfort with uncertainty," as Alan Sears (2014, p. 112) puts it, and accept that we will only come to know by owning up to what we do not actually know—and by listening to others' experiences.

Learning from the Struggle and Teaching in the Classroom

So what lessons can those working, learning, and teaching in formal education settings take from non-formal and informal movement learning? Over time many people have critiqued the function and impact of the institutions of formal education. Many have criticized schooling for reproducing rather than addressing social and economic inequalities linked to class, race, and gender relations. One important critique of formal education is that articulated by Bowles and Gintis (1976), who contend that the repressive and unequal aspects of schooling derive from the need to supply a labour force that is compatible with the social relations of capitalist production. Other scholars since then have urged that scholarship on schooling re-engage with Marx (e.g., Cole, 2008; Anyon, 2011). Many who teach and work in such settings are attentive to how teaching and learning there do not meet the needs of many students. Some strive to "mix up" the way education is delivered in both non-formal and formal education contexts, using techniques adapted from popular education practices, consciously or not, that acknowledge not everyone learns from reading textbooks, course packs, and online materials or by being lectured at for a class period. This does not necessarily mean, however, that educators take action for change beyond how they talk about learning. Interventions in the name of social justice, equity, and human rights often stop at the rhetorical or discursive rather than challenging dominant power relations, let alone being connected to forms of action to change them.

As noted, there are many pressures on education today, particularly the focus on "standards" and "outcomes" in an increasingly commodified sector, reflecting the free market capitalist imperatives of the economies in which they exist. Perhaps schools and universities need to learn from these other experiences precisely because pedagogical experimentation and approaches to and practices of education and learning outside of formal education contexts have been born from the shackles of the old system. Vio Grossi's (1983, p. 109) observation is relevant here: "It is widely known that participation is sometimes allowed only to give the impression that things are managed collectively, rather than in an authoritarian way, but in fact that participation has so many limits that it helps to consolidate domination." Put another way, Neville Alexander (1990, pp. 63–64) cautioned, "We *must* learn the rudimentary lesson that in a class-divided society the dominant ideas are the ideas of the dominating classes and that 'education' that doesn't challenge these ideas is simply reinforcing the reproduction of the status quo, no matter what fancy names we give it." Academics are indeed quite prolific in producing fancy words and phrases, some of which typically include claims about transformation, participation, and empowerment. Questioning the extent to which these are self-proclaimed properties or illusory claims should not be a heresy.

Throughout this book, I have tried to show practical and historical examples of ways in which learning and knowledge take place and circulate reflexively in movement contexts. Major disconnects often remain, though, between most formal education contexts and the learning and education that occur in practice in struggles outside them. I have suggested that challenging the dominant tendency to overlook the intellectual contributions of activism and to devalue or instrumentalize experiential knowledge (Bofelo, Shah, Moodley, Cooper, & Jones, 2013; Cooper & Harris, 2013), and insisting upon recognizing the lineage of ideas and theories that have been forged outside of academia, often incrementally, collectively, and informally, is a start. Many people are conscientized

FIGURE 5.2: Participant in a climate justice march during the US Social Forum in Detroit in 2010. (Photograph by Orin Langelle)

and politicized through their experience of powerful movement mobilizations that inspired them, and through which they have developed commitment, skills, and confidence. But for others, this happens in less visible, mundane daily struggles—or perhaps both. Reflecting on movements in the United States, scholar-activists Rose Brewer and Walda Katz-Fishman (2010, pp. 329–330) suggest that "[w]henever our struggles converged into a powerful movement, it was because people united theory and practice—they acted, reflected, and were intentional about the intellectual and subjective side of the movement as well as the action side." Moreover, some of the most radical critiques and understandings about our societies, our world and its power structures and dominant ideologies, and the fragility of the environment—indeed the most powerful visions for social change—emerge from ordinary people coming together and working for such change. In turn, these sources of knowledge can enrich our analysis and understandings of the world as well as help us to think through, in our own lives and locations, the possibilities and ways to change it.

REFERENCES

Africa, S. (2013). Philippine NGOs: Defusing dissent, spurring change. In A. Choudry & D. Kapoor (Eds.), *NGOization: Complicity, contradictions and prospects* (pp. 118–143). London: Zed Books.

Ahmad, A. (2000). *Lineages of the present: Ideology and politics in contemporary South Asia.* London: Verso.

Alexander, N. (1990). Liberation pedagogy in the South African context. In *Education and the struggle for national liberation in South Africa: Essays and speeches by Neville Alexander (1985–1989)* (pp. 52–70). Braamfontein: Skotaville Publishers.

Allman, P. (2010). *Critical education against global capitalism: Karl Marx and revolutionary critical education.* Rotterdam: Sense.

Anderson, S., & Cavanaugh, J. (1996, 25 September). *The rise of corporate global power.* Washington, DC: Institute for Policy Studies.

Anyon, J. (2011). *Marx and education.* New York: Routledge.

Arendt, H. (2006). *Eichmann in Jerusalem: A report on the banality of evil.* London: Penguin Books. (Original work published 1963).

Armstrong, E., & Prashad, V. (2005). Exiles from a future land: Moving beyond coalitional politics. *Antipode, 37*(1), 181–185. http://dx.doi.org/10.1111/j.0066-4812.2005.00482.x

Austin, D. (2013). *Fear of a black nation: Race, sex, and security in sixties Montreal.* Toronto: Between the Lines Press.

Austin, D. (2009). Education and liberation. *McGill Journal of Education, 44*(1), 107–117. http://dx.doi.org/10.7202/037774ar

Baldwin, J. (1985). White man's guilt. In *The price of the ticket: James Baldwin collected nonfiction 1948–1985* (pp. 409–414). New York: St. Martin's.

Bannerji, H. (2011). *Demography and democracy: Essays on nationalism, gender and ideology.* Toronto: Canadian Scholars' Press.

Bannerji, H. (1995). Beyond the ruling category to what actually happens: Notes on James Mill's historiography in the history of British India. In M. Campbell & A. Manicom (Eds.), *Knowledge, experience and ruling relations: Studies in the social organization of knowledge* (pp. 49–64). Toronto: University of Toronto Press.

Bargh, M. (Ed.). (2007). *Resistance: An indigenous response to neoliberalism.* Wellington: Huia.

Bayat, A. (1997). *Street politics: Poor people's movements in Iran.* New York: Columbia University Press.

Bazán, C., Cuellar, N., Gómez, I., Illsley, C., Monterroso, I., Pardo, J., Rocha, J.L., Torres, P., & Bebbington, A. (2008). Producing knowledge, generating alternatives? Challenges to research oriented NGOs in Central America and Mexico. In A. Bebbington, S. Hickey, & D. Mitlin (Eds.), *Can NGOs make a difference? The challenge of development alternatives* (pp. 174–195). London: Zed Books.

Bench Marks Foundation. (2012). *Resources for community monitors.* Johannesburg: Bench Marks Foundation.

Berger, D., & Dixon, C. (2009). Navigating the crisis: A study group roundtable. *Upping the Ante: A Journal of Theory and Action, 8,* 159–177.

Bevington, D., & Dixon, C. (2005). Movement-relevant theory: Rethinking social movement scholarship and activism. *Social Movement Studies, 4*(3), 185–208. http://dx.doi.org/10.1080/14742830500329838

Biel, R. (2015). *Eurocentrism and the Communist movement.* Montreal: Kersplebedeb.

Biko, S. (1978). *I write what I like: A selection of his writings.* London: Heinemann.

Bleakney, D. (2012, November/December). Conventions of labour: Movement or paralysis? *Briarpatch.* http://briarpatchmagazine.com/

Bleakney, D., & Morrill, M. (2010). Worker education and social movement knowledge production: Practical tensions and lessons. In A. Choudry & D. Kapoor (Eds.), *Learning from the ground up: Global perspectives on social movements and knowledge production* (pp. 139–155). New York: Palgrave Macmillan.

Bob, C. (2005). *The marketing of rebellion: Insurgents, media and international activism.* New York: Cambridge University Press. http://dx.doi.org/10.1017/CBO9780511756245.

Bofelo, M., Shah, A., Moodley, K., Cooper, L., & Jones, B. (2013). Recognition of prior learning as "radical pedagogy": A case study of the Workers' College in South Africa. *McGill Journal of Education, 48*(3), 511–530. http://dx.doi.org/10.7202/1021917ar

Bogad, L.M. (2005). *Electoral guerrilla theatre: Radical ridicule and social movements.* New York: Routledge. http://dx.doi.org/10.4324/9780203401033

Boron, A. (2005). *Empire and imperialism: A critical reading of Michael Hardt and Antonio Negri.* London: Zed Books.

Boughton, B. (2013). Popular education and the "party line." *Globalisation, Societies and Education, 11*(2), 239–257. http://dx.doi.org/10.1080/14767724.2013.782189

Bowl, M., & Tobias, R. (2010). Learning from the past, organizing for the future. *Adult Education Quarterly, 62*(3), 272–286. http://dx.doi.org/10.1177/0741713611403830

Bowles, S., & Gintis, H. (1976). *Schooling in capitalist America: Educational reform and the contradictions of economic life.* New York: Basic Books.

Brewer, R.M., & Katz-Fishman, W. (2010). Feminism: Gender, race and class—Lessons learned and today's moment. In USSF Book Committee (Ed.), *The United States social forum: Perspectives of a movement* (pp. 319–325). Chicago: Changemaker.

Buck-Morss, S. (2009). *Hegel, Haiti and universal history.* Pittsburgh: University of Pittsburgh Press.

Burgmann, V. (1995). *Revolutionary industrial unionism: The Industrial Workers of the World in Australia.* Cambridge: Cambridge University Press.

Burgmann, V., & Ure, A. (2004). Resistance to neoliberalism in Australia and Oceania. In
Polet, F., & CETRI (Eds.). *Globalizing resistance: The state of struggle* (pp. 52–67). London: Pluto.

Burrowes, N., Cousins, M., Rojas, P.X., & Ude, I. (2007). On our own terms: Ten years
of radical community building with Sista II Sista. In INCITE! Women of Color
against Violence (Eds.), *The revolution will not be funded: Beyond the non-profit
industrial complex* (pp. 215–234). Boston: South End Press.

Cabral, A. (1973). *Return to the source: Selected speeches of Amilcar Cabral*. New York: Monthly
Review Press.

Canadian Union of Postal Workers. (2009). Instructor training course—phase 2: Facilitator's
binder.

Cancian, F. (1993). Participatory research and alternative strategies for activist
scholarship. In H. Gottfried (Ed.), *Feminism and social change: Bridging theory and
practice* (pp. 187–205). Urbana: University of Illinois Press.

Carpenter, S., & Mojab, S. (2012). Introduction: A specter haunts adult education:
Crafting a Marxist-Feminist framework for adult education and learning. In
S. Carpenter & S. Mojab (Eds.), *Educating from Marx: Race, gender and learning*
(pp. 3–18). New York: Palgrave MacMillan.

Carroll, W.K. (2013). Networks of cognitive praxis: Transnational class formation from
below? *Globalizations, 10*(5), 691–710.

Carroll, W.K. (2006). Marx's method and the contributions of institutional ethnography. In
C. Frampton, G. Kinsman, A.K. Thompson, & K. Tilleczek (Eds.), *Sociology for changing
the world: Social movements/social research* (pp. 232–245). Black Point, NS: Fernwood Press.

Casas-Cortés, M.I., Osterweil, M., & Powell, D. (2008). Blurring boundaries: Recognizing
knowledge-practices in the study of social movements. *Anthropological Quarterly,
81*(1), 17–58. http://dx.doi.org/10.1353/anq.2008.0006

Choudry, A. (2012). Avec nous dans la rue! pedagogy of mobilization, university
of the streets. Wi: Journal of mobile media, 6 (2). http://wi.mobilities.ca/
avec-nous-dans-la-rue-pedagogy-of-mobilization-university-of-the-streets/

Choudry, A., Hanley, J., & Shragge, E. (2012). Introduction: Organize! Looking back,
thinking ahead. In A. Choudry, J. Hanley, & E. Shragge (Eds.), *Organize! Building
from the local for global justice* (pp. 1–22). Toronto: Between the Lines Press.

Choudry, A., & Kapoor, D. (Eds.). (2013). *NGOization: Complicity, contradictions and
prospects*. London: Zed Books.

Choudry, A., & Kapoor, D. (Eds.). (2010). *Learning from the ground up: Global perspectives
on knowledge production in social movements*. New York: Palgrave MacMillan.

Church, K., Shragge, E., Fontan, J., & Ng, R. (2008). While no one is watching:
Learning in social action among people who are excluded from the labour
market. In K. Church, N. Bascia, & E. Shragge (Eds.), *Learning through community:
Exploring participatory practices* (pp. 97–116). Amsterdam: Springer. http://dx.doi
.org/10.1007/978-1-4020-6654-2_6

Clark, R., & Ivanic, R. (1997). *The politics of writing*. New York: Routledge.

Coben, D. (1998). *Radical heroes: Gramsci, Freire, and the politics of adult education*. New York:
Garland.

Cockburn, A., & St Clair, J. (2002). So who did win in Seattle? Liberals rewrite history.
In E. Yuen, G. Katsiaficas, & D. Burton Rose (Eds.), *The battle of Seattle: The new
challenge to capitalist globalization* (pp. 93–98). New York: Soft Skull Press.

Cohen, J.L., & Arato, A. (1994). *Civil society and political theory*. Cambridge, MA: MIT Press.

Cole, M. (2008). *Marxism and educational theory: Origins and issues*. London: Routledge.

Cooper, L., & Harris, J. (2013). Recognition of prior learning: Exploring the "knowledge question." *International Journal of Lifelong Learning, 32*(4), 447–463. http://dx.doi.org/10.1080/02601370.2013.778072

Cox, L., & Nilsen, A. (2007). Social movements research and the "movement of movements": Studying resistance to neoliberal globalization. *Social Compass, 1*(2), 424–442. http://dx.doi.org/10.1111/j.1751-9020.2007.00051.x

Croteau, D., Haynes, W., & Ryan, C. (Eds.). (2005). *Rhyming hope and history: Activists, academics and social movements*. Minneapolis: University of Minnesota Press.

CSIS. (2000, 22 August). Anti-globalization: A spreading phenomenon. Report # 2000/08. Retrieved from http://www.csis-scrs.gc.ca/eng/miscdocs/200008_e.html

CSIS. (1997, 29 October). The terrorist threat to APEC. Presentation to ICSI.

Daulatzai, S. (2012). *Black star, crescent moon: The Muslim International and black freedom beyond America*. Minneapolis: University of Minnesota Press.

Davis, A. (2007, 21 May). Grinnell College commencement address. www.c-span.org/video/?198220-1/grinell-college-commencement-address

Dawson, M.C., & Sinwell, L. (2012). *Contesting transformation: Popular resistance in twenty-first century South Africa*. London: Pluto.

DeFilippis, J., Fisher, R., & Shragge, E. (2010). *Contesting community: The limits and potential of local organizing*. New Brunswick, NJ: Rutgers University Press.

Dixon, C. (2014). *Another politics: Talking across today's transformational movements*. Oakland: University of California Press.

Dixon, C. (2012). Building "another politics": The contemporary anti-authoritarian current in the US and Canada. *Anarchist Studies, 20*(1), 32–60.

Douglass, F. (1985). The significance of emancipation in the West Indies. In J.W. Blassingame (Ed.), *The Frederick Douglass papers. Series One: Speeches, Debates, and Interviews. Vol. 3: 1855–63*. New Haven, CT: Yale University Press. (Original speech given on August 3, 1857, Canandaigua, New York)

D'Souza, R. (2006). *Interstate disputes over Krishna Waters: Law, science and imperialism*. New Delhi: Orient Longman.

D'Souza, R. (2002). Sustainable development or self-determination? Asking hard questions about the World Summit on Sustainable Development (WSSD). *Social Policy, 33*(1), 23–26.

Dunayevskaya, R. (1958). *Marxism and freedom: From 1776 until today*. New York: Bookman Associates.

Dykstra, C., & Law, M. (1994). Popular social movements as educative forces. In M. Hyams, J. Armstrong, & E. Anderson (Eds.), *Proceedings of the Annual Adult Education Research Conference* (May 20–22, 1994) (pp. 121–126). Knoxville: University of Tennessee.

Ellsworth, E. (1989). Why doesn't this feel empowering? Working through the repressive myths of critical pedagogy. *Harvard Education Review, 59*(3), 297–324.

Eschle, C. (2001). Globalizing civil society? Social movements and the challenge of global politics from below. In P. Hamel, H. Lustiger-Thaler, J. Nederveen Pieterse, & S. Roseneil (Eds.), *Globalization and social movements* (pp. 61–85). Basingstoke, UK: Palgrave.

Fals-Borda, O. (1979). Investigating reality in order to transform it: The Colombian experience. *Dialectical Anthropology*, 4(1), 33–55. http://dx.doi.org/10.1007/BF00417683

Fanon, F. (1968). *The wretched of the earth*. New York: Grove Press.

Faraclas, N. (2001). Melanesia, the banks, and the BINGOs: Real alternatives are everywhere (except in the consultants' briefcases). In V. Bennholdt-Thomsen, N. Faraclas, & C. von Werlhof (Eds.), *There is an alternative: Subsistence and worldwide resistance to corporate globalization* (pp. 67–76). London: Zed Books.

Flacks, R. (2005). The question of relevance in social movement studies. In D. Croteau, W. Haynes, & C. Ryan (Eds.), *Rhyming hope and history: Activists, academics and social movements* (pp. 3–29). Minneapolis: University of Minnesota Press.

Flacks, R. (2004). Knowledge for what? Thoughts on the state of social movement studies. In J. Goodwin & J.M. Jasper (Eds.), *Rethinking social movements: Structure, culture, and emotion* (pp. 135–153). Lanham, MD: Rowman and Littlefield.

Flinn, A., & Stevens, M. (2009). 'It is noh mistri, wi mekin histri'. Telling our own story: Independent and community archives in the United Kingdom, challenging and subverting the mainstream. In J. Bastian & B. Alexander (Eds.), *Community archives: The shaping of memory*. London: Facet Publishing.

Foley, G. (1999). *Learning in social action: A contribution to understanding informal education* (pp. 2–28). London: Zed Books.

Frampton, C., Kinsman, G., Thompson, A.K., & Tilleczek, K. (2006). Social movements/social research: Towards political activist ethnography. In C. Frampton, G. Kinsman, A.K. Thompson, & K. Tilleczek (Eds.), *Sociology for changing the world: Social movements/social research* (pp. 1–17). Black Point, NS: Fernwood Press.

Freire, P. (1970). *Pedagogy of the oppressed*. New York: Continuum.

Freire, P., & Shor, I. (1987). *A pedagogy for liberation*. London: Macmillan.

Friedman, T.L. (1999, 1 December). Senseless in Seattle. *New York Times*. Retrieved from http://www.nytimes.com/library/opinion/friedman/120199frie.html

Germino, D. (1990). *Antonio Gramsci: Architect of a new politics*. Baton Rouge: Louisiana State University.

Gramsci, A. (1985). *Selections from cultural writings*. D. Forgacs & G. Nowell-Smith (Eds.). London: Lawrence and Wishart.

Gramsci, A. (1971). *Selections from the prison notebooks of Antonio Gramsci*. New York: International Publishers.

Guha, R. (1983). *Elementary aspects of peasant insurgency in colonial India*. New Delhi: Oxford University Press.

Guha, R. (Ed.). (1982). *Subaltern studies 1*. New Delhi: Oxford University Press.

Hale, C. (Ed.). (2008). *Engaging contradictions: Theory, politics, and methods of activist scholarship*. Berkeley: University of California Press.

Hall, B. (1978). Continuity in adult education and political struggle. *Convergence: An International Journal of Adult Education*, 11(1), 8–15.

Hall, B., & Turay, T. (2006). State of the field report: Social movement learning. Vancouver: University of British Columbia. http://www.nald.ca/library/research/sotfr/socialmv/socialmv.pdf

Hanhardt, C.B. (2013). *Safe Space: Gay neighbourhood history and the politics of violence*. Durham and London: Duke University Press.

Heiner, B. (2007). Foucault and the Black Panthers. *City: Analysis of Urban Trends, Culture, Theory, Policy, Action, 11*(3), 313–356.

Hewitt, S. (2010). *Snitch: A history of the modern intelligence informer.* New York: Continuum.

Hewitt, S., & Sethna, C. (2012). Sex spying: The RCMP framing of English-Canadian women's liberation groups during the Cold War. In D. Clement, L. Campbell, & G. Kealey (Eds.), *Debating dissent: Canada and the 1960s* (pp. 134–151). Toronto: University of Toronto Press.

Hilary, J. (2013). *The poverty of capitalism: Economic meltdown and the struggle for what comes next.* London: Pluto.

Holford, J. (1995). Why social movements matter: Adult education theory, cognitive praxis and the creation of knowledge. *Adult Education Quarterly, 45*(2), 95–111. http://dx.doi.org/10.1177/0741713695045002003

Holloway, J. (2002). *Change the world without taking power.* London: Pluto.

Holst, J.D. (2002). *Social movements, civil society, and radical adult education.* Westport, CT: Bergin and Garvey.

Holtzman, B. (2010). Challenging power and creating new spaces for possibility: A discussion with Robin D.G. Kelley. In Team Colors Collective (Ed.), *Uses of a whirlwind: Movement, movements and contemporary radical currents in the United States* (pp. 317–329). Oakland, CA: AK Press.

Horton, M., & Freire, P. (1990). *We make the road by walking: Conversations on education and social change.* Philadelphia: Temple University Press.

Howard, S. (2010). *Shane Howard: Lyrics.* Melbourne: One Day Hill.

Hsia, H. (2010). The subjectivation of marriage migrants in Taiwan. In A. Choudry & D. Kapoor (Eds.), *Learning from the ground up: Global perspectives on social movements and knowledge production* (pp. 101–118). New York: Palgrave Macmillan.

Hudson, P.J. (2014). Research, repression and revolution—On Montreal and the black radical tradition: An interview with David Austin. *CLR James Journal, 20*(1), 197–232.

INCITE! Women of Color Against Violence (Eds.). (2007). *The revolution will not be funded: Beyond the non-profit industrial complex.* Boston: South End Press.

Iton, R. (2008). *In search of the black fantastic: Politics and popular culture in the post-civil rights era.* New York: Oxford University Press. http://dx.doi.org/10.1093/acprof: oso/9780195178463.001.0001

Jackson, M. (1999). Impact of globalization on marginalized societies and the strategies by Indigenous People. In A. Tujan (Ed.), *Alternatives to globalization: Proceedings of International Conference on Alternatives to Globalization* (pp. 101–106). Manila: IBON Books.

Johnson, R. (1979). "Really useful knowledge": Radical education and working class culture. In J. Clarke, C. Crichter, & R. Johnson (Eds.), *Working class culture: Studies in history and theory* (pp. 75–102). London: Hutchinson.

Jordan, S. (2003). Who stole my methodology? Co-opting PAR. *Globalisation, Societies and Education, 1*(2), 185–200. http://dx.doi.org/10.1080/14767720303913

Juris, J. (2007). Practicing militant ethnography with the Movement for Global Resistance in Barcelona. In S. Shukaitis & D. Graeber (Eds.), *Constituent imagination: Militant investigations/collective theorization* (pp. 164–178). Oakland, CA: AK Press.

Kapoor, D. (2009). Participatory academic research (par) and people's participatory action research (PAR): Research, politicization, and subaltern social movements in India. In D. Kapoor & S. Jordan (Eds.), *Education, participatory action research, and social change: International perspectives* (pp. 29–44). New York: Palgrave Macmillan. http://dx.doi.org/10.1057/9780230100640.

Katsiaficas, G. (2002). Seattle was not the beginning. In E. Yuen, G. Katsiaficas, & D. Burton Rose (Eds.), *The battle of Seattle: The new challenge to capitalist globalization* (pp. 29–35). New York: Soft Skull Press.

Kauffman, L.A. (2015). The theology of consensus. *Berkeley Journal of Sociology.* http://berkeleyjournal.org/2015/05/the-theology-of-consensus

Kelley, R.D.G. (2002). *Freedom dreams: The Black radical imagination.* Boston: Beacon Press.

Kelsey, J. (1999). *Reclaiming the future: New Zealand and the global economy.* Wellington: Bridget Williams Books. http://dx.doi.org/10.7810/9781877242014

Kelsey, J. (1995). *The New Zealand experiment: A world model for structural adjustment?* Palmerston North: Dunmore Press. http://dx.doi.org/10.7810/9781869401306

Kinsman, G. (2010). Queer liberation: The social organization of forgetting and the resistance of remembering. *Canadian Dimensions, 44*(4). https://canadiandimension.com/articles/view/queer-liberation-the-social-organization-of-forgetting-and-the-resistance-o

Kinsman, G. (2006). Mapping social relations of struggle: Activism, ethnography, social organization. In C. Frampton, G. Kinsman, A.K. Thompson, & K. Tilleczek (Eds.), *Sociology for changing the world: Social movements/Social research* (pp. 133–156). Black Point, NS: Fernwood Press.

Kinsman, G., Buse, D.K., & Steedman, M. (Eds.). (2000). *Whose national security? Canadian state surveillance and the creation of enemies.* Toronto: Between the Lines Press.

Kinsman, G., & Gentile, P. (2010). *The Canadian war on queers: National security as sexual regulation.* Vancouver: UBC Press.

Krebbers, E., & Schoenmaker, M. (2002). Seattle '99: Wedding party of the left and right? In E. Yuen, G. Katsiaficas, & E. Burton Rose (Eds.), *The battle of Seattle: The new challenge to capitalist globalization* (pp. 209–214). New York: Soft Skull Press.

Kress, G. (1982). *Learning to write.* London: Routledge.

Kumar, R. (1993). *The history of doing: An illustrated account of movements for women's rights and feminism in India, 1800–1990.* London: Verso.

Lave, J., & Wenger, E. (1991). *Situated learning: Legitimate peripheral participation.* Cambridge: Cambridge University Press. http://dx.doi.org/10.1017/CBO9780511815355

Le Bon, G. (1960). *The crowd: A study of the popular mind.* New York: Viking Press.

Lenin, V.I. (1977). On slogans. In *Lenin: Collected works* (Vol. 25, pp. 185–192). Moscow: Progress Publishers. (Original work published 1917)

Long, D.A. (1997). The precarious pursuit of justice: Counterhegemony in the Lubicon First Nation coalition. In W.K. Carroll (Ed.), *Organizing dissent: Contemporary social movements in theory and practice* (pp. 151–170). Toronto: Garamond Press.

Lynd, S. (2010). Intellectuals, the university and the movement. In A. Grubacic (Ed.), *From here to there: The Staughton Lynd reader* (pp. 144–151). Oakland, CA: PM Press.

Lynd, S., & Grubacic, A. (2009). *Wobblies and Zapatistas: Conversations on anarchism, Marxism and radical history.* Oakland, CA: PM Press.

Magnien, N. (2012). Neville Alexander. South African History Online. Retrieved from http://www.sahistory.org.za/people/dr-neville-edward-alexander

Maira, S. (2014). Surveillance effects: South Asian, Arab, and Afghan American youth in the War on Terror. In S. Perera & S. Razack (Eds.), *At the limits of justice: Women of color theorize terror* (pp. 86–106). Toronto: University of Toronto Press.

Malcolm, J., Hodkinson, P., & Colley, H. (2003). The interrelationships between formal and informal learning. *Journal of Workplace Learning, 15*(7/8), 313–318. http://dx.doi.org/10.1108/13665620310504783

Martin, E., & Tremblay-Pepin, S. (2011). *Do we really need to raise tuition fees? Eight misleading arguments for the hikes.* Montreal: Institut de recherche et d'informations socio-économiques.

Marx, K. (1984). *The civil war in France: The Paris Commune.* New York: International Publishers.

Marx, K., & Engels, F. (1976). *The German ideology.* Moscow: Progress Publishers.

Mathew, B. (2010). Conversations on the M60: Knowledge production through collective ethnographies. In A. Choudry & D. Kapoor (Eds.), *Learning from the ground up: Global perspectives on knowledge production in social movements* (pp. 157–172). New York: Palgrave MacMillan.

Mathew, B. (2005). *Taxi! Cabs and capitalism in New York City.* New York: New Press.

Mathew, B. (2003). The politics of self-absorption: Experience versus solidarity in movement dynamics. *SAMAR (South Asian Magazine for Action and Reflection), 16.* http://samarmagazine.org/archive/articles/144

McAdam, D., McCarthy, J.D., & Zald, M.N. (Eds.). (1996). *Comparative perspectives on social movements: Political opportunities, mobilizing structures and cultural framings.* New York: Cambridge University Press. http://dx.doi.org/10.1017/CBO9780511803987

McCarthy, S. (2015, 17 February). 'Anti-petroleum' movement a growing security threat to Canada, RCMP say. *Globe and Mail.* Retrieved from http://www.theglobeandmail.com/news/politics/anti-petroleum-movement-a-growing-security-threat-to-canada-rcmp-say/article23019252/

McNally, D. (2011). *Global slump: The economics and politics of crisis and resistance.* Oakland, CA: PM Press.

McNally, D. (2002). *Another world is possible: Globalization and anti-capitalism.* Winnipeg: Arbeiter Ring.

Melucci, A. (1989). *Nomads of the present: Social movements and individual needs in contemporary society.* Philadelphia: Temple University Press.

Melucci, A. (1980). The new social movements: A theoretical approach. *Social Sciences Information/Information sur les Sciences Sociales, 19*(2), 199–226. http://dx.doi.org/10.1177/053901848001900201

Meyer, D.S., & Rohlinger, D.A. (2012). Big books and social movements: A myth of ideas and social change. *Social Problems, 59*(1), 136–153. http://dx.doi.org/10.1525/sp.2012.59.1.136

Mignolo, W.D. (2000). *Local histories, global designs: Coloniality, subaltern knowledges and border thinking.* Princeton, NJ: Princeton University Press.

Monbiot, G. (2002, 30 April). Stealing our clothes: The far right is trying to hijack the green and anti-globalisation agenda. *The Guardian*. Retrieved from http://www.theguardian.com/politics/2002/apr/30/globalisation.thefarright

Moore, M. (2003). *A world without walls: Freedom development, free trade and global governance*. Cambridge: Cambridge University Press.

Moore, M. (1999, 28 September). Challenges for the global trading system in the new millennium. Speech to the Council on Foreign Relations, Washington, DC. Retrieved from http://www.wto.org/english/news_e/spmm_e/spmm08_e.htm

Moore, M. (1997, 25 August). International liberalisation. Speech to University of Canterbury seminar, Christchurch, NZ.

Naples, N. (1998). Women's community activism and feminist activist research. In N. Naples (Ed.), *Community activism and feminist politics: Organizing across race, class and gender* (pp. 1–27). New York: Routledge.

Narayan, S., & Scandrett, E. (2014). Science in community environmental struggles: Lessons from community environmental monitors, Cuddalore, Tamil Nadu. *Community Development Journal, 49*(4), 557–572.

Nawrocki, N. (2012). Listen to the music: Work the music, organize the community. In A. Choudry, J. Hanley, & E. Shragge (Eds.), *Organize! Building from the local for global justice* (pp. 96–110). Oakland, CA: PM Press.

Neigh, S. (2012). *Resisting the state: Canadian history through the stories of activists*. Halifax, NS: Fernwood Press.

Newman, M. (2006). *Teaching defiance: Stories and strategies for activist educators*. San Francisco: Jossey-Bass.

Newman, M. (2000). Learning, education and social action. In G. Foley (Ed.), *Understanding adult education and training* (pp. 59–80). Sydney: Allen and Unwin.

Novelli, M. (2010). Learning to win: Exploring knowledge and strategy development in antiprivatization struggles in Colombia. In A. Choudry & D. Kapoor (Eds.), *Learning from the ground up: Global perspectives on social movements and knowledge production* (pp. 121–138). New York: Palgrave Macmillan.

NZSIS. (1998, 30 September). Declassified document: Government and public order: Miscellaneous protests: AGM of CAFCA. (Declassified 14 August 2008).

Ollman, B. (1998). Why dialectics? Why now? *Science and Society, 62*(3), 338–357.

Petras, J., & Veltmeyer, H. (2005). *Social movements and state power: Argentina, Brazil, Bolivia, Ecuador*. London: Pluto Press.

Petras, J., & Veltmeyer, H. (2003). *System in crisis: The dynamics of free market capitalism*. Black Point, NS: Fernwood Press.

Petras, J., & Veltmeyer, H. (2001). *Globalization unmasked: Imperialism in the 21st century*. New Delhi: Madhyam.

Phelps, C., & Rudin, J. (1995). Lenin, Gramsci, and Manzani: Response to Toporowski. *Monthly Review, 47*(6), 53–54. http://dx.doi.org/10.14452/MR-047-06-1995-10_6

Phillips, M. (2003). Obituary: Lenford (Kwesi) Garrison. 1943–2003. *History Workshop, 56*(1), 295–297.

Piven, F.F., & Cloward, R.A. (1977). *Poor people's movements: Why they succeed, how they fail*. New York: Pantheon.

Quijano, I. (2012, 12 October). Laguna Lake fishers at the mercy of "development." Pesticide Action Network Asia and the Pacific. http://www.panap.net/en/fs/post/food-sovereignty-wfd-2012/1284

Raghavan, C. (1990). *Recolonization: GATT, the Uruguay Round and the developing world.* London: Zed Books.

Ramamurthy, A. (2013). *Black star: Britain's Asian youth movements.* London: Pluto Press.

Rodriguez, R.M. (2010). *Migrants for export: How the Philippine state brokers labor to the world.* Minneapolis: University of Minnesota Press.

Routledge, P. (1996). The third space as critical engagement. *Antipode, 28*(4), 399–419. http://dx.doi.org/10.1111/j.1467-8330.1996.tb00533.x

Ryan, C. (2005). Successful collaboration: Movement building in the media arena. In D. Croteau, W. Haynes, & C. Ryan (Eds.), *Rhyming hope and history: activists, academics and social movements* (pp. 115–136). Minneapolis: University of Minnesota Press.

Ryan, C. (2004). Can we be compañeros? *Social Problems, 51*(1), 110–113.

Sainte-Marie, B. (1992). Bury my heart at Wounded Knee. On *Coincidence and Likely Stories* [CD]. Ensign Records.

Sangari, K., & Vaid, S. (Eds.). (1989). *Recasting women: Essays in colonial history.* New Delhi: Kali for Women.

Sarkar, S. (1998). *Writing social history.* New Delhi: Oxford University Press.

Sarkar, S. (1983a). *Modern India 1885–1947.* New York: St Martin's Press.

Sarkar, S. (1983b). *Popular movements and middle class leadership in late colonial India: Perspectives and problems of a "history from below."* Calcutta: Centre for Studies in Social Sciences.

Scandrett, E. (2012). Social learning in environmental justice struggles—political ecology of knowledge. In B.L. Hall, D.E. Clover, J. Crowther, & E. Scandrett (Eds.), *Learning and education for a better world: The role of social movements* (pp. 41–55). Rotterdam: Sense. http://dx.doi.org/10.1007/978-94-6091-979-4_3

Scheper-Hughes, N. (1995). The primacy of the ethical. *Current Anthropology, 36*(3), 409–420.

Scott, D., & Barnett, C. (2009). Something in the air: Civic science and contentious environmental politics in post-apartheid South Africa. *Geoforum, 40*(3), 373–382.

Sears, A. (2014). *The next new left: A history of the future.* Halifax, NS: Fernwood Press.

Sears, A. (2005a). *A good book, in theory.* Toronto: University of Toronto Press.

Sears, A. (2005b). Creating and sustaining communities of struggle. *New Socialist, 52*, 32–33.

Shragge, E. (2013). *Activism and social change: Lessons for community organizing* (2nd ed.). Toronto: University of Toronto Press.

Sitrin, M.A. (2012). *Everyday revolutions: Horizontalism and autonomy in Argentina.* London: Zed Books.

Smith, A. (2013). Unsettling the privilege of self-reflexivity. In F.W. Twine & B. Gardener (Eds.), *Geographies of privilege* (pp. 263–280). London: Routledge.

Smith, G. (2006). Political activist as ethnographer. In C. Frampton, G. Kinsman, A.K. Thompson, & K. Tilleczek (Eds.), *Sociology for changing the world: Social movements/social research* (pp. 44–70). Black Point, NS: Fernwood Press.

Smith, L.T. (1999). *Decolonizing methodologies: Research and Indigenous Peoples.* London: Zed Books.

Speed, S. (2006). At the crossroads of human rights and anthropology: Toward a critically engaged activist research. *American Anthropologist, 108*(1), 66–76. http:// dx.doi.org/10.1525/aa.2006.108.1.66

Staggenborg, S. (2011). *Social movements.* Oxford: Oxford University Press.

Tarrow, S. (1998). *Power in movement: Social movements and contentious politics* (2nd ed.). Cambridge: Cambridge University Press. http://dx.doi.org/10.1017/CBO 9780511813245

Tavares, P. (1992). Hegel et Haiti, ou le silence de Hegel sur Saint-Domingue. *Chemins Critiques, 2,* 113–131.

Taylor, V. (1989). Social movement continuity: The women's movement in abeyance. *American Sociological Review, 54*(5), 761–775. http://dx.doi.org/10.2307/2117752

Thobani, S. (2002). War frenzy. *Atlantis, 27*(1), 5–11.

Thompson, A.K. (2006). Direct action, pedagogy of the oppressed. In C. Frampton, G. Kinsman, A.K. Thompson, & K. Tilleczek (Eds.), *Sociology for changing the world: Social movements/social research* (pp. 99–118). Black Point, NS: Fernwood Press.

Thompson, J. (1997). *Words in edgeways: Radical learning for social change.* Leicester, UK: NIACE.

Tilly, C. (2004). *Social movements: 1768–2004.* Boulder, CO: Paradigm.

Tilly, C. (1988). Social movements, old and new. *Research in Social Movements, Conflicts and Change, 10,* 1–18.

Tilly, C., & Tarrow, S. (2007). *Contentious politics.* Boulder, CO: Paradigm.

Togliatti, P. (1949). *Gramsci.* Milano: Milano Sera.

Touraine, A. (1981). *The voice and the eye.* Cambridge: Cambridge University Press.

UNESCO. (1997). *International standard classification of education. ISCED 1997.* Paris: UNESCO.

United Nations Conference on Trade and Development. (1995). *World investment report 1995: Transnational corporations and competitiveness.* New York: United Nations.

Vally, S., wa Bofelo, M., & Treat, J. (2013). Worker education in South Africa: Lessons and contradictions. *McGill Journal of Education, 48*(3), 469–490. http://dx.doi .org/10.7202/1021915ar

Veltmeyer, H. (2007). *Illusions and opportunities: Civil society in the quest for social change.* London: Zed Books.

Venne, S. (2001). Same beast, new name. Colours of resistance. http://www .coloursofresistance.org/418/same-beast-new-name/

Venne, S. (2004). See must be civilized: She paints her toenails. In S. Greymorning (Ed.), *A will to survive: Indigenous essays on the politics of culture, language, and identity* (pp. 126–139). New York: McGraw-Hill.

Vio Grossi, F. (1983). Adult education and rural development: Some comments on convergence and divergence from Latin America. *Adult Education and Development, 20,* 103–111.

Von Kotze, A. (2012). Composting the imagination in popular education. In B.L. Hall, D.E. Clover, J. Crowther, & E. Scandrett (Eds.), *Learning and education for a better*

world: The role of social movements (pp. 101–112). Rotterdam: Sense. http://dx.doi
.org/10.1007/978-94-6091-979-4_7

Walia, H. (2013). *Undoing border imperialism.* Oakland, CA: AK Press.

Wood, E.M. (1998). Labor, class and state in global capitalism. In E.M. Wood,
P. Meiksins, & M. Yates (Eds.), *Rising from the ashes? Labor in the age of "global"
capitalism* (pp. 3–16). New York: Monthly Review Press.

Wood, L. (2012). *Direct action, deliberation, and diffusion: Collective action after the WTO
protests in Seattle.* New York: Cambridge University Press. http://dx.doi
.org/10.1017/CBO9781139105859

Youngman, F. (1986). *Adult education and socialist pedagogy.* Beckenham, UK: Croom
Helm.

Yuen, E. (2002). Introduction. In E. Yuen, G. Katsiaficas, & D. Burton Rose (Eds.), *The
battle of Seattle: The new challenge to capitalist globalization* (pp. 3–20). New York:
Soft Skull Press.

Yuen, E., Katsiaficas, G., & Burton Rose, D. (Eds.). (2002). *The battle of Seattle: The new
challenge to capitalist globalization.* New York: Soft Skull Press.

Zald, M.N., & McCarthy, J.D. (Eds.). (1987). *Social movements in an organizational society.*
New Brunswick, NJ: Transaction Books.

Zibechi, R. (2003). *Genealogía de la revuelta. Argentina, una sociedad en movimiento.* La
Plata: Letra Libre.

INDEX

DATE DUE

12/14/16		
		PRINTED IN U.S.A.